How to Do Everything with Your Scanner

Jill Gilbert

Osborne/McGraw-Hill

New York   Chicago   San Francisco   Lisbon
London   Madrid   Mexico City   Milan   New Delhi
San Juan   Seoul   Singapore   Sydney   Toronto

Osborne/McGraw-Hill
2600 Tenth Street
Berkeley, California 94710
U.S.A.

To arrange bulk purchase discounts for sales promotions, premiums, or fund-raisers, please contact **Osborne/McGraw-Hill** at the above address. For information on translations or book distributors outside the U.S.A., please see the International Contact Information page immediately following the index.

How to Do Everything with Your Scanner

Screenshot of Yahoo.com reproduced with permission from Yahoo! Inc. © by Yahoo! Inc. YAHOO! and the YAHOO! logo are trademarks of Yahoo! inc.

Visioneer Product image used by permission from Visioneer, Inc. 2001

Polaroid instant camera image used with permission from Polaroid Corporation and Gary Sloan.

HP Scanjet3400c scanner image used with permission from Hewlett-Packard Company.

Epson scanner image used with permission from Epson America, Inc 2001.

4567890 FGR FGR 0198765432

ISBN 0-07-219106-6

Publisher
Brandon A. Nordin

Vice President & Associate Publisher
Scott Rogers

Editorial Director
Roger Stewart

Acquisitions Editor
Megg Bonar

Project Manager
Deidre Dolce

Freelance Project Manager
Laurie Stewart

Acquisitions Coordinator
Alissa Larson

Copy Editor
Laura Ryan

Proofreader
Andrea Fox

Indexer
Jack Lewis

Illustrators
Jeff Wilson, Beth Young, Lyssa Wald, Michael Mueller

Computer Designer
Maureen Forys, Happenstance Type-O-Rama

Series Design
Mickey Galicia

Cover Design
Dodie Shoemaker

This book was composed with QuarkXPress 4.11 on a Macintosh G4.

To my husband, Dan, and my little scanning
buddies Tara, Julia, and Daniel Welytok

About the Author

Jill Gilbert strayed from a career as a tax attorney, succumbing to the lure of technology. She holds a law degree, is a CPA, and is completing a master's degree in computer science in furtherance of a career in patent law. She has three grade-school children who learned to read from a computer screen and now prefer scanners and image-editing software to crayons.

Jill, shown below, wearing one of the stylish project templates included with PhotoSuite 4, has written eight computer books and never leaves home without a laptop and digital camera.

Contents

PART III   **Practical Uses for Your Scanner**

Acknowledgments

My thanks to the terrifically creative and knowledgeable staff at Osborne, particularly acquisitions editor Megg Bonar and acquisitions coordinator Alissa Larson for their responsiveness and flexibility. Special thanks to technical editor Steve Bain, not only for his insight and attentiveness to accuracy, but also for actively coming up with many ideas for content. Credit for the great idea of covering useful shareware belongs to him. Sincere thanks to Laurie Stewart, and the able assistance of Beth Young, Lyssa Wald, and Michael Mueller, and to Maureen Forys, Laura Ryan, Andrea Fox, and Jack Lewis for all their efforts in getting this book to your shelves.

Special thanks to my husband, Dan Welytok, and to all the friends and family members who served as tireless models for the photos that were the raw material for the scanning projects you see in this book.

Thanks go out to a few folks who helped us with the images for the book's cover, specifically:

- Epson America and Darryll Harrison Jr. at Walt & Company

- Hewlett-Packard Company and Nikki Riordan at Porter Novelli

- Polaroid Corporation and Rachel Street

- Gary Sloan, photographer (www.garysloan.com)

- Visioneer Inc. and Mike Griffith

Introduction

Scanners are powerful imaging devices that are now inexpensive enough to be used for fun and recreation as well as business applications. Once regarded as exotic, complex design tools, scanners are now simple enough to allow even young children to experiment and unleash their creativity. Better yet, benevolent market forces have unleashed inexpensive image-editing software that allows us all to create things in our homes that were once the exclusive domain of graphic artists. You and your family can cut, crop, combine, correct, mail, and post your photos electronically. You just need someone to guide you through the dazzling array of tools you suddenly have at your disposal—and that, my scanning friend, is the purpose of this book.

Who Should Read this Book?

Everyone who wants to add a visual component to their communication, be it stationery, greeting cards, or email. This includes small-business owners, hobbyists, and basically anyone old enough to click a mouse and read the menu options on his or her screen. Scanning and image editing, with the help of this book, are indeed that simple.

What's in Each Part of the Book?

The book is divided into four parts to help you complete a course of self-study that will make you a scanning pro:

Part I explains the basics of how scanning technology works, how to buy a good scanner, and how to install it and recognize its parts once you get it home.

Part II makes the learning curve for conducting your first scan as brief as possible. It also gives you a wealth of troubleshooting tips and tricks that will help everyone from novices to experts. This part concludes by teaching you the basics of editing scanned images—how to select an image-editing program and how to use the tools within it.

Part III expands your scanning horizons toward instantly developed photos (taken with popular Polaroid cameras), negatives, and slides. It also tells you how to scan a text document and convert it to a file format, such as Microsoft Word, that you can edit.

Part IV assumes you are ready to turn your scanned photos into works of art, and to send them to far-flung corners of the world by emailing them and posting them on the Web. This section even tells you everything you need to know to create your own website to display your scanned photos.

What Features and Benefits Are Included in this Book?

Many helpful editorial elements are presented in this book, including a checklist of how-to topics at the beginning of each chapter to let you know what's covered. Skim through these lists to find out what is relevant and interesting to you. Feel free to skip anything that isn't. The chapters of this book are fairly self-contained, and a detailed index is provided to help you review specific terms and concepts.

You'll also find step-by-step instructions, figures, and illustrations to guide you every step of the way. The illustrations themselves are also worth skimming to gauge and review your familiarity with the topics covered.

Other useful elements include:

- *Tips* that point out easier and more efficient ways to do projects and tasks under discussion

- *Cautions* that warn you of common errors and pitfalls

- *Notes* that highlight additional relevant concepts

- *How To* and *Did You Know sidebars* that contain useful additional information about the scanning process and equipment

The following conventions are used in this book:

- *Click* means to click an item once using the left mouse button.

- *Double-click* means to click an item twice in rapid succession using the left mouse button.

- *Right-click* means to click an item once using the right mouse button.

- *Work area* means the area on your computer screen in which an open project appears for editing.

Let Me Hear from You

If you have any comments about how to make this book better or you want to arrange to share some of your family photos and scanning projects with me for possible inclusion in a subsequent edition of this book, by all means drop me a line at my email address: taxtalks@wi.rr.com. I practice strict antivirus procedures, so I will not open attachments, but I will provide you with an address to mail printouts of interesting scanning projects that you'd like me to consider.

Part I

The Basics of Scanning

Chapter 1

How To...

- ■ Figure out what projects you can use your scanner for

- ■ Survey the tools and capabilities associated with scanning

- ■ Set project goals for yourself and your scanner

- ■ Start learning what you need to know to accomplish different projects

A scanner shares the lure of most items that drop in price enough to be accessible to the home consumer and small-business market. Unlike a VCR or a widescreen television, however, a scanner is a creative tool. It's a means to an end, allowing you to transform a bunch of family photos mildewing in a shoebox to digitally organized albums and images posted on websites. It can allow you to add a high-tech flair to your correspondence, presentations, and just about any other communication that has a visual component. This chapter gives you an overview of some of what you can accomplish with your scanner.

Scanners Transform Paper Images into Digital Ones

Scanners are relatively inexpensive, yet powerful, imaging devices. Perhaps you wonder what's so great about the capability to scan photos, especially if you can use your office copier for free.

A scanner is much more than a device that allows you to make copies. A scanner allows you to transform what appears on a piece of paper to a digital image that can be stored and edited on your computer.

Why Scanned Images Are Better than Paper Ones

The photos that capture your most precious memories can be made a lot more poignant when you convert them to digital images. Business graphics, logos, and visual presentations can work ever so much more effectively if they, too, are captured in a digital format. For starters, scanned images can be manipulated, edited, stored, emailed, and posted on the Web.

You Can Touch-Up and Correct a Scanned Image

Taking a photo can be a maddening process. Kids don't sit still, and adults blink at the wrong time. Even if everyone does cooperate, there's that horrific red-eye effect that

1

ruins many a perfect portrait. Scanning is a benevolent technology that allows you to correct the unfortunate flaws that otherwise ruin a perfectly captured memory.

For example, PhotoSuite and PhotoDeluxe, two image-editing programs commonly included with scanners, both allow you to correct the red-eye effect with a click of your mouse. Other tools allow you to correct blurry images, and fix flaws such as a milk mustache or an awkwardly hanging tree branch. For example, Figures 1-1 and 1-2 illustrate how this technology can be used to air-brush the braces on the model's teeth and smooth her uncombed hair.

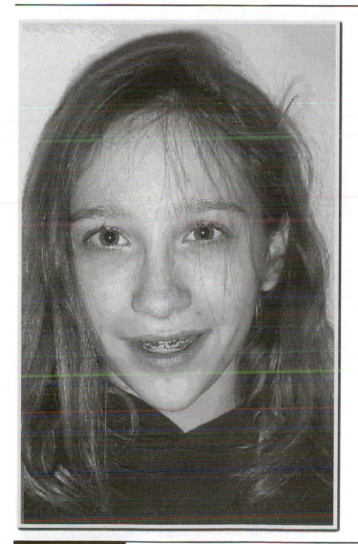

FIGURE 1-1   This model is wearing braces, and her hair needs combing.

FIGURE 1-2   PhotoSuite tools airbrush the braces and tame the hair.

You can use scanning technology to compensate for bad lighting at the time you took the photo. Most image-editing programs have features that allow you to correct a digital image to compensate for under- and overexposure. Figure 1-3 shows a photo with both under- and overexposed areas. For examples, areas where the sun is reflecting off a rock and behind the subject are overexposed (too light) while the majority of the photo appears underexposed (too dark). Figure 1-4 shows the same photograph after the tools in the PhotoSuite 4 program have been used to correct the effects of both the under- and overexposure. The PhotoSuite Enhance feature simultaneously adjusts all the light and dark areas of the photo to achieve the optimum effect with literally a single mouse click.

FIGURE 1-3   This photo has both under- and overexposed areas.

FIGURE 1-4   The PhotoSuite Enhance tool adjusts the lightness and darkness of all areas.

Colors in a scanned photo can also be corrected. Have you ever taken a photo where the lighting makes everyone appear jaundiced? Or had a photo turn a reddish color from poor developing? Once you've scanned the off-color photo, you can apply simple-to-use color-correction tools, like the ones shown in Figure 1-5.

NOTE   *Chapter 10 tells you which image-editing tools to use for specific tasks.*

FIGURE 1-5   Some color-correction tools from PhotoSuite 4, a program commonly used after scanning

You Can Cut and Crop a Scanned Image

There's a lot to worry about when you take a photo—the subject, the lighting, the background, and so on—and just when you get everyone perfectly positioned against the sunset beach, some unwanted passerby plunks down in the background with a beach umbrella. The ability to crop an image can solve this problem. You might simply be able to crop out that umbrella.

The ability to crop an image allows you control over your subject matter. You can concentrate on getting the shot, and worry later about what's in the background.

Cropping also allows you to emphasize the important parts of a photo. Figures 1-6 and 1-7 illustrate how getting rid of some extraneous background focuses attention on the subjects. Figures 1-8 and 1-9 illustrate how scanning and cropping allow you to turn a spontaneous photo into a portrait of your intended subject.

FIGURE 1-6   Lots of extraneous background detracts from this shot.

FIGURE 1-7   Cropping cleans up the background and focuses attention
on the subjects.

FIGURE 1-8   This spontaneous photo captures a smiling subject.

FIGURE 1-9   Cropping creates a portrait.

You Can Combine Multiple Scanned Photos

Most image-editing programs that are used with scanners allow you to cut out and combine portions of a photo. You can create interesting collages, composites, and artistic scenes using these features. Figures 1-10 and 1-11 show how the subject from one image can be superimposed on another photo.

Chapter 10 tells you how to create cutouts from scanned images and provides ideas for interesting applications of this tool.

FIGURE 1-10   A subject can be cut from this photo.

FIGURE 1-11   The subject superimposed on another photographic background

You Can Import Scanned Photos into Project Templates

A project template is a pre-existing design format you can use for a project. Depending on which templates are included with your image-editing program, here are some examples of the types of projects you can create:

Greeting cards   Most image-editing programs come with a variety of templates that you can import your scanned photos into to create personalized greeting cards, like the one shown in Figure 1-12.

FIGURE 1-12   A greeting card created from a scanned photo

Calendars and other useful objects   Photo calendars, like the one shown in Figure 1-13, bookmarks, recipe cards, and other useful objects have become a popular application for scanning technology.

Business cards, brochures, and promotional items   Scanning technology has useful business applications. Templates created by professional graphic artists, like the one shown in Figure 1-14, can place your cards, brochures, and promotional items on the cutting edge at a fraction of the usual printing and design costs.

FIGURE 1-13   Calendars created from scanned images make popular gifts.

ADVENTURE SPORTS

NORMAN SINGLER
dive instructor

675 Monterey Rd. Franklin, CX54872

FIGURE 1-14   Scanning technology has useful business applications.

1

Stationery and note paper   Stationery sends its own message. Whether you use if for personal or business applications, scanning technology can help you create highly stylized writing material, like the sample shown in Figure 1-15.

FIGURE 1-15   Used scanned photos to create personalized stationery and note paper.

Signs and tags   Why rely on a plain piece of paper and some unobtrusive text when you can convey a message using a graphically illustrated sign or tag, as shown in Figure 1-16?

Place photo of your dog here.

BEWARE OF DOG

FIGURE 1-16   Importing scanned images gives signs and tags visual impact.

Novelty items such as fake magazine covers, IDs, and posters   Professionally created templates and layouts help you create sophisticated novelty items, like the million-dollar bill with the imported photo shown in Figure 1-17.

FIGURE 1-17   Novelty items such as fake magazine covers are a popular application of scanning technology.

Chapters 15 and 16 tell how to make the projects described above, including where to find templates for them.

You Can Email Scanned Photos and Post Them on the Web

Once of the biggest benefits of scanning is that it makes your images portable. Sure, you can go to a photo lab and pay to have a few extra copies made for your friends and relatives, but using a lab to copy and share photos is inefficient, if not downright expensive.

Your new scanner offers you the following options for sharing photos:

You can make your own copies.   With a scanner, a decent printer, and some good-quality paper, you don't need to resort to a lab to make a simple copy. There are times when you might want to use a lab to achieve a higher level of quality, but scanning gives you the option to autonomously reproduce your photos.

You can scan negatives.   Some printers afford you the capability to scan negatives. Chapter 12 tells you more about this optional feature.

You can email a photo.   If you know how to email, your scanner gives you the capability to send your photos electronically. This medium offers the advantages of instant delivery, and your recipients can print, forward, edit, and delete the pictures you send to them. Chapter 17 provides you with time- and space-saving tips for emailing your photos.

You can post photos to a communal website.   There are many services on the Web that allow you to post your scanned photos to a communal website. After you upload your photos (as explained in Chapter 17), you can give friends and family a password. This allows them to access and view your photos without having to download and store them on their own computers.

You can create your own website.   Even if you have no prior experience doing anything like website creation, you too can be the master and designer of your own website featuring scanned photos you upload. Chapter 17 covers a range of different products, features, and services that allow you to do this.

Of course, after you get your scanner, you might still want to send pictures via the U.S. postal service (sometimes referred to as "snail mail"). The next time you do, however, you have the option of mailing them on a disk or CD!

You Can Organize Images into Easily Accessed Databases

What good is a photo you can't find? Scanning photos allows you to organize your memories into digital databases—sometimes called albums. You can give photos and albums descriptive names, and use search tools within a program to access them quickly.

> **TIP**   *Chapter 14 tells you about the features in PhotoSuite 4 and Photoshop for accessing and archiving photos.*

Other Uses for Your Scanner

Scanning allows you to come as close to editing reality as any technology in history. It also makes sharing photos with family and friends inexpensive and efficient—but don't forget some other important applications for your scanner:

Business applications   Scanning makes it easy to share and send promotional items, and to create impressive logos from digital images to stylize all your business communications.

Creating trees, charts, diagrams, and other compositions   Scanning allows you to create family trees and organizational charts, combining multiple scanned photos and sizing them to the exact proportions you need, as shown in Figure 1-18.

FIGURE 1-18   It's easy to create trees, charts, and diagrams using scanned photos.

PowerPoint presentations and slide shows   You can use the PhotoSuite digital-imaging program to create slides from scanned image files, as explained in Chapter 14. You can also import them, as you would any other image file, into PowerPoint. If you want to learn more about how to use Power Point to create presentations from scanned photos, *PowerPoint 2000: Get Professional Results* (Osborne/McGraw-Hill, 1999) provides an excellent reference.

A Logical Approach to Getting Started

Scanners are sophisticated technology, but they're simple to learn. If you're wondering the best way to start mastering your new tool, try this approach:

Shop for the right scanner.   Identify a scanner model that best meets your needs, paying close attention to the differing features of various models and which software comes bundled with them. Chapter 3 provides tips to help you select the right scanner in your price range.

Become familiar with your scanner and its parts.   Try several test scans before attempting any projects. Chapters 4 and 5 will help you with this phase of the learning process.

Choose an image-editing program.   Decide which image-editing program allows you to accomplish your planned projects and has an interface you're comfortable with. Chapter 9 provides information about different types of image-editing programs, their features, and their level of difficulty to master.

Familiarize yourself with image-editing tools.   Chapter 10 explains common image-editing tools, and how to select the right ones for the project tasks you want to accomplish.

Begin your projects.   Experiment with different projects, perusing Chapters 15–17 of this book for ideas.

Within a matter of days, you can expect to become familiar and proficient with sophisticated image-editing tools that were once the domain of professional photographers. The learning process begins in Chapter 2!

Chapter 2

How Scanning Technology Works

How To...

- Understand the process of converting photos and text to digital images you can edit

- Maximize the performance of your computer, monitor, and printer in the scanning process

- Compare resolution and bit-depth specifications provided for different scanners

- Determine the best scanning techniques for various types of original media

- Optimize the software that comes with your scanner

Currently most scanners are owned and operated in homes rather than offices; but don't let that make you think scanning technology is simplistic. While scanners are becoming more user-friendly with each truckload of inventory, these unobtrusive desktop devices perform incredibly sophisticated imaging functions. Today's scanners enable home hobbyists to give seasoned graphic artists real competition.

The Scanning Cycle

Paper is a versatile substance, but it has its limitations. You can't email a paper document. Attempts to photocopy graphic images can yield visually unappealing results. More importantly, you can't freely edit what appears on paper, or easily repair damage such as spills, tears, and scratches.

A scanner allows you to transform the image on your printed page (or from other media, such as film or transparencies) into bits of coded information that your computer can interpret and display on your monitor. Once you've used your scanner to convert a paper image to one that appears on your computer screen, the repairing and editing possibilities are limited only by your imagination and software.

After editing, you can share your scanned image with the world by printing, emailing, or using it in a visual presentation such as PowerPoint. Figure 2-1 summarizes tasks your scanner, computer, modem, and monitor perform in the scanning process.

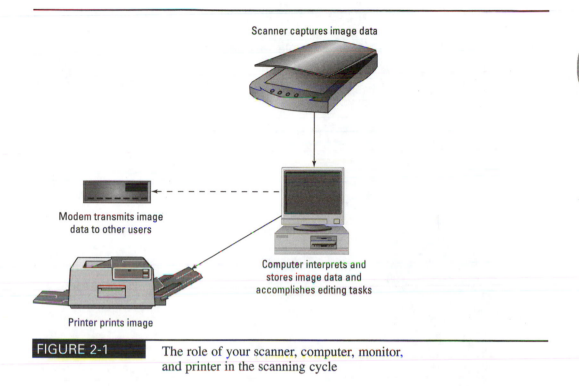

Scanner captures image data

Modem transmits image
data to other users

Computer interprets and
stores image data and
accomplishes editing tasks

Printer prints image

FIGURE 2-1   The role of your scanner, computer, monitor,
                  and printer in the scanning cycle

The Science Behind a Scan

In many ways, a scanner is similar to a camera. Both cameras and scanners are based on an underlying technology of exposing sensitive substances to a light source to reproduce an image. Your camera exposes light-sensitive film by opening and closing a shutter. Similarly, your scanner uses tiny light-sensor devices to grab information about each tiny dot of color that makes up the text or graphic image on paper.

Images Consist of Pixels

All printed and digital images are made of tiny rectangular dots of color, called *picture elements,* or *pixels.* Each pixel is a tiny, rectangular building block of color.

When you look at an image on your computer monitor, the dots are so close together that your eye views them as a continuous, seamless image. Just as you don't see the molecules that make up an actual apple, you don't see the pixels that make up the image of an apple. Figure 2-2 shows an image of a bunch of grapes as it appears to you on your computer screen, and Figure 2-3 shows an enlarged version of a section of the picture, in which the color gradations of the pixels are apparent.

FIGURE 2-2   A photograph of a bunch of grapes

Pixels Contain Image Data

Each individual pixel contains information, or data, stored in the form of *bits*. Bits are the smallest unit of information processed by the computer. Each pixel contains a predetermined number of bits, depending on the type of original you've scanned. Bits are represented by sequences of zeros and ones—the universal language of computers.

The simplest kind of pixel, for a black-and-white image with no shades of gray, contains only two bits: one that represents black, and one that represents white.

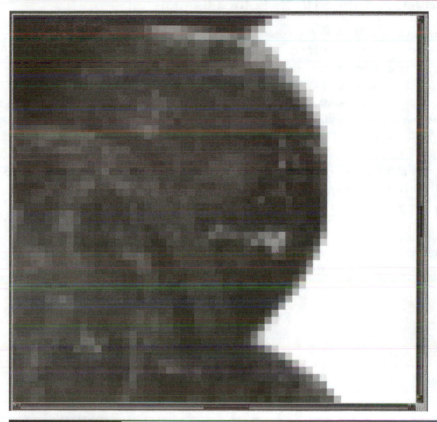

FIGURE 2-3   The photograph scanned and enlarged to display individual pixels of a single grape

Bit Depth

The number of bits of information in a pixel is called *bit depth* (also referred to as *color depth*). Pixels with greater bit depth can store a wider variety of shades of gray and color. Pixels of greater variety create richer, more detailed images.

A pixel having a bit depth of two can produce only a black-and-white image, with no intervening shades of gray. An image with shades of gray, aptly called *grayscale*, requires eight bits of information per pixel, or a bit depth of eight. Reproducing a color image requires a 24-bit depth. (This particular bit depth is often referred to as 256-color, since that is the number of colors 8-bit pixels are capable of producing.)

Red, Green, and Blue (RGB) Color Channels

In kindergarten you learned you could create nearly every conceivable color by mixing amounts of the primary colors red, blue, and yellow. In the world of computer graphics, however, the primary colors are red, blue, and *green*. A color image is actually made of three layers of 24-bit pixels. Each layer is called a *color channel*.

There is a separate color channel for red, green, and blue. The color channels each have their own numeric value, and are superimposed on top of each other to create a precise mathematical "recipe" of red, green, and blue.

The MGI PhotoSuite program, for example, allows you to use the dialog box shown in Figure 2-4 to adjust the three channels individually, creating different colors to be displayed on your computer monitor. The following table shows you some of the numeric values the program assigns to each color channel to produce various color results:

Color that Appears on Screen	Green Channel Value	Red Channel Value	Blue Channel Value
Blue	0	0	254
Chartreuse	255	0	19
Violet	0	219	255
Magenta	0	255	213

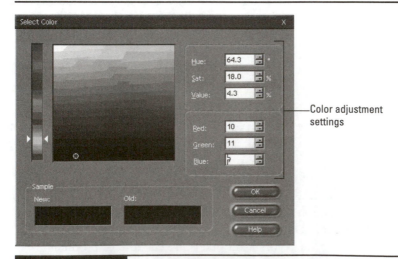

Color adjustment settings

FIGURE 2-4   Imaging software allows you to create colors by adjusting separate color channels.

CMYK Color Channels

A scanner or device with a 32-bit depth is capable of creating images containing four layers of 8-bit pixels, or four different color channels. These are called CMYK channels for the primary colors of cyan, magenta, yellow, and black. By combining these four-color channels, a device can create 16.7 million colors.

Cyan is a sort of aqua-blue color. The K is used to represent black in the acronym because a letter B could be erroneously assumed to stand for the color blue.

How a Scanner Interprets Pixels

There is actually no such thing as a color scanner! A 24-bit scanner reads each pixel in a color image, and interprets it as one of 256 shades of gray. In other words, you're actually capturing a color image as a grayscale image every time you scan.

Your monitor and computer graphics card generate the color that you see on your screen when it interprets the scanner's grayscale. Similarly, the color you get from your printer is a product of the printer's software interpreting the grayscale, not of information conveyed directly by your scanner.

> **NOTE** *Your computer graphics card determines the detail and depth of color rendered by your monitor. The graphics card is an expansion board within your computer that converts images contained inside your computer to electronic signals that can be interpreted by your monitor. The card contains memory to store color data information.*

Decide How Much Bit Depth You Actually Require

Nearly all scanners on the market today have the minimum 24-bit depth necessary to create color images. You also see scanners advertising 30-, 40-, or even 46-bit capacity. Are these better than 24-bit capacity?

The general rule is that the more bits used to store a color, the more colors can be stored. The higher the bit levels, the truer to the original the scan will be.

But the human eye can discern only so many colors. A 24-bit scanner can actually combine 256 shades of gray to capture about 16.7 million colors. This is already great quality, as the human eye is capable of discerning only about 5,000 colors. A 30-bit scanner (10 bits per color) can capture more than 1 billion colors, and a 36-bit scanner can capture more than 6.8 trillion colors. These high bit-depth scanners are useful for scanning slides and negatives that have a greater range of colors and tones than ordinary paper prints. They give you a lot more to work with in the editing process. Also, extra bits ensure the accuracy of the scanned image, since not all bits are flawlessly captured in the sampling process. Extra bits provide insurance for sharper, more accurate images.

In the final analysis, should you spring for a 30- or 42-bit scanner? It depends on the type of image you're scanning, as discussed in the "Different Originals Require Different Scan Techniques" section later. Also, it's important to keep in mind that because there are so many other factors affecting the quality of a scan, simply opting for a 42-bit depth as opposed to 30-bit depth might not give you dramatically better results.

The Difference Between Pixels, Dots, and Samples

Manufacturers often use the terms pixels, dots, or samples interchangeably to indicate how much data a scanner can process. While all these terms are adequate for giving consumers information about the capabilities of a scanner, they do not mean precisely the same thing. Pixels are a measurement associated with computer monitors, while dots per inch are most accurately used to convey the capabilities of a particular printer. Here is a summary of the precise information each of these terms actually conveys:

Pixels per inch (ppi) Technically, a pixel is the smallest display unit on a monitor, arranged in rows and columns called a bitmap. The bitmap is reflected as of series memory addresses that keep track of where the color data associated with each pixel is stored in the computer's memory.

Dots per inch (dpi) Dots per inch is an industry specification for printer capabilities, indicating how densely the printer places individual dots of color in a one-inch square area. For example, a 300-dpi printer generates 90,000 dots in a one-inch square area.

Samples per inch (spi) This is a term that pertains specially to scanners, and refers to how many color samples per inch the CCD (charge-coupled device) on the scanner samples as it moves across a page. It is the most accurate term with respect to a scanner, but one that's seldom used.

Recognize the Common Parts All Scanners Have

Scanner design and efficiency are constantly evolving, but the basic technology remains as constant as that of the camera. The role of a scanner is to capture an image you can observe with your naked eye so that your computer can convert it into a series of numeric values representing the color channels for each pixel. In its most primitive form, scanning requires a light source and sensor device. Everything else is there to enhance the quality.

The Charge-Coupled Device (CCD)

Not surprisingly, the most important part of your scanner for determining its price and quality is the device that contains the sensors that read and convert the data. This component is called a charge-coupled device, or CCD.

The CCD is an array of tiny sensors, or photosensitive cells, which are highly reactive to light. The CCD moves across the page of an image or text you're scanning, line-by-line, and converts the light levels from each pixel into digital data.

Generally, the quality of the CCD determines the quality of your scanned image. Manufacturers measure CCD quality in terms of how many pixels per inch (ppi), dots per inch (dpi), or samples per inch (spi). These measurements, often used interchangeably, refer to how much data the CCD can record. For example, a 300-ppi scanner can transmit 300 color samples, or data from 300 different pixels, as it travels across each line of a page.

Other Key Scanner Components

Looking briefly at the physical make-up of your scanner can give insight as to how the device actually works. Although there are specialized types of scanners for reading film and transparencies, most of the scanners you find in homes and offices today are of the *flatbed* variety, like the one shown in Figure 2-5.

Flatbed scanners come with a variety of options, but all must contain the following essential components:

Sensor   Light-sensitive photocells attached to a moving carriage device that take color samples of the image. As discussed earlier in "The Difference Between Pixels, Dots, and Samples" sidebar, this component is called a CCD.

Internal processing components   Electronic devices inside your scanner translate what the scanner's sensors "see" into digital data your computer can interpret.

FIGURE 2-5   A flatbed scanner

Light source   Scanning requires a lot of light. Every scanner contains a light source that illuminates the scanned object to help the sensor do its job.

Glass surface   Images and objects to be scanned rest on the glass surface of the scanner, which also serves as a protective barrier between the image and the sensor device.

Power cable connector   Every scanner needs an electrical power source and a cable to provide a connection to the source.

Computer cable connector   Your scanner needs a cable to connect it to your computer so the scanner can transfer the image data that has been recorded during each scanning operation.

Lid   A scanner lid protects the photosensitive elements of your scanner, and maximizes the efficiency of your light source.

In addition to the foregoing parts, your scanner might have one or more of the following bells and whistles:

Slide or negative adapter   Some flatbed scanners come with devices that allow you to adapt the scanner so that it can be used to reproduce images on slides and negatives.

External buttons   A popular feature of some of today's newer scanners are external buttons that enable you to access scanner features without having to pull up and select options from menus on your computer screen.

Sheet-feed devices   These convenient additions allow you to scan more than one original at a time.

Chapter 3 explains how parts and options vary from scanner to scanner.

The Role of Resolution

The term *resolution* refers to how well your scanner captures detail. It's a sort of catchall term for image quality, and used imprecisely by manufacturers. Nevertheless, it's important to understand the factors that contribute to resolution ratings so that you can make accurate comparisons among different types of scanners. You must be especially careful to distinguish between *optical* and *interpolated* resolution specifications when making comparisons, as explained in the following section.

Factors that Determine Resolution

How well a scanner perceives and translates image detail depends on the number and quality of sensors packed into the scanner's CCD sensor device. The following CCD characteristics determine the scanner's resolution:

The quality of the optic sensors themselves   High-quality sensors will achieve a better result than low-quality, cheaply manufactured optics. This is analogous to the difference between a camera with a high-quality lens, and a cheap disposable.

The number of optic sensors   The more sensors packed onto the CCD devices, the greater the amount of information that can be obtained to reconstruct the detail of the image.

Samples per inch   As the CCD moves the image, it takes samples of the color data. The greater number of *samples per inch (spi)*, the more image data is available.

Vertical resolution   This is the distance the CCD moves between lines. The smaller this distance, the greater the amount of image data the scanner conveys.

Be Sure to Look at the Optical Resolution of a Scanner

Optical resolution is the most commonly used specification to compare the capabilities of different scanners. It refers to how many pixels, dots, or samples per inch the scanner's sensors can detect. Generally, the higher the resolution, the better the quality of the scanned image. Low-end scanners have a resolution of 300 ppi, while high-end scanners can detect as many as 4,000 ppi.

The 300-ppi variety will provide adequate resolution for computer-screen images, since most computer graphics cards can't handle much more detail than this. (You can learn more about how a graphics card functions in Chapter 4.) On the other hand, if your objective is a nice copy from a laser or color printer, the results from a scanner with a 300-ppi optical resolution are likely to disappoint you. A 400 to 600 resolution will probably give you the quality you're looking for in a printed copy.

TIP   *Optical resolution is most important when you need to print good-quality photos to include in publications such as books, magazines, newsletters, or scrapbooks. If you need good-quality printed photos, choose as high a resolution as you can afford. Economize with a lower optical resolution if you're producing images to be viewed on a computer monitor or in PowerPoint presentations.*

Avoid Comparisons of Interpolated Resolution

Suppose you have a choice of two scanners in your price range, one advertising a resolution of 300 dpi (or spi or ppi) and another boasting a 600-ppi resolution. The 600-ppi resolution is a better deal, right? Not necessarily.

A recent trend has been for manufacturers to market their scanners based on *interpolated,* or software-enhanced, resolution. Based on some technical guesswork, interpolation uses a mathematical algorithm to add more pixels to the ones the scanner has sampled with its sensors. The result is an image with more pixels or dots per inch, but not necessarily more accuracy as to detail.

Interpolated resolution produces good results for images on the Web, but is less satisfactory for scanning photographs for archiving or publication. Generally, it is not a good option if you need to scan negatives, since negatives require a resolution capability of at least 1,200 ppi.

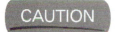 *When comparing the resolution of various scanners in your price range, make sure you're comparing apples to apples. Do not compare the optical resolution of one model to the interpolated resolution specifications of another.*

Testing the Tonal Sensitivity

Not all 30-bit scanners are created equal. A scanner might be able to detect a large number of colors, but over a relatively narrow range. Also, bit depth doesn't tell you how well scanners distinguish among similar shades. This is called *tonal sensitivity*, and is not disclosed by manufacturers. Generally, high-end, more expensive scanners exhibit greater tonal sensitivity.

 *You can evaluate the tonal sensitivity of different scanners by comparing the scanning results using the same original. Skin tones are particularly useful for comparing tonal sensitivity between scanner models. Certain models of scanners often cast a slight greenish tinge to skin tones, which can significantly alter the appearance of your subject.*

How to ... Read the Manufacturer's Resolution Rating

When you check the optical resolution of a particular scanner, you find it expressed in two numbers. For example, a scanner might have a 300×600 ppi resolution, or a 400×800 ppi capability. The first number refers to the number of pixels that can be sampled horizontally, and the second number specifies the vertical sampling.

The number of samples for the vertical sampling is greater, but because of the blurring effect that occurs as the scanner moves vertically from line to line, not all of the sampled data is useful for reconstructing the image. For this reason, when you are shopping for a scanner, it is most useful to compare scanners based on the their horizontal resolution, or the lower of the two numbers.

Coordinating Your Scanner with Your Printer and Monitor

An issue that causes constant confusion is that of coordinating the capabilities of your scanner with those of your printer and monitor to get the best final image. Although your scanner might have the capability to detect large amounts of color data, your printer might not have the capability to print it, and your monitor likely cannot display all of it.

Measuring the Monitor's Resolution

Computer monitors have resolution specifications all their own, usually provided to you by the manufacturer in horizontal and vertical pixels. A common monitor resolution is 800×600 pixels, or 800 pixels horizontally and 600 pixels vertically. Another common monitor resolution is 1024×768.

The higher the resolution setting on your computer, the more detail you can display from a scanned image on your computer screen. In contrast, lower resolutions do not make full use of all the image data your scanner might have captured.

The Effect of Changing the Monitor and Scanner Resolution Settings

Increasing the resolution setting on your monitor makes images, such as the icons on your screen, appear smaller because the pixels display closer together. The overall image at a higher resolution level is more detailed, and appears seamless. Figures 2-6 and 2-7 show images displayed at monitor resolution settings of 1024×768 and 640×480, respectively.

 *Higher resolutions—1024×768 or greater—usually work better on a larger monitor. If you currently have a 17-inch monitor, you might want to invest in a 19- or 21-inch one if you plan on doing a lot of graphics work.*

The effect of increasing or decreasing the resolution settings on your scanner also has a marked effect on what you see on your screen. For example, suppose you create two different scans of the same original image. You scanned the first using a resolution of 600 ppi, and the second using 100 ppi, as shown in Figures 2-8 and 2-9. When viewed, the 600-ppi scanned image appears physically larger than its 100-ppi counterpart. This is due to the fact that while the original image was the same, the amount of pixel information scanned and displayed has increased. So, your monitor simply has *more* pixels to display.

FIGURE 2-6   An image displayed on a monitor set at a resolution of 1024×768 appears smaller.

FIGURE 2-7   An image displayed on a monitor set at a resolution of 640×480 appears larger.

FIGURE 2-8   An image scanned at 100 ppi

FIGURE 2-9   An image scanned at 600 ppi

Most scanners today have multiple resolution settings for scanning different media such as text or photos. Check the instructions for your scanner to adjust the scan settings.

2

How to Change the Resolution Settings on Your Monitor

You can actually easily change the resolution settings on your monitor using the Windows Display Properties dialog box. To adjust the resolution of your monitor follow these steps:

1. From the Windows Start menu, go to Settings and then Control Panel. The Control Panel window appears on your desktop.

2. Double-click the Display icon to open it. The dialog box shown in Figure 2-10 appears.

3. Click the Settings tab to display the options shown in Figure 2-11, which allow you to set the color depth and monitor resolution higher or lower.

4. Be sure to click OK after you've adjusted the settings. A dialog box prompts you to view the new resolution settings prior to confirming them.

FIGURE 2-10   Select the Display icon from the Control Panel window.

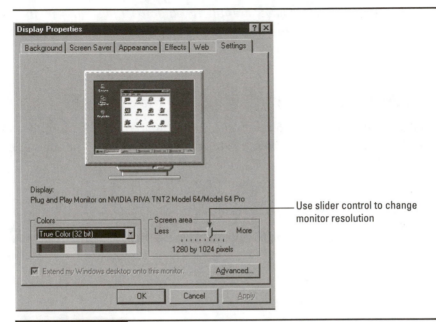

Use slider control to change
monitor resolution

FIGURE 2-11   Use the slider control in the dialog box to adjust monitor resolution.

Matching Scanner and Printer Specifications

Your first impulse might be to match the resolution specifications of your printer and scanner. After all, if your scanner captures 600 ppi, wouldn't it seem that a 600-dpi printer should be able to do a great job with it? This isn't necessarily the case.

Generally, aim to scan an image at a higher resolution than your output device. For example, if you have a 600-dpi printer, scanning at 800 ppi is probably your best bet. Scanning at 1,200 ppi might also be a good tactic. Extra pixels capture added detail, enabling you to apply effects with more precision, and maximizing printer output quality; however, if your image is destined for a specific purpose, such as offset printing or Web use, be sure to reduce the resolution to the necessary size as a final step.

Downsides of scanning at higher resolutions are that the scan takes longer to complete, and creates larger image files that take up more space on your hard drive. More importantly, scanning at too high a resolution can cause your printer software to crash. Since there is not a one-to-one ratio between your scanner's ppi setting and the printer's dpi setting, the printer does not place dots on the page in the same ratios and proportions as the scanner records them. The printer takes the dpi data from your scanner, and employs an entirely different mathematical algorithm to decide how densely to place the dots on the paper to arrive at its own dpi. Extremely high image-scanning relative to printer capability can put a real burden on the software that was never designed to handle such a disproportionate conversion.

Different Originals Require Different Scan Techniques

Not all originals are created equal when it comes to scanning. The type of original media you're scanning is a big factor in determining the optimum resolution settings for your scanner.

Original scanned images and media fall into five basic categories, each of which calls for a distinct scanning technique:

Color photos   Reproducing color photos presents the special challenge of capturing color accurately, and without a red, green, or blue cast. This process, called calibration, is covered in detail in Chapter 6. Color scans require a bit depth of 24 or greater.

Grayscale   These images are black-and-white representations, and do not require as high a bit depth as color scans. Loss of detail from scans that are too light or too dark is a common problem encountered when working with grayscale. Proper calibration, as discussed in Chapter 6, is a must when working with these images.

Line art   Line art is images with solid edges, usually line drawings. Examples of line art include logos, pencil drawings, black-and-white clip art, and other simple graphics. Since line art is in only two colors (black and white), the main focus when scanning line art is reproducing the edges or lines of the image to be as faithful as possible to the original. Resolution requirements for line art are generally higher than for color and grayscale media.

Transparency (including film)   A *transparency* is an image that exists on film. When you scan a transparency, light is captured as it passes through the film. With other types of media, light is reflected off the surface of the image. As with grayscale images, scanners must be carefully calibrated to avoid reproductions that are too light or too dark. Color balance is also an issue, since transparencies are prone to greenish and yellowish casts. You can learn more about scanning film and transparencies in Chapter 12.

Text   Scanning text documents is similar to scanning line art, and requires high-resolution capability to preserve the sharpness and readability of the original. You also need to install special optical character recognition (OCR) software. Text scanning is discussed in Chapter 13.

Software to Optimize Your Scan

Your scanner and other hardware devices are only half the equation in creating a good scan. The scanner software that directs and calibrates your scanner, and the image-editing program tools you apply after scanning, also control the finished scanning product.

Types of Scanner Software

Most scanners come with several different types of software. Generally, the better the quality of your scanner, the better the software that comes along with it. The following software is usually bundled with a new scanner:

Drivers   This is the basic software required to run your scanner device, enabling it to communicate with your computer. You don't need to do any comparison shopping on this particular software, other than checking that the scanner you want to purchase is compatible with your computer's operating system software (for example, whatever version of Windows you're using.)

Scanner program   This is the program that interfaces with your scanner driver, enabling you to view and store the recorded information, or in some cases, apply editing changes to the newly-scanned image before committing to saving the resulting scan. Not all scanner programs are created equal. Compare them on the basis of the tools they provide, such as cutting, cropping, brightness, contrast, and sharpening. It is particularly useful if your scanner provides you a sophisticated color adjustment tool called a *histogram*, which is discussed in Chapter 10.

Imaging or photo-editing software   Today most scanners come with image-editing software that not only allows you to correct flaws in scanned images, but also to do many fun and creative projects. Image-editing software enables you to do things after the scan such as combining images from different photos into one; adding special effects; applying filters and colorizing techniques; adding frames, borders, and props to photos; and creating greeting cards and novelty items.

Optical character recognition (OCR) software   This is a task-specific type of software that gives your scanner the ability to read documents and text, and create a text file on your computer.

This book covers steps specific to the software programs most commonly bundled with today's scanners; however, you can do most projects covered using a wide variety of image-editing or OCR programs on the market. It's simply a matter of checking the specific instructions for your particular software product, and referring to the figures and illustrations.

The Important Role of Software During a Scan

A basic principle of good scanning technique is that you perform most of your image adjustments and correction chores during the scanning process. Image-editing software allows you to correct and enhance photos for which the original was defective, but you might have to spend a lot of time correcting something your scanner software would have avoided in the first place.

Most scanner software allows you to efficiently perform the following tasks during the scanning process:

Cutting and cropping   You can specify which portions of a photo you want to appear in the finished scan. For example, you can eliminate a stray passerby from the background, or crop a headshot of your subject.

Controlling resolution   Most scanners have several settings to vary the ppi (or dpi) of your scan. You might, for example, want to scan and save a photo to be sent over the Internet at a lower resolution than one you plan to publish in a magazine. (Scanning at higher resolutions creates much larger, more cumbersome files than images scanned at lower resolutions.)

Color correction   Color-correction tools, previously the exclusive domain of image-editing software, are now included with many scanners to allow you to correct for various factors as you scan.

Become familiar with the image-correction tools your scanner offers. You save time and end up with a better-quality scanned image by performing as many image-editing and color-correction tasks as possible during the scan.

Chapter 3

Selecting the Right Scanner

How To...

- Decide which scanner features you'll actually use

- Find a scanner that matches your PC interface

- Match the resolution of your scanner to your printer and monitor capabilities

- Shop on line for a good deal on a scanner

- Test a scanner before you buy it

Scanners can be like those exercise bikes with all the flashing lights monitoring your vital signs. You can spend a lot of money on high-end features, with every intention of putting them to good use, but their value lies in whether you actually give them a good workout, and how often. The key to selecting a scanner is identifying the features you actually need for the types of projects you plan to do. You want to purchase the greatest level and range of capability for the features you use, and avoid paying for those you don't. For example, if you don't plan on scanning transparencies, you might be better off skipping that capability and opting to spend more for a another feature, such as push-button email or better editing software.

A Basic Shopping List of Scanner Features

Shopping for a scanner is a lot easier once you figure out what types of projects you plan on doing, and what features you need to accomplish them.

 *A basic, good-quality scanning device might be the best use of your budget, particularly if your printer and graphics adapter card can't take full advantage of the more sophisticated features available on some scanners.*

Here's a preliminary shopping list of features to commit to memory before setting foot in an office-equipment store or logging on to an online shopping site:

Interface   The hardware interface of a scanner determines how it connects to your computer—what type of port and cable your scanner must have. Most computers have parallel ports and USB ports. Others might be configured for SCSI interfaces or the new FireWire. The next section, "Pick the Right Port Connection," tells you what all of these options are and how to figure out which one you need for your computer.

3

Resolution   Resolution is the capacity of a scanner to capture image detail. You need dramatically different resolution capabilities, depending on the end product you're planning to produce. This chapter tells you which resolution is required for which types of projects. (Chapter 2 covers the topic of resolution in depth.)

Bit depth   This measurement tells you how well the scanner is able to discern between subtly different shades. It's covered in the "Deciding on the Right Bit Depth" section.

Image sensors   The more sophisticated a scanner's sensor is, the higher the overall image quality will be—and the more expensive the scanner. While a CIS sensor is less expensive, a CCD type is worth the additional cost. The "What to Consider When You Compare Sensors" section tells you why.

External buttons   External buttons are the latest user convenience. Previously, all scanners required that you operate them by opening your scanner's software and executing commands through your mouse and keyboard. Now, a new generation of scanners, such as the Visioneer One Touch series, allows you to initiate and even email a scan simply by pressing buttons on the scanner itself. You never have to open and search for a command in a scanner application. This is a clear upgrade.

Scanner speed   It's hard to gauge the speed of a scanner, and there are few standard measurements available. If speed is important to you, by all means avoid purchasing a three-pass scanner. This type of scanner actually scans an image three times—one pass for each of the colors magenta, cyan, and yellow. Opt for a one-pass scanner if you want to minimize your minutes per scan.

Bundled software   Comparison-shop the software that comes with a scanner. In addition to the basic drivers that make the scanner work with your computer, scanners might come bundled with software that allows you to make corrections during a scan, image-editing software for after the scan, and optical character recognition (OCR) software that allows you to scan text and edit it using a word-processing program such as Microsoft Word or WordPerfect. Chapter 2 tells you about the functions of all the different software that can come with a scanner.

TIP   *You might also want to do a bit of comparison-shopping to see which versions of a particular software are bundled. Several scanners might offer the same bundled software, but some might offer later versions than others.*

Film adapters   Film and transparency adapters that allow you to scan negatives. You need special hardware for this because light must shine through the transparency image to be captured. The "Adding a Film Adapter" section gives you some tips on how to select one of these devices.

Automatic sheet-feed device   This handy gadget allows you to feed multiple sheets to your scanner the way you would a printer or copier. Some high-end scanners can accept 100 sheets or more at a time, scanning images consecutively. This is particularly useful for scanning long documents using OCR software.

If you opt for a sheet-feed device, it's crucial to get as much information as is available about the speed of the scanner that comes with this feature. Testing a model at your local office-equipment store might be the best way to speed-test a scanner.

Pick the Right Port Connection

Your PC and scanner each come equipped with connector sockets referred to as ports. These ports enable hardware peripherals such as your scanner, printer, mouse, and keyboard to communicate with your computer via input/output cards. Typically, a cable transfers the data between the ports on each of these devices.

Depending on the age and price of your PC, it might be equipped with any of four different types of ports: parallel, USB, SCSI, and possibly even FireWire. You want to select a scanner that gives you the fastest, most reliable connection, with the least hassle to install. Figure 3-1 shows an illustration of the rear view of a typical PC, having both parallel and USB connections.

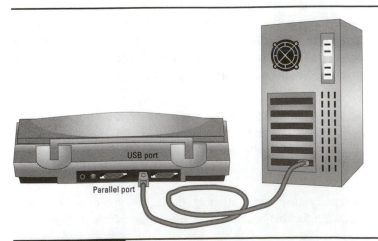

FIGURE 3-1   Most scanners offer both USB and parallel port connections.

The Common Contenders: Parallel and USB Connections

Most PCs and scanners today have two types of ports: parallel and USB. Your scanner requires a compatible cable to connect to either of them. Scanners usually include one or both of the parallel or USB port cables, but sometimes you have to purchase a cable separately at an added cost of anywhere from $12 to $30.

> **TIP** *When comparing two closely priced scanners, make sure they both include a cable, and that it is compatible with your PC's interface.*

A parallel port is actually a printer port. Most PCs have a single parallel port; a few PCs boast a second one. Herein lies the downside of a parallel port: it's the port you usually use to connect your printer. This might mean that if you have only one parallel port, every time you want to use your scanner you need to disconnect your printer and restart the computer. Fortunately, most recent parallel port scanners allow you to connect your printer to your scanner, which is then directly connected to your PC. This way, you can use them both at the same time.

On the other hand, if you have a USB connection, you don't have to keep shutting down your computer to disconnect and reconnect your printer. You might even plug in and unplug the USB device without having to restart your computer.

> **TIP** *Many scanners, such as those manufactured by Visioneer, include both a parallel and a USB cable.*

Most newer computers and scanners have USB ports, and the scanners come with USB cables. A new, faster USB cable—USB 2.0—has recently made its market debut. This new generation of USB cable offers faster data transfer speeds, and connects to existing USB ports. Scanner manufacturers currently including USB cables are expected to switch to this second-generation cabling.

> **TIP** *All things being equal, opt for USB 2.0 cabling over standard USB if it's available for your scanner.*

SCSI Connections

High-end scanners might offer another type of connection called a SCSI, which stands for Small Computer System Interface. SCSI connections offer faster and more reliable data transfer. Usually only high-end high-resolution professional-caliber scanners offer SCSI connections (for example, the Kodak Professional RFS 3600).

With a SCSI interface, you can connect several peripheral devices using only one PC port and "host adapter" device, as shown in Figure 3-2. You don't need to purchase a separate hub to connect multiple devices, as you do with a USB port. The SCSI components are carefully designed so performance is not compromised for any of the devices in the "daisy chain."

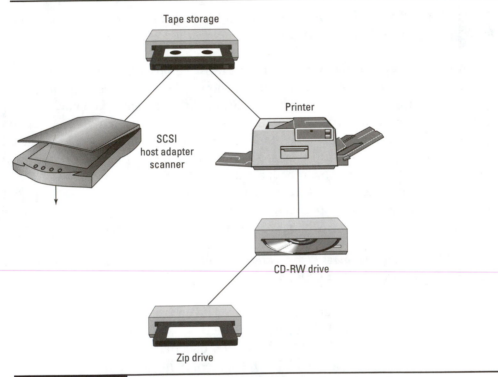

FIGURE 3-2   SCSI interfaces allow devices to be connected to each other using one PC port.

The Furor over FireWire

FireWire is a brand of connection interface and cabling introduced by Apple Computers to compete with the very popular USB ports and cables—and compete it does. There is no question that FireWire technology dramatically increases transmission speeds—as much as 400 million bits per second.

As far as scanners go, FireWire might be overkill. It's really designed for devices that need fast, real-time data transmission, such as video from video cameras. You don't need anything approaching this speed for a scanner, mouse, or joystick, all of which are considered low-speed peripherals.

While you might want to spring for a FireWire port (also known as an IEEE 1394 port) on a new PC so you can accommodate high-speed data transfer from devices that require it, paying extra for a scanner with this type of connection is probably not a good idea. Scanners simply do not require high-speed data transfer.

Be Realistic about the Kind of Resolution You Need

Resolution is the main reason one scanner costs more than another. The marketplace views resolution as the ultimate determining factor of a scanner's quality.

While you should note more of a scanner's resolution statistics when you go shopping, resolution capability is indeed a good a place to start.

Chapter 2 tells you all about the nuances of resolution. This section provides you with just enough information to do some informed comparison-shopping.

As you might recall from Chapter 2, a scanner's resolution is usually measured and disclosed on the outside of the box in terms of dpi, or dots per inch. (Pixels per inch and samples per inch are also valid measurements, which for the moment, we'll equate with dpi.)

Scanners range in resolution capability from 100 to 4,000 dpi. A resolution capability for 400×600 is pretty good for most hobbyists and general business purposes. Professional scanners usually have a resolution of about 1,200 to 2,400 dpi. This is the resolution you'll require if you're doing a lot of work with negatives or other transparencies.

What the Resolution Numbers Mean in a Scanner Description

Generally, you'll see resolution expressed as two numbers, for example, 800×600 or 1024×768. The first number reflects the number of dots per horizontal inch, and the second number reflects the vertical measurement. It's that second number you want to look at because it's a more valid measurement of the ppi you're actually capturing.

The number for vertical resolution is lower than for horizontal resolution because the scanning devices must travel across each line and than down to the next line. The more sophisticated the sensor device, the smaller the distance between lines.

You Can Skip the Interpolated Resolution Specs

As you learned in Chapter 2, manufacturers provide information about both optical resolution and interpolated resolution. You want to be sure, as you comparison-shop, to consistently look for the optical resolution. Optical resolution, in a nutshell, tells you how much data the scanner's sensors are actually capturing and recording. Interpolated resolution is a software-enhanced version of your image, where the scanner's software adds extra pixels to the ones its sensor has captured. The added pixels are a product of guesswork, and don't add more detail to the image.

Pay Only for the Resolution You Really Need

How much resolution is enough? The answer depends on what you're going to be doing with your scanner. If you're going to being doing a lot of work with negatives and graphic layouts for magazines, you're going to need relatively high-resolution capabilities.

If you're strictly an email photo buff, your resolution requirements are quite low. In fact, high resolution can be disadvantageous on the Web. Increased resolution increases the size of the files that must travel over the Internet. This can slow the transfer considerably.

> **TIP** *Make sure to consider the capability of your output devices—the printer and monitor—as you consider paying more for higher resolution.*

Another downside to higher-resolution scanners is that they cost more. The added expense might or might not be worthwhile. Consider, for example, the capabilities of your printer. Take into account that you want to scan at a somewhat higher resolution than your printer can actually print—more information is better—but you don't want to go for overkill. Scanning at too high a resolution can cause your printer to behave oddly. When you scan at dramatically different resolutions, you can tax the conversion feature of your printer's software. Scanning at 2,400 dpi on a 600-dpi printer isn't going to give you a better final product than scanning at 800 to 1,200 dpi. The added resolution is simply a waste of money.

 *Scanning at higher-than-necessary resolutions wastes time and storage space. The higher the resolution, the more pixels your scanner must read and store. The resulting image file also takes up extra space on your computer and can take ages to email.*

Match the Resolution to What You Actually Do

When shopping for a scanner with the adequate resolution capabilities for your particular needs, the goal is to pay for what you need—and then some. It's always a good idea to store a little more information than can be displayed on your output device, without going overboard and creating huge files that don't noticeably improve appearance.

To assist you on your shopping trip, the following table summarizes the resolution requirements for the various uses you might want your scanner for:

Your Use	Minimum dpi	Recommended dpi
Image files destined for the Web	72	96
Printing photos	300	600
Enlarging photos	600	1,200
Line art	300	600
Slides and negatives	1,200	2,400
Text (OCR software)	150	300

How Resolution and Hard-Drive Space Affect Each Other

Storing your scanned images can require a lot of hard-drive space. When you scan photos, you create image files on your hard disk drive. The requirements of the image file increase with the size of the photo or the amount of resolution. For example, if you scan a 5×7-inch photo with a 600×1200 scanner, you might need as much as 72 megabytes of free disk space. If your storage space is limited, you might want to reconsider paying for a scanner that offers you the capability to scan at very high resolutions. Your output devices might not display all of the added resolution, and your hard drive simply might not have the room to store it.

Did you know?

Why Different Images Require Different dpi

Knowing a little bit about what different image types are and why they require different resolutions can help you shop for the scanner capabilities you need—and keep you from being sold on the ones you don't need.

Web images   Images you email are stored as JPEG or GIF files and generally require a lower resolution. (You can learn more about different file types in Chapter 8.) The capabilities of the monitor (usually a range of 800×600 to 1024×768) mean that you can't see a difference on screen by using the higher resolution. Scanning at a lower resolution keeps image files small so they travel across the Web quickly. If the recipient plans on printing images, however, you should patiently scan at a higher resolution.

Standard-size color pictures   Photos you plan to reproduce at the size you've scanned require about 300–600 ppi. Added detail at higher resolutions is usually not apparent to the naked eye.

Black-and-white photos   These can be scanned at a slightly lower resolution than color photos with good results.

Enlarged and edited photos   If you're going to enlarge photos, you want to try to scan them at about twice the normal resolution (600×1200) to avoid "pixel spread," which makes the photo look grainy. This effect results when the same number of pixels per inch needs to be spread over a larger area, increasing the amount of space between pixels. The solution is to add more pixels per inch with higher resolution.

Line art   Line art is a nonphotographic image. Drawings and blueprints are examples. Usually line art is black and white, but it can also be reproduced from a color original. Here you want a relatively high resolution, not to capture color but to ensure the sharpness of the lines and detail created with the lines.

Slides and negatives   These types of media capture far more color data than ordinary paper, and you need high-resolution capability to capture it— at least 1,200 dpi.

Text   Capturing text requires a lot of image detail. Your optical character recognition software has to compare the image of each character it reads with the ones stored in its template. Increasing the resolution is like giving your scanner reading glasses.

Deciding on the Right Bit Depth

A scanner's resolution determines how many dots per inch the scanner can capture. In contrast, bit depth determines the richness of the information contained in each pixel or dot.

When a scanner captures an image, it stores the information as colored dots called *pixels*. Each pixel stores data in information units called bits. The quality of an image depends on how many bits are stored in each pixel.

The minimum bit depth you find on low-end scanners is eight bits, but there are few of these on the market anymore. An 8-bit scanner is primitive by today's standards. It barely produces the colors necessary to recognize the image, and can give you a lot of muddy tones.

The minimum you usually see these days is 24-bit depth, and scanners in the 30- to 42-bit range are neither uncommon nor exorbitantly expensive. Your printer might not, however, be able to reproduce images at this bit depth. Nevertheless, it's a good investment to opt for the highest bit depth your budget allows since printers are constantly improving. You might not notice the increased bit depth initially, but there is no downside to scanning at 30- to 42-bit depth other than increased file size.

What to Consider When You Compare Sensors

The image sensor is the most important component of your scanner—and the most important factor in determining its price. There are two main types: the charge-coupled device (CCD) and the contact image sensor (CIS).

Both types of sensors will do the job for you, and the type is not as important as the resolution and bit depth specifications; however, the CCD is the more advanced device, and what you find in most high-end scanners.

Usually, manufacturers don't provide specifications on image sensors other than which type you're purchasing. Occasionally, however, a manufacturer will make the *optical density* ratings for the particular scanner available. This rating tells you how sensitive a scanner is to the brightness values of an image.

Most scanners on the market, as of the writing of this book, have OD, or *optical density*, ratings in a range of 2.8 to 4.0, with the higher values being better. The 3.0 range is fine for most scanning purposes, but if you scan film or negatives you should look for an OD rating of at least 3.2.

 *If you scan negatives only occasionally, you might be better off opting for a service, rather than spending a lot of money on a negative adapter that you could budget for features you use more often. KodakPhotoCD service inexpensively produces your vacation and holiday negatives on a high-resolution CD.*

Research and Shop for a Scanner on Line

In this day and age, it's almost unthinkable that someone would invest in computer peripherals without doing at least some preliminary research on the Web. Even if you're short on time and anxious to get your scanner, it takes only a few minutes to get a comprehensive and current picture of what's on the market and at what price.

Survey the Market with CNET

A good place to start your scanner search is the CNET website, located at http://computers.cnet.com/hardware. Click on the Scanners link to display a page like the one shown in Figure 3-3, which provides you with the following information:

Scanner reviews   CNET conducts research and provides you with reviews of what it deems to be the top five moderately priced scanners on the market. The reviews provide you with "the good, the bad, and the bottom line." The site also provides a separate link to reviews of high-end scanners.

Product comparisons   The CNET site enables you to create your own comparison chart, selecting up to five different scanners in which you're interested to compare their features.

Rebates   The site provides information about rebates currently being offered by scanner manufacturers.

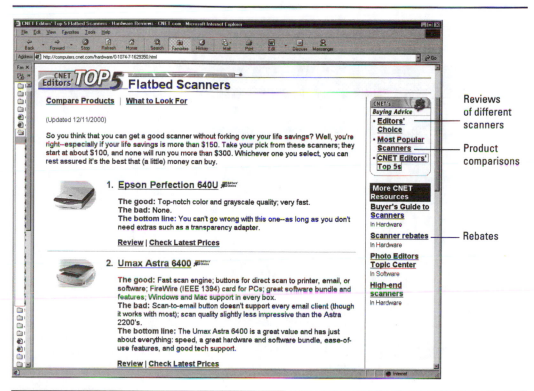

FIGURE 3-3   The CNET website is a good place to start your scanner search.

Compare Prices and Features on ZDNet

The ZDNet website, located at www.zdnet.com, allows you to run a quick and fairly exhaustive search for just the right scanner. This site, shown in Figure 3-4, offers the following search criteria for its comprehensive database of scanners:

Price range   You can select from a drop-down menu or price categories ranging from less than $140 to more than $4,500.

Type   You can search for flat-bed, sheet-fed, or film scanners.

Interface   Another drop-down menu lets you specify whether you want a parallel port, USB, SCSI, FireWire, or other type of interface.

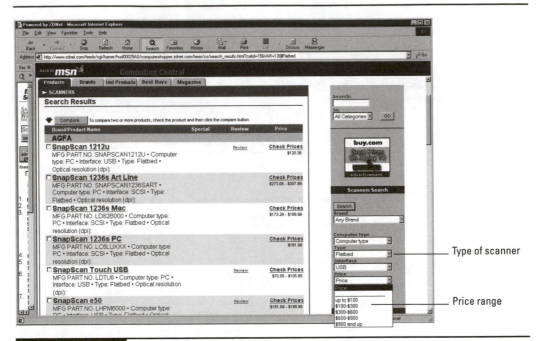

FIGURE 3-4   The ZDNet website allows you to search for a scanner meeting your criteria.

After you've selected your search criteria from the drop-down menus, the ZDNet site compiles a list of scanners meeting your criteria.

Get Details from the Scanner Manufacturer Sites

Scanner manufacturers maintain their own websites to promote their products. Once you've surveyed the market and decided on a particular scanner in your price range, it's a good idea to visit the manufacturer's site for precise specifications and more comprehensive information about scanner features. The Hewlett-Packard website, located at www.image-acquire.com, is shown in Figure 3-5. The Visioneer site, at www.visioneer.com, is shown in Figure 3-6.

Bargains at Overstock.com

Looking for a bargain on a scanner? Who isn't? The Overstock.com website, located at www.overstock.com, is a bargain hunter's dream.

Link to
technical
support

FIGURE 3-5   The Hewlett-Packard website

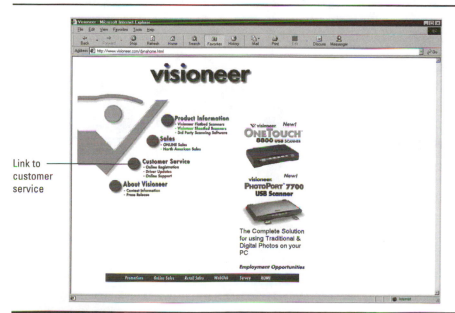

Link to
customer
service

FIGURE 3-6   The Visioneer website

3

For example, as of the writing of this book, I found a scanner with 600×1200 dpi optical resolution and a 30-bit depth for only $50.

The Overstock.com site, shown in Figure 3-7, offers good service as well. You have access to customer support, both by telephone and email. There's also a fairly liberal return policy.

FIGURE 3-7 The Overstock.com website is for bargain hunters.

Precaution: Check the Service Record of the Online Vendor

When shopping on line, you can find out about the service and privacy reputation of the online vendor. The Gomez.com website, at www.gomez.com, shown in Figure 3-8, provides a consumer rating service for online vendors. The supplier sites are evaluated based on customer support and service, reliability, and adherence to privacy standards for your credit-card information.

FIGURE 3-8   Gomez rates online computer vendors for consumers.

Gomez also certifies online vendors that meet the minimum performance standards it has set, as shown in Figure 3-8.

Buying a Scanner in Person

After you've exhausted the Internet resources in your scanner search, you're faced with the decision of whether go one step further and order your scanner with a click of your mouse. It's certainly convenient to do so, but actually visiting an office equipment store and making your purchase in person offers several advantages:

Savings on shipping costs   Most vendors charge separately for shipping, so you have to factor in the added cost when comparison-shopping. Overnight or next-day freight can be downright pricey—as much as $30.00.

Ease of testing   This is a definite advantage, and you should be prepared to avail yourself of it by bringing a few photos.

Immediate delivery   No waiting for the delivery. You can drive off with your new purchase in your trunk.

Returns are easier   Most people are more comfortable taking a defective product back to the store for immediate credit rather than shipping it back and waiting for credit.

Narrowing Down the Choices

This chapter helped you assess your scanning needs and identify the features in a scanner that might help you accomplish them. You also learned which scanner information and specifications to compare, and some websites that can save you research time in doing so. You even learned how to test a sample scanner in the store, and where to go on the Web to look for a bargain if you choose to order one on line. The next chapter helps you become familiar with the operation of your scanner once you've purchased it.

How to ...

Test a Scanner

Many of the larger office equipment and supply stores have scanners on their sales floor that they invite you to test before making a purchase. Usually, the manufacturer provides a test shot for you to scan, but I suggest you bring your own photo.

Select a test shot with people in it. Skin tones are hardest to replicate accurately. Scanning skin tones allows you to see the relative color depth capacities of different scanners, since a hint of green or a yellow tinge on a person's face is pretty noticeable.

You should also look at the light and dark areas of the picture. Do these areas retain their detail, or do they appear to be a single shade? Generally, the higher the color depth, the more detail you retain in the light and dark areas of the photo.

Scanner speed is another issue. Speed specifications usually aren't provided by the manufacturer. Store testing allows you the opportunity to pit two scanners on your short list in an actual race to see which offers you a faster scan.

Did you know?

Some Scanners Have Memory Card Readers for Digital Camera Photos

Have you ever thought, "Wouldn't it be great if I had a single way to get my scanned and digital camera photos into the computer?" One leading manufacturer, Visioneer, has recently introduced the first scanner with built-in CompactFlash and SmartMedia high-speed memory card readers. (A memory card stores photos from a digital camera or other device and can store a lot more high-resolution photos than an ordinary floppy disk). The new Visioneer PhotoPort 7700 USB scanner transfers images up to 40 times faster than serial

Continued on next page

Did you know?

Some Scanners Have Memory Card Readers for Digital Camera Photos

cameras equipped for image transfer, and 30 percent faster than dedicated memory card readers. The scanner automatically transfers the images from the memory card inserted into one of the built-in readers.

This scanner, now a personal favorite of mine, allows you to store, load, email, fax, and upload all of your digital images using its five "OneTouch" buttons. Even better, the software included with the scanner automatically creates a thumbnail of each image that allows you to instantly organize, locate, and use all of your photos in other applications. The scanner offers a 600×1200 dpi optical resolution, and 42-bit color.

Surprisingly, the Visioneer PhotoPort 7700 USB, shown in Figure 3-9, retails at about $149 as of the writing of this book, making it one of the best deals on the market. This price is particularly attractive, considering the scanner comes with some terrific bundled software: MGI PhotoSuite III SE and TextBridge Pro 9.0 (enabling you to scan and edit text documents as discussed in Chapter 3).

FIGURE 3-9   The new Visioneer PhotoPort 7700 USB scanner has high-speed memory card readers.

Chapter 4

Install Your Scanner and Inventory Your Hardware

How To...

■ Evaluate and update your hardware for scanning projects

■ Decide what kind of printer you need

■ Install your scanner

■ Get help and troubleshoot the installation process

Hardware Requirements for Successful Scanning

Scanning projects are amazingly fun and easy for *you*, but play havoc on your hardware. This is mostly because image files can be big—much larger than text or database files. This makes the size and speed of your PC components more noticeable when you're doing image-editing than for other tasks.

Speed and Power

Little metal slivers called *chips* are the driving force in the computer industry—and in your computer. Chips are teeny, "microminiaturized" electronic circuits, or pathways, that are specially designed for use inside PCs and other electronic products such as microwave ovens.

Chips contain millions of tiny transistors used for transmitting information. The more transistors on a chip, the greater its information-processing and storage capabilities. The two most important chips in your computer, for determining its speed and power, are the microprocessor and the memory chips, called RAM, which are discussed later in the "RAM" section.

The Microprocessor

The computer's microprocessor is the computer's main memory chip. It's also sometimes called a *CPU*, which is short for *central processing unit*. It's the brain of your computer.

The speed of a microprocessor has traditionally been measured in megahertz, or MHz, which are equivalent to 100 cycles per second. Think of it as the heartbeat of your computer—the faster the pulse, the faster the performance. The MHz value measures the rate at which a microprocessor "thinks," or performs calculations. For example, a Pentium III computer might have an 866 or 933 MHz processor. The 933 MHz processor is obviously faster, but you probably wouldn't notice the additional speed. You would certainly notice, however, the difference between a 233 and a 933 MHz computer.

Recently, Pentium 4 processors have been introduced, with speeds that are measured in gigahertz, or GHz, which are a billion cycles per second.

How to Find Your Processor Speed

You can easily determine the speed of your processor, but you need to be quick about it. Most PCs literally flash their processing speed for a few seconds as they're booting up. For example, you might see "Pentium III 750 MHz" fleetingly appear across the black screen, just before the familiar Windows desktop appears. This information only stays on your screen for a couple of seconds, so you really have be looking for it.

How Much Processing Speed Do You Need?

How fast is fast enough for your processor? The difference between an 866 or 933 processor is negligible. Mere fractions of seconds. Those fractions of seconds can add up over a number of tasks—but probably not enough to make a real difference to you.

On the other hand, you probably wouldn't even want to attempt image-editing with a processor of less than a Pentium processor with a 200 to 400 MHz capability. That, of course, is a bare and stingy minimum.

Generally, it's not economical to upgrade your microprocessor. If you find yourself in need of additional processing speed, it's probably time to start shopping for another computer.

RAM

RAM can be even more significant than your processor for determining the speed of your computer. RAM, which is a type of computer chip, is an acronym for random access memory. It's temporary memory that your computer uses in the course of processing and performing tasks. The more RAM your computer has, the more imaging and processing tasks it can perform simultaneously. Simultaneous performance of tasks, called *multitasking,* increases the speed at which you can complete a project.

These days, most scanner manufacturers recommend you have a minimum of 32 megabytes of RAM. (A megabyte is one million bytes of stored information.) Of course, more RAM is better. You might find a computer equipped with 32 megabytes of RAM annoyingly slow, and decide that $100 to $250 more to upgrade to anywhere from 64 to 256 RAM is well spent.

As with microprocessors, it's difficult to discern the difference from incremental increases in RAM—you need to increase it a lot to notice a significant difference in performance. For example, you might or might not be able to notice an impact by upgrading to 128 megabytes of RAM from 96. But that boost from 96 to 256 gives your computer a real shot of adrenalin.

How Much RAM Do You Currently Have?

Are you wondering how much RAM you currently have? It's easy to check. Just follow these steps:

1. Right-click the My Computer icon on your Windows desktop, and select Properties from the pop-up menu. The System Properties dialog box appears.

2. Click the Performance tab in the System Properties dialog box to display the amount of RAM installed on your computer as shown in Figure 4-1.

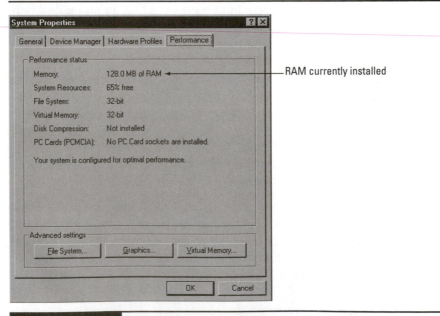

FIGURE 4-1   This computer currently has 128 megabytes of RAM installed. Plenty!

Installing Additional RAM

You can install additional RAM in your computer provided your computer has the necessary *expansion slots* to accommodate it. Expansion slots are places inside a computer that allow you to insert additional RAM chips or cards containing additional RAM chips.

If you're not sure if you have the expansion slots in your computer to upgrade the RAM, check the documentation that came with your computer. You can hire a professional to actually install the RAM, or consult a resource such as *How to Do Everything with Your PC* (Osborne/McGraw-Hill, 2000).

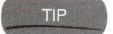 *You definitely will notice increased speed and performance from additional RAM. If your computer has the necessary expansion slots to upgrade your RAM, it's usually very cost effective to do so. Buy as much RAM as you can afford.*

Storage Space for Your Images

In addition to RAM, which is temporary memory, you computer also has permanent memory. This is the memory that saves information and projects after you've turned your computer off. It's referred to as *hard disk* or *permanent storage.* It includes your computer's hard drive (usually the C drive), your floppy disk, and CD-ROM drives.

How Much Hard Drive Space Do You Need?

Image files consume a lot of space. A single image file, scanned at high resolution, can take up to 100 megabytes of space. You'll find yourself very cramped if you have only one or two gigabytes of hard drive space. In fact, when you try to store images, you might get a message telling you that there is insufficient space on your designated drive.

Most computers today come with hard drives of 10 gigabytes or more. A driving force behind this is the industry recognition that users are doing things such as digital imaging that require a lot more space—both for the programs and the files.

How to Check the Available Space on Your Hard Drive

You can you tell in advance of beginning a scanning project how much space is available on your hard drive and whether you're going to run into a problem. Follow these steps to see exactly how much room you have to work with:

1. Double-click the My Computer icon on your Windows desktop. This displays a window listing all of your computer's available drives, similar to the one shown in Figure 4-2.

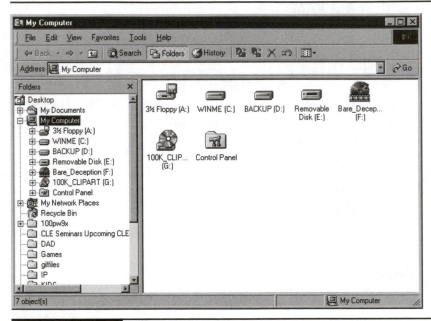

FIGURE 4-2   Your computer's drives

2. Right-click the icon for the C drive, and select Properties from the pop-up menu. A Properties dialog box, similar to the one shown in Figure 4-3, appears.

3. Click OK, Cancel, or the × button in the upper righthand corner of the dialog box to exit once you've finished viewing the hard drive space.

As a rule of thumb, I usually figure on about a megabyte for each image. Also, keep in mind that your scanner software and image-editing programs, themselves, take up a lot of hard drive space—as much as 40 or 50 megabytes apiece.

As with memory, more is better when it comes to hard drive space. Something in the 8 to 20 gigabyte range should be nice and roomy. Experts recommend that you plan to use 10 percent of the total capacity for temp files to be created when editing image files.

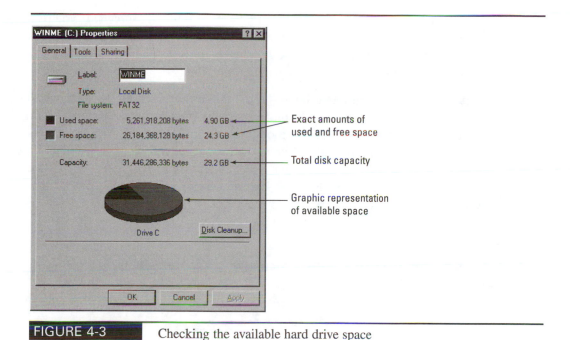

FIGURE 4-3   Checking the available hard drive space

The Limitations of Floppy Disks

If you have only a standard floppy disk drive to supplement the storage available on your computer, this probably isn't enough. A standard floppy disk holds 1.44 megabytes of information. A single high-resolution image can consume 2 megabytes, which is well beyond the capabilities of that floppy. Although most images at standard resolutions are less than 1 megabyte, you can't get more than one on a floppy even if you do compromise the quality of the image by decreasing the resolution. Floppy disks are a pretty inconvenient way to supplement the space available on a cramped hard drive.

Adding Disk Storage Space

If you have a small hard drive, it might be time to think about supplementing it with one of the following options:

Adding a larger hard drive   You can replace the existing hard drive on your computer with a larger one. It's a matter of backing up everything on your existing hard drive, and unscrewing and screwing in a few mounting screws. If you're comfortable doing this sort of thing, you can find a terrific tutorial on installing a new internal hard drive at the HardwareCentral website, www.hardwarecentral.com/hardwarecentral/tutorials/31/1/, shown in Figure 4-4.

Installing an external hard drive   If the thought of opening up your computer makes you queasy, you can add more space by purchasing an external hard drive like the External Solutions model shown in Figure 4-5. You simply plug the device into your computer, like any other peripheral device. External hard drives cost about $150 to $200, and you can add up to 18 gigabytes of space. You can find several models at the External-Solutions website, located at www.external-solutions.com.

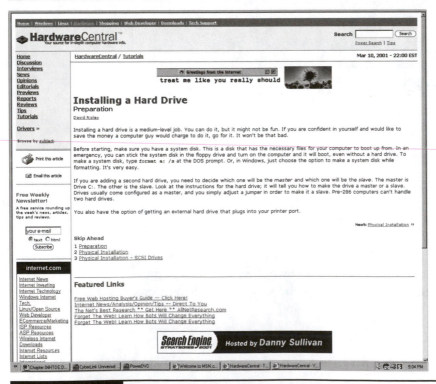

FIGURE 4-4   Get help installing a new hard drive on the HardwareCentral website.

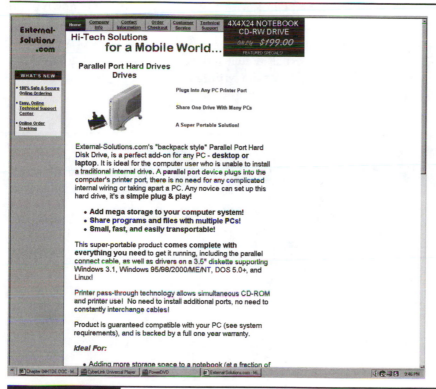

FIGURE 4-5   An external hard drive is an easy solution.

A high-capacity disk drive   Zip drives and Jaz drives are external devices that allow you to add a drive to your computer. They use special, high-capacity diskettes. Figure 4-6 shows a Zip drive, and Figure 4-7 shows you what a Jaz drive looks like. Both of these devices use high-capacity storage disks. Using a Zip disk, you can store an additional 100 to 250 megabytes of information. Jaz drives afford you 1 or 2 gigabytes of extra storage. Iomega is the market leader for these devices, and you can find their extensive website at www.iomega.com/jaz.

A recordable CD-ROM drive   The advantage of CDs is that they are remarkably portable high-capacity storage devices. Since nearly everyone with a PC has (or will eventually have) access to a CD drive, CDs are a great way to store and share lots of image data. CD-R and CD-RW drives have recently come down in price considerably. (The latter allows you to rewrite a disk you've previously recorded on.) As with hard drives and high-capacity disk drives, a CD-R drive can be either internal or external. The external models are easier to install, but aren't otherwise significantly less expensive. As of the writing of this book, you can find many excellent CD-R drives for less than $400.

FIGURE 4-6   A Zip drive stores 100 to 250 megabytes on a disk.

FIGURE 4-7   A Jaz drive adds 1 or 2 gigabytes of storage space to your PC.

Where to Shop for Additional Storage Devices

Once you decide you do need to add some more storage space to your PC before scanning and image-editing full swing, it's a straightforward task. The Microsoft Network shopping site offers you excellent resources for comparing features and prices of all types of external drives. The site, located at www.eshop.msn.com, shown in Figure 4-8, allows you to specify search criteria as to the type of peripheral you want (for example, a new CD-R drive), as well as your price range. You can even do a detailed comparison of the features of the models you decide you like best, based on your initial search.

FIGURE 4-8   Comparison-shop for storage devices on the MSN website.

Printer Capability

Unless you're content to view images on screen, you're pretty much dependent on your printer to do your carefully scanned and edited image final justice.

This book assumes you're currently using—or are going to be purchasing—an inkjet printer, rather than a laser printer for your color photos. The reason for this is that color laser printers are expensive. In fact, too expensive to be serious contenders for the home-based user. More importantly, you can get a result that is, for all practical purposes, just as good as a color laser printer using an inkjet printer.

CMYK vs. Photo-Quality Printers

That being said, there are two varieties of inkjet printers—standard and photo-quality. Either of them is a solid investment, but the photo-quality printer is designed specifically to produce great color photographs. On the other hand, a standard inkjet printer (also called a CMYK printer) might be quite adequate if you scan a lot of black-and-white images or text since you don't need the capacity to reproduce a wide range of colors.

How the CMYK Printer Works   The standard type inkjet printer uses two cartridges. The first one contains only black ink, and the second contains three colors of ink: cyan, yellow, and magenta. Hence the moniker CMYK printers; the K stands for black since the letter B could be mistakenly assumed to refer to blue. These four colors can be combined to produce nearly every color imaginable, as explained in Chapter 2.

There are also "three-color" printers on the market that don't contain black ink. Instead, they produce black by combining the other colors. The result is inferior, and most users don't feel that the cost savings are worth skimping on the black ink.

The Photo-Quality Printer   Photo-quality printers are specially designed to give you great results when printing color photos. This printer uses six different colors of ink, as opposed to the four colors used in standard CMYK printers. Why are more ink colors better? Because it means you can reproduce the colors of an image more accurately when you're scanning at lower resolutions.

   The major downside to a photo-quality printer is—you guessed it—price. They're generally 30 to 40 percent more expensive than their CMYK counterparts. Additionally, the replacement cartridges are about 30 percent more expensive.

Shopping for a Printer

Shopping for a printer on line has the advantage of convenience, and being able to compare lots of prices and specifications with a click of your mouse. A great place to start an online search is the ZDNet site at www.zdnet.com/products/ shown in Figure 4-9.

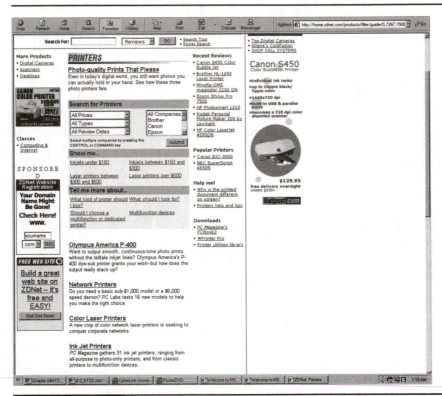

FIGURE 4-9   The ZDNet website is a great place to shop for a printer.

Looking for a bargain on a printer? Don't forget to check the Overstock.com website, located at www.overstock.com, shown in Figure 4-10. This site capitalizes on the mistakes of other Internet-based businesses—close-outs, overstocks, and even bankruptcies. You can get surprisingly up-to-date merchandise at a steal of a deal.

Shopping in an office-equipment store has some advantages, too. The biggest one is that you can test the output of the printer. To make the most of this opportunity, go to one of the larger office supply stores that are likely to have several printers on display. Take a photograph with you that has lots of people in it. Accurate skin tones are some of the hardest shades to replicate and the easiest to discern if they're a little bit off. You'll notice a slightly greenish or yellow tinge on a face a lot faster than whether the t-shirt or lawn is off a shade or two.

FIGURE 4-10   The Overstock.com website offers great printer bargains.

When shopping for a printer, here are a few other features to compare:

Cost   A printer is one product it pays to shop around for. Printers of the same quality can vary in price by as much as 30 percent.

Speed   Most printer manufacturers disclose how many pages per minute their printers are capable of producing. Sometimes they disclose speeds for both black-and-white and color output, so make sure you're comparing apples to color apples.

Print quality   Generally the more dots per inch (dpi) a printer is capable of producing, the higher the quality of the image. (See Chapter 2.)

Ease of use   This is not a factor to be underestimated in any peripheral device. Look for smoothly running sheet feeds, external buttons, and lights that give you clear operational indications.

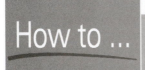

Select the Right Paper for a Good Finished Product

If it's worth printing, it's probably worth putting on good paper. Generally, paper is a pretty nominal cost in the grand scheme of things, and can really impact your finished product. There are dozens of different grades and brands of paper, but generally you can categorize them into three types:

Standard-quality copy paper   This is low-grade, inexpensive paper that works fine for text. However, if you're printing a color image you've scanned, the result can be smeary or smudged. This is because this grade of paper is simply ill-suited to absorb all of the ink from the dots your printer needs to put out to reproduce an image at decent resolution. The solution, if you absolutely must resort to low-grade copy paper, is to set your printer on draft mode when producing a color image.

Ink-jet paper   This paper is slightly more expensive, but offers better ink absorption. It's the minimum quality you should consider when working with high-resolution color images.

Photographic paper   It can be twice as expensive as other grades of paper, but it's well worth the price if you truly care about what you're printing. Use this type of paper for photographs you want to frame, greeting cards, and other finished products you expect to be examined in some detail.

Other media   You can purchase other interesting media for scanned images such as stuff for iron-on transfers, decals, and transparencies. The mySimon website, located at www.mysimon.com carries a wide range of papers and products that you can browse and order on line.

Installation Made Easy

Installing a scanner is painless, although some manufacturer's instruction booklets seem to try their best to confuse you. They're pretty cryptic, and offer only bare bones step-by-step instructions. It helps the process along if you understand what you're connecting at each step and why.

Although scanners come in widely varying shapes, sizes, and capabilities, the process of installing any of them is more similar than it is different. The tips and tricks in this portion of the chapter will have you up and scanning in less than 20 minutes.

4

Step 1: Inventory Your Scanner Components

There's nothing more frustrating than starting a project—such as installing a scanner—only to find you don't have everything you need. This is particularly irritating if you're just about hooked up, and you realize the manufacturer has forgotten to enclose the film-scanning attachment or a disk for an image-editing program you're supposed to receive. To save yourself the aggravation of unhooking, uninstalling, and repacking, run through the following checklist of what you *should* have before you begin the setup process:

Driver disk   Your scanner must have driver software to enable it to talk to your computer. Usually it comes on a diskette or CD labeled "installation disk."

> **TIP**   *If you lose or damage your driver disk, you can download the driver software by logging on to the manufacturer's website. Look for a link on the website that says "drivers."*

Cables   You need to have a cable compatible with your computer interface to connect your scanner to your PC. There are two primary types of interfaces—USB and parallel port. A USB cable connection looks like the one shown in Figure 4-11, and a parallel port cable is shown in Figure 4-12. Make sure that the backside of your computer has ports to accommodate the type of cable you've received. Many vendors provide you with both types of cable, and you can choose which connection to use. (You can find more information about ports and cable connections in Chapter 2.)

FIGURE 4-11   A USB cable connector

FIGURE 4-12	A parallel port cable connector

Power source   It's not enough to be able to plug your scanner into your PC. Your scanner needs its own electrical power source. Your scanner should come with a cord that plugs into an electrical outlet.

Optional connection cables   Some scanners include special types of cabling. You want to make sure those are in the box, too. For example, a high-end scanner might require a SCSI interface connected to a single port on your computer. The SCSI interface enables you to connect several peripheral devices in a daisy-chain arrangement, avoiding the requirement of additional ports.

Bundled software   The image-editing and OCR software that comes with your scanner adds value to it. In the case of the OCR software, you won't be able to read text documents without it. So inventory the CDs that come with your scanner carefully, and request copies of any missing ones from the manufacturer.

Step 2: Connect Your Cabling and Power Source

Your computer and scanner communicate via a cable that runs between them. Image data travels through the cable, as well as messages to adjust and control your scanner.

If you're using a parallel port connection, you must first connect the cable and restart your computer before installing the software driver. When you shut down your computer, connect your power cord to the scanner by plugging it into the wall.

If you're using a USB connection, hook up the power cord to your scanner and start your computer. You'll probably be prompted during the installation of the driver to attach your scanner to the USB port. With a USB connection, you don't have to restart your computer before you begin scanning!

Step 3: Install the Driver

A driver is a software program that links your scanner to your Windows or other operating system software. You can't do anything with your scanner prior to installing the driver software. This is because your computer's operating system simply doesn't know how to talk to your scanner without the driver.

The driver is located on the installation CD that comes with the scanner. (The installation disc might contain help resources and other features as well as the driver.) If the CD-ROM drive doesn't automatically read the installation CD, you can prompt it as follows:

1. Click the Start icon usually found at the bottom of your Windows screen and select Run from the pop-up menu. The dialog box shown in Figure 4-13 appears.

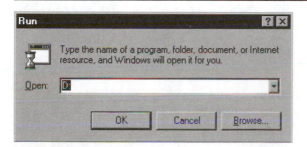

FIGURE 4-13   Use this dialog box to start your driver software.

2. Enter the letter of the drive that contains the installation disc, followed by a colon.

Alternatively, you can initiate the driver installation by locating and running the executable file on the CD. To do this:

1. After inserting the installation CD in your CD-ROM drive, click the My Computer icon on your desktop.

2. Click the icon for your CD-ROM drive. A list of files located on the installation disc appears.

3. Look for an executable file that has a name ending in .exe and click it. This should initiate the installation of your driver.

Did you know?

Plug and Play

The standard today for installing scanners and other peripheral devices to your PC is something called Plug and Play—or Plug and Pray as the punsters have dubbed it. Plug and Play is a special proprietary design for Intel *expansion boards*, which are the components that plug into slots inside a PC and allow it to connect to outside devices.

The idea behind Plug and Play is that you can add new peripheral devices— such as a scanner—to your computer without the need to perform any special technical analysis or procedure. (It's not always perfect, hence the Plug and Pray jibe.)

The Plug and Play software in your computer automatically searches for new hardware. Then it checks to see if the correct device driver is installed. This feature is useful to know about if you think you might have accidentally un- installed or corrupted the driver for your scanner or aren't sure you installed it correctly.

To activate the Plug and Play feature:

1. Click the Start icon on your Windows taskbar and select Settings, Control Panel to open the Control Panel dialog box.

2. Click the Add New Hardware icon. This initiates the Add New Hardware wizard. The wizard will search for new hardware, which means any hardware a driver is not presently installed for.

3. When prompted, select the manufacturer and model number of your scanner. The Add New Hardware wizard will search for the driver on the system, or prompt you to enter a disc with the driver.

4. Install the driver disc if necessary, and complete the wizard to reinstall your scanner.

Step 4: Check the Status of Your Scanner

Most of us experience a small sense of relief when we install a new peripheral—such as a scanner or printer—and get it to work just right. Scanner manufacturers know this, and most of them offer you little breadcrumbs along the installation path. These might include icons that appear on your Windows taskbar, and special wizards that facilitate your first test scan.

Most scanning-software installations automatically add an icon to the Windows taskbar at the bottom-right corner of your computer screen, like this one:

This icon lets you know your scanner is correctly installed. Sometimes these taskbar icons even let you know if your scanner is correctly connected and activated. For example, the Visioneer One Touch scanners display a red X through the scanner icon if the cabling has come loose or the scanner has otherwise become disconnected.

Some scanners also have a special wizard that takes you through the process of your first scan, step by step. These wizards are usually directed toward novices; however, it's a good idea to use this wizard the first time, even if you're a scanning pro. The wizard is usually designed to help you diagnose problems that might have occurred during installation, as well as orient you to the scanning process.

Troubleshooting the Installation Process

From time to time, a perfectly good, undamaged scanner refuses to perform its scanning duty. This means it's troubleshooting time. Here's a checklist of possible killjoys and culprits:

Make sure the scanner is plugged in. Seriously. It's easy to forget your scanner needs its *own* electrical power source.

Is the cable connecting your scanner to your computer loose? Even if you thought you'd plugged in the cable connection to your computer, check again. It's one of life's great mysteries as to how a cable suddenly comes loose on a device you haven't moved or jostled.

Is your computer an older one, with serial as well as parallel ports?   If your computer is an older one, it might have connections for older-type serial ports as well as parallel ports. These two types of ports are really easy to confuse, because they both have 24-pin connectors. Today's scanners uniformly use parallel, USB, and FireWire connections—serial ports are dinosaurs. Check to see if you've accidentally connected your scanner to a serial port, and if so, reconnect it to a parallel port.

Did you restart the computer after connecting the scanner?   If you're using a parallel port, you need to restart the computer before it will recognize your new scanner. To do this using Windows, choose Start, Shutdown to view the Shutdown dialog box, click the Restart option, and click OK. To perform a Restart using a Macintosh, choose Special, Restart from the Finder menu.

Did you restart the computer after installing the software?   Regardless of whether you're using a USB or parallel port connection, you need to restart your computer after installing the scanner software.

If you try all of the above troubleshooting strategies to no avail, it's possible you have a malfunctioning scanner. It's rare, but it happens. Before you take it back to the store, however, it's worth a call to the technical support phone number provided by the scanner manufacturer. You can usually find this number by checking the instructions that came with your scanner.

How to Get Help

Scanner manufacturers are pretty good about supporting their products. In addition to the directions that come with your scanner, you can get help from the following three sources:

The Help menu for your scanner software   You can usually search the Help menu by keyword or using a topical table of contents. This is usually the best place to start if you know what's wrong, but it might be hard to think of a search request if you don't.

Telephone support   Most scanner manufacturers maintain a telephone support line. You might even be able to select an automated help option for troubleshooting the installation process. Automated help for common problems is often preferable to holding "for the next available representative."

Websites   In addition to a phone number you can call, scanner manufacturers maintain websites to provide technical support to their customers. The Visioneer customer support website is shown in Figure 4-14, and you can find it at www.visioneer.com. The Hewlett-Packard website (see Figure 4-15) allows you to search for help using a keyword. This site is located at www.hp.com/cposupport. Most technical support sites provide a surprising range of services—providing quick answers to technical questions and an online library of downloadable drivers, patches, and updates for your scanner.

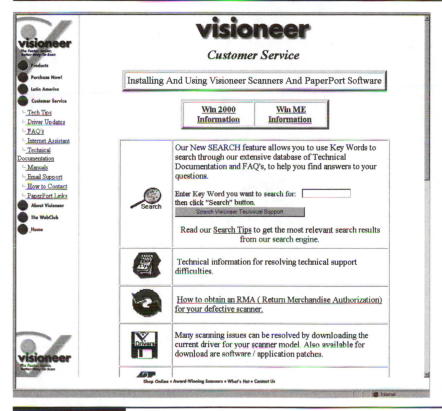

FIGURE 4-14   The Visioneer customer support website

4

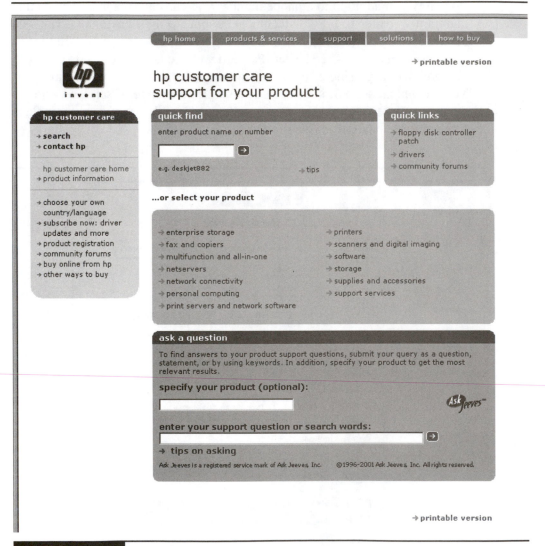

FIGURE 4-15   The Hewlett-Packard technical support website

Part II

The Techniques of Scanning and Editing

Chapter 5

The Basics for Your First Scan

How To...

- Use and program the buttons on your scanner

- Start a scan

- Decide on an output setting

- Save an image

- Print and send a scanned image

If you've never used a scanner before, it can look like an intimidating piece of equipment. Even computer professionals will tell you that it's daunting to use a brand-new peripheral device for the first time. With technology changing so rapidly, there are always new features, functions, and interfaces to learn. This chapter gives you the bare-bone basics you need to take that first scanning plunge with today's most popular models.

Overview of the Scanning Process

After you've properly connected your scanner and familiarized yourself with its external buttons, it's time to scan your first image. Whether you have a high-end or basic scanner, the process is remarkably similar. With *any* flatbed scanner you need to

- Position your original on the scanner and close the cover

- Initiate the scanning process using the external buttons on the scanner or the correct command in the scanner software

- Send your scanned image to an image-editing, email, or facsimile program

Be Sure to Unlock Your Scanner Carriage

I recently called Hewlett-Packard technical support to find out what problems users most frequently encounter on their first scan. I actually wasn't surprised to learn that the number-one source of calls is confusion about unlocking the scanner carriage. This issue is not unique to Hewlett-Packard. Most scanners have carriage locking mechanisms you need to be aware of.

A scanner's carriage (the device the moving sensors are attached to) is so sensitive, it can be damaged by something as simple as turning your scanner upside down to check the serial number. Oddly, many scanner manufacturers install the carriage lock switch on the underside of the scanner, like the one shown in Figure 5-1, or in other equally hidden places. Sometimes you really have to look for it!

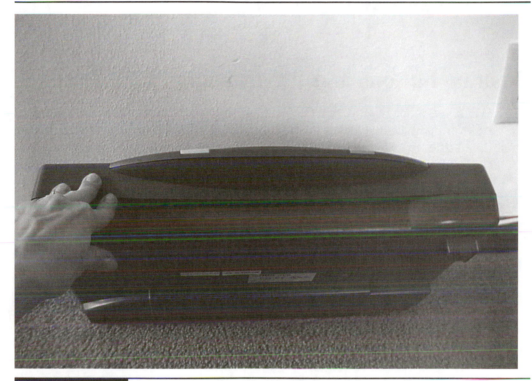

FIGURE 5-1   Sometimes the carriage lock switch is underneath.

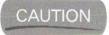 *Whenever moving, jostling, or turning a scanner, make sure that the carriage lock mechanism is in the lock position.*

What happens if you don't unlock your carriage? Unfortunately, most scanner software isn't sophisticated enough, as of the writing of this book, to communicate with your scanner and give you a specific message telling you this is a problem. No wonder technical support gets all those calls! For example, on the Hewlett-Packard scanner, the lamp on the device begins flashing in a sort of Morse code SOS signal, but you can't assume the flashing lamp always indicates a locked carriage because the lamp is programmed to flash other error messages as well.

 *You definitely want to check the carriage lock if you've installed your scanner properly but it's not functioning correctly. This is an easy feature to forget about, and a locked carriage can cause your scanner to behave in a number of strange ways.*

Pushing Buttons and Programming Commands

When you think about it, most devices and appliances have some sort of push-button or lever interface that makes them intuitive to use. Until recently, scanner interfaces didn't offer this convenience. You had to place your original on the scanner, then turn your attention back to the computer screen. To scan a document, you had to open your scanner's software program and search for the menu option that allowed you to perform a scan.

Why Have Manufacturers Added External Buttons?

Today's scanners make the process of capturing an image as intuitive as turning on your television or using your electric can opener. Buttons, like the ones shown in Figure 5-2, replace the need to remember how to locate software menu options before you can perform basic scanning tasks. Oddly enough, most scanners on the market don't label their scanners with words, and the icons are not always intuitive. For example, one scanner on the market comes with buttons labeled with different shapes and arrows. Other scanners, such as the Hewlett-Packard 5300 series and the Visioneer OneTouch models, have opted to put illustrative icons on their buttons.

External buttons

FIGURE 5-2 External buttons are the latest enhancement to scanner interfaces.

How to Identify What the Buttons Do

The process of using buttons becomes easier to master when you realize that most scanners on the market have buttons that perform the same three to five functions. The shapes, sizes, and appearance of external scanner buttons might vary, but you can expect that they all perform the following three tasks:

Initiate a basic scan   All scanners with external buttons allow you the luxury of initiating a basic scan using whatever default settings exist. While pushing a button is simple for *you*, the process that your scanner initiates is fairly complex. This unobtrusive little button launches your scanner's software, looks at the image, determines its size and type, and adjusts color settings to capture the contrasts and variations.

Email a scanned image   This button opens your scanner's software and performs a scan. Then it opens your email program and attaches the image.

Copy a document   Today's scanners often do double duty as copy machines. You can program your scanner to make copies using settings you specify for this purpose. For example, you might want to use the black-and-white setting or a low-resolution setting, which saves time by capturing less extensive image data.

Additional external buttons might allow you to

Open scanner software to adjust settings   External buttons generally operate by using the default settings you've specified; however, some models allow you to press a button to open the software and modify the settings without having to resort to a mouse and menu.

Fax a scanned image   If your scanner has this option, you can capture an image and send it directly to your faxing software.

TIP   *Once you have some sense what scanner buttons accomplish, it's easy to sit down at an unfamiliar scanner and perform scanning tasks. You can just look at the icons or button names, and pretty much figure out what to do with the device.*

Programming Your Scanner's Buttons

Scanner buttons perform specific operations according to default settings in your scanning software. Your installation software initially specifies settings such as size, resolution, and tonal quality. You can program and modify these settings to make the process even more convenient.

Scanners differ as to how you are permitted to change the settings and customize the buttons. You can usually find out how to make your buttons yield the result you want. Try searching the online help menu for your particular scanner. You can usually figure out how to customize the performance of the scanner's buttons using the key phrase "customize buttons."

Does Your Scanner Have a Button for Modifying Settings?

The popular Visioneer 8100 series actually allows you to customize your scanner buttons by clicking the Customize button. This feature automatically launches your scanner software and opens the dialog box shown in Figure 5-3, which enables you to adjust your resolution, image type, and other settings.

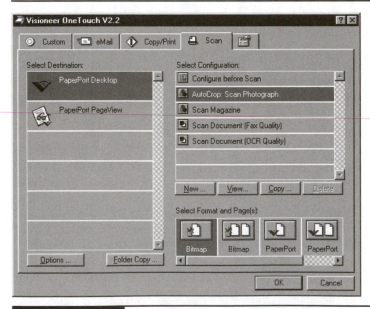

FIGURE 5-3   Visioneer OneTouch allows you to customize button settings using a dialog box like this.

An extremely convenient feature of the Visioneer OneTouch scanner series is an external button that allows you to open your software to change your scanner settings without using your menu or mouse.

Using the Control Panel to Configure Button Settings

Hewlett-Packard scanners allow you to customize your scanner buttons using the Windows Control Panel dialog box. If you have a Hewlett-Packard scanner, just follow these steps to modify the initial configuration:

1. Click the Start icon on your Windows taskbar, select Programs, then HP ScanJet Software, then ScanJet Utilities, then Scanner Button Settings, as shown in Figure 5-4.

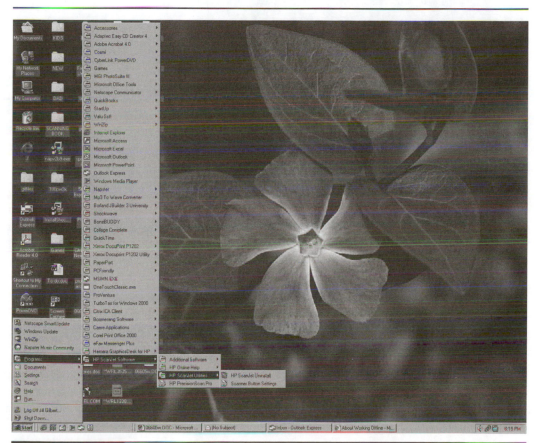

FIGURE 5-4   Recent Hewlett-Packard scanners allow you to customize external button settings.

2. The dialog box shown in Figure 5-5 appears, which enables you to customize the settings for the fax and email buttons.

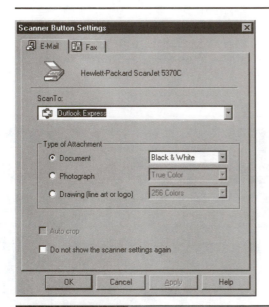

FIGURE 5-5   The Hewlett-Packard fax and email configuration dialog box

Choose the Best Original

Regardless of the make, model, year, or cost of your scanner, it helps to start with the best possible quality original. Here are a few tips on choosing original media (assuming you have a choice):

Use the largest version.   If you have a choice between scanning a 3×5-inch original and an 8×7-inch original, pick the larger size. Scanned at the same resolution, the larger original will result in a more detailed scan. Flaws such as uneven ink coverage are more noticeable when you're scanning from the smaller original.

Opt for an original rather than a photocopy.   Uneven ink deposits make photocopies undesirable for photos. The problem is compounded if you're working with text, since optical character recognition (OCR) software is highly sensitive and has a hard time reading fuzzy-edged characters. If you absolutely have to scan a fax, have it sent to you using a large type size, and the Fine rather than Standard resolution setting.

Develop an eye for which defects can be repaired.   Don't panic about a few specks of dust, or a slight blurring. The paint and sharpen tools in your image-editing software will enable you to attend to these sorts of things. If you have a torn or wrinkled photo, however, try to locate an original in better condition. After working on scanning and image-editing projects for a while, you get a feel for how much work it takes to fix certain things.

Overexposed is better than underexposed.   If you have a choice between an overexposed image and an underexposed one, pick the overexposed version. Overexposed photos contain more image data and are much easier to fix using your image-editing software.

The Two Ways to Perform a Scan

Just as you can open or copy a file more than one way in Windows, you can usually accomplish a scanning task by more than one method. The method you choose—pushing a button or selecting the scan option from the software menu—won't affect your finished result. It's strictly a matter of user preference.

   *Although most new models of scanners offer external push buttons, older and less expensive models might not. If this is the case, you have no choice but to execute a scan by opening the scanner's software.*

Open Your Scanner Software

To start a scan using the software, you must first open the software by selecting it from your Programs menu, or clicking an icon installed on your desktop. Once you open the software, you can usually begin your scanning operation via a dialog box or command menu. Figure 5-6 shows the software bundled with the Hewlett-Packard 5370C scanner. Commands listed under the Scan menu enable you to view and save your scanned images.

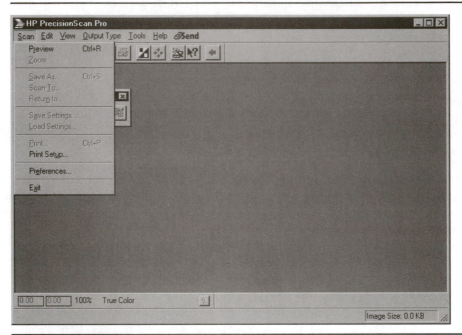

FIGURE 5-6   The software bundled with the Hewlett-Packard 5370C scanner

Use the External Buttons

The advantage of having external buttons on your scanner is that you don't have to open your software program to start a scan. This saves you a few seconds. Many scanners open the software program when you push the button to allow you to edit the image or select the program you want to send the scanned image to.

Select the Right Image Output Type

This chapter is confined to the basics, and avoids having you do a lot of configuring for your first scan. Your scanner software does a pretty good job of selecting default settings for scanning an image. This means you don't have to provide it with a lot of image information prior to your first scan. To get optimum results, however, you need to identify an image output type for the image you're scanning. Most scanners prompt or allow you to select from some or all the following types of image output:

Black and white/line art   This type of image format supports only black and white—similar to the appearance of a pen-and-ink drawing. It can include patterns and lines to give the effect of shaded areas, but the lines are drawn in only one shade. Your scanner uses a high resolution to produce this sort of output so the lines appear clear and sharp.

Grayscale   This type of image contains a continuous range of black, gray, and white tones. Professional photographers and graphic artists think of grayscale in terms of many "steps" or shades of gray. Your scanner and printer use a process called *half-toning* to reproduce the continuous image using a series of dots. When you select grayscale on your scanner as your image output type, you're configuring it to produce the dotted, or half-toned, image.

True color   This output setting, which is also referred to as 8-bit color, sets your scanner to reproduce millions of shades. As with grayscale, true color sets your scanner to produce a digital half-tone image.

256 color   This setting outputs 256 colors or shades of gray for a half-tone image composed of colored dots.

Text   During your scan your text is formatted to readable, ASCII characters. ASCII is a system of coding letters to numeric values that can be interpreted by your computer. The acronym stands for American Standard Code for Information Interchange.

Text and image   If this sophisticated option is available on your scanner, you can preserve both the text and image in a single scan.

Chapter 6 tells you more about these different image types.

Sending Your Image to Its Final Destination

An image that's just been scanned is sort of in limbo. After your scanner has captured an image, it needs to send it to another software application somewhere on your computer to be saved as a file within that application.

Scanners differ as to how they allow you to specify the "destination application" for a scanned image. For example, Hewlett-Packard scanners allow you to click the icon shown in Figure 5-7 and access a menu of applications your scan can be sent to.

You can also select the Save As option from the File menu to save your image in a default application you've specified.

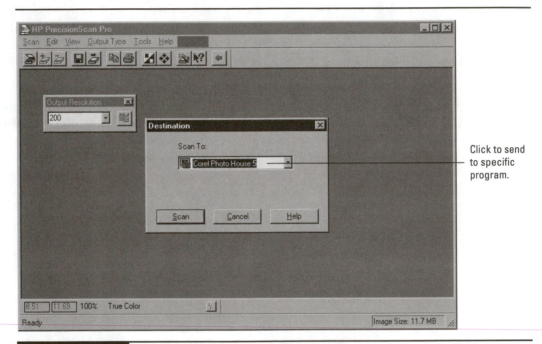

FIGURE 5-7   Sending an image to a specific program

   *If you are not sure how to specify destination software for your image, or you need to change it, try searching your scanner's online help menu using a query such as "saving."*

Chapter 6

Scanning Techniques for Different Types of Images

How To...

■ Recognize line art, grayscale, and different types of color images

■ Clearly scan line art

■ Capture a grayscale image to its best advantage

■ Scan vibrant color images

Human beings have an instinctive desire to produce images. Only a couple hundred thousand years after our ancestors first began scrawling on cave walls, our species has evolved the ability to reproduce digital images with scanners and PCs.

Images captured in digital form fall into five general categories: line art, black and white, color, half-tone, and text. This chapter tells you how to recognize and differentiate different types of images, and how to adapt your scanning techniques to best capture them.

Overview of the Different Types of Images

If you're serious about scanning, you need to know about the different kinds of originals. There are five types of images you can expect to be working with:

Line art   Line art is an image consisting of a single color (such as black) against a single-color background (such as white), or vice versa. The term is a little misleading because the image doesn't necessarily need to be lines. For example, a solid black circle on a uniform white background is considered line art. Figure 6-1 is an example of line art.

Grayscale   A black-and-white photo (like most of the figures in this book) is an example of a grayscale image. A grayscale image appears to have smooth, continuous shading gradations ranging from black to white, with all the shades of gray in between.

Color   When graphic artists refer to a color image, they usually mean an image such as a photograph or transparency that's made up of a continuous range of color tones.

Half-tones   When you scan a photograph that's been printed in a color magazine or newspaper you're actually scanning a type of image called a *half-tone*. Color photographs are reproduced on a printing press using a process called half-toning, in which continuous tones are translated either manually or digitally into a matrix of dots that emulate the tones in the original. The technique allows a printing press to produce the continuous tones of a color photo using black, yellow, cyan, and magenta dots. Figures 6-2 and 6-3 show an original image, and the same image reproduced using a particular half-toning technique and resolution that make the normally indiscernible dots visible to the naked eye.

Text   Scanning text requires the use of optical character recognition (OCR) software, discussed in Chapter 13.

All the foregoing images require you to take a slightly different approach to scanning to get the optimum result.

FIGURE 6-1   This blue jay is an example of line art.

 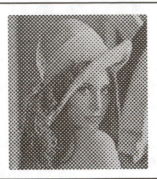

FIGURES 6-2 AND 6-3   An original color image (left) and a scanned half-tone showing the dots that compose the image (right)

Scan Clear, Clean, Line-Art Images

When you're working with line art, the operative words are sharpness and clarity. The goal is to produce clean lines that lend a professional quality to your line art–scanning project. You can achieve this by scanning at the right resolution and choosing the correct color setting on your scanner.

Scan Line Art at a High Resolution

The rule of thumb for resolution when scanning line art is quite simple: the higher the better. The higher the resolution setting, the clearer and sharper your final image will be. Increasing resolution increases the density of the pixels that make up an image.

Denser pixels along the edges of each line of an image make the image appear sharp and clear. Too low a resolution, and the lines of the image have a fuzzy, jagged effect. Line-art images are particularly prone to this effect when enlarged, as illustrated in Figure 6-4, which shows a portion of an enlarged line-art image. Enlarging has the effect of reducing the resolution of the image and decreasing the density of the pixels.

FIGURE 6-4   The lines of the blue jay (shown in Figure 6-1) when the photo is enlarged

When you scan line art, start by scanning at a resolution that matches the dpi (dots per inch) setting on your printer. For example, if you're working with a 600 dpi printer, try scanning at 600 ppi (which stands for pixels per inch). Test your results by printing a copy of the image, then compare the result by scanning at a slightly higher or lower resolution. You might find that scanning at 1,200 ppi makes your file very large, but doesn't improve the quality of your image very much.

CAUTION   *It's very important to print a test copy of your image at the size you'll actually be producing. When you view an image on screen, the tendency is to zoom in and blow up the image to a much larger size than you actually need for your printed copy. When you enlarge any image three or four times, you can get it to appear fuzzy and jagged.*

How to Capture Black-and-White Bitmaps and Vectors

The lines that make up a line-art image might be thick or thin, and placed at different intervals; however, all the lines have one color of dots, usually black.

Availability of Black-and-White Settings

Since the only color you need to capture is black, it makes sense to set your scanner to capture as few colors as possible. Scanners capture the line art as something called *single-bit* or *binary images*. Some old scanners don't have settings for less than 16 different shades, while virtually all new scanners have specific black-and-white settings for capturing two-shade binary images.

Many scanners offer you a choice between two types of black-and-white settings. They allow you to select either a bitmap or vector for your black-and-white image. Figure 6-5 shows the drop-down menu for the Hewlett-Packard Precision Scan Pro, which offers such a choice.

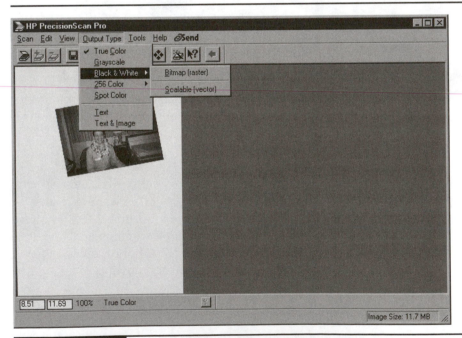

FIGURE 6-5   Some scanners offer you both bitmap and vector options for black-and-white scans.

Bitmap Versus Vector Images

Line art can be categorized as either a bitmap or vector image.

A *bitmap* image (sometimes called a *raster*) is created from differently colored rows of pixels. Figures 6-6 and 6-7 provide an illustration of how a bitmap image works. The image that appears on your computer monitor is a bitmap.

A *vector* image is constructed using complex mathematical formulas that describe shape, color, and placement. A vector image doesn't consist of dots. It's made of curves, lines, and other shapes, defined with mathematical precision. It's the job of the graphic artist to combine the shapes to get the desired image.

FIGURE 6-6   A bitmap image at the resolution it's normally viewed at

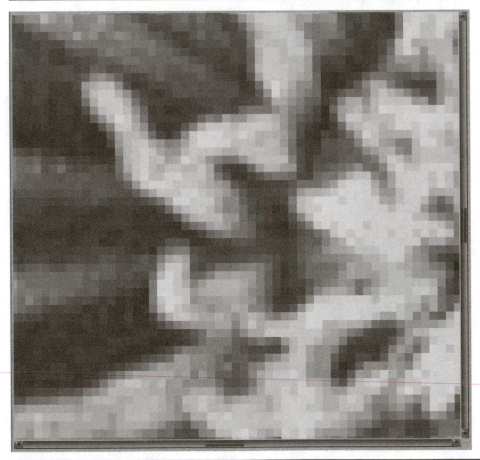

FIGURE 6-7   An enlarged image showing the rows of pixels that make up the image

You can convert a vector file into a bitmap file. Doing so will save some space, because vector files are generally much smaller than bitmap files. Vector files are often used for line art, but aren't appropriate for reproducing complex images such as photos.

On the other hand, it's very difficult to convert a bitmap file to a vector file, but most likely you won't want to. Vector files are often used for line art because they are easier to alter than bitmap files. Bitmap files can appear jagged if you enlarge them, or fuzzy if you shrink them, while vector files are easy to resize because the mathematical proportions that make up the various shapes are precisely changed.

Produce High-Quality Grayscale Images

A grayscale image is one that's made of continuous shades of gray, ranging from pure black to pure white. The photos of Ansel Adams are good examples of grayscale. Adams was famous for his ability to capture subtle detail and shadows. This effect is achieved by reproducing hundreds of different shades of gray. The more shades of gray that can be produced, the more detailed a grayscale image. Figure 6-8 is an example of an image captured using a setting that reproduces 256 shades of gray.

FIGURE 6-8   An image capturing 256 shades of gray

When scanning a grayscale image, use the grayscale setting on your scanner. If you're planning on printing the image, scan at a resolution setting of 150 to 300 spi (or samples per inch). Opt for something at the higher end of that range if you're planning on enlarging the photo. If you plan to view the image only on the Web, scan at a lower resolution of 72 to 75 spi, or 96 dpi. A higher resolution will increase file size considerably, without producing a noticeably better result on screen.

Capture Vibrant Color Images

Today's scanners and printers allow you to create vivid color prints. To scan color images successfully, you need to pay attention to both the resolution and color-capture settings of your printer.

Rules of thumb for color resolution are similar to those for grayscale. If you're planning on printing a color photo, scan at a resolution setting of 150 to 300 spi. If you're planning to enlarge the photo or reproduce it in a publication, don't scan at a lower resolution than 300 spi. For Web images, scan at a resolution of 72 to 75 spi, or 96 dpi. A higher resolution will increase file size, without producing a better result on screen.

Your scanner might offer several different capture settings for color photos, including true color, 256 color, and spot color. All these settings serve distinct color-capture functions.

Maximize Quality with the True-Color Setting

This setting is capable of producing 16,777,216 colors, referred to as 16.7 million colors. This is sometimes referred to as 24-bit color. Of course, the human eye cannot discern anywhere near 16 million colors, and this option might result in unnecessarily large files. Use this format only when you need to store as much image data as possible.

Optimize Your 256-Color Images

The 256-color setting, sometimes referred to as 8-bit color, allows you to capture up to 256 colors. Your scanner might have the following selections under this choice:

Web Palette   This setting uses a 216-color format that can be displayed by all Web browser software. Web browser software is the program on your computer that allows you to view images sent over the Internet.

System Palette   This option uses the 240 colors used by the Windows program. It's meant for images that will be displayed using a Windows-based program.

Optimized Palette   This option creates a set of the best possible 256 colors to represent your image to its best advantage. It selects from the 16,777,216 true colors that are available. This option is often associated with GIF or other fixed-palette image formats restricted to 256 colors. By optimizing an image's palette colors, only the minimum number of colors needed to reproduce the image are stored in the palette of the image file. For example, if only two are required, only two are stored.

Save File Space with the Spot-Color Option

The spot-color setting scans a limited range of colors. Solid colors are represented as single color data, rather than a gradation of hues. Spot color is great for scanning logos and graphics with limited color.

Working with Half-Tone Images

Laser printers and many commercial printing presses reproduce images such as grayscale and color photographs (sometimes called continuous-toned images) using a technique called half-toning.

Why You Need to Know about Half-Toning

Although half-toning can be done during the scanning process, it's usually a function performed by your printer. Most color printers have sophisticated drivers that perform the process; however, you need to be aware that image data is reordered and discarded in the process of creating a half-tone (printable) image from a continuous-toned color photograph or grayscale piece. As image detail and complexity increases, there might be a trade off between the amount of color data that can be saved and the resolution of the photo.

Images are divided into half-tone cells, each of which contains an appropriate number of color dots. The more dots than can be stored per cell, the more color combinations that can be produced. As you use printer dots to create color combinations, however, you decrease the amount of printer dots available to re-create other image detail. Thus, the increased color quality can decrease the overall resolution of the image, making it appear grainy.

How to Scan Previously Half-Toned Images

When you scan a previously half-toned image, you're working off a medium that has less data than the original photograph. Some of the valuable data was discarded at the time the photo was converted by the half-toning process. Scanning at lower resolutions or selecting an optimized palette option often yields good results when scanning previously half-toned images. You can also opt to capture the previously half-toned image as black and white, following the guidelines for such images given earlier in this chapter.

Scanning Text and Images that Contain Text

Text is a different animal to scan than an original that contains *both* images and text. Most scanners have separate settings for scanning both types of originals. Text is scanned using optical character recognition (OCR) software. This topic of scanning text is covered in depth in Chapter 13.

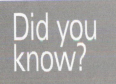

How Interpolation Works

Interpolation is a process that's used when you increase or decrease the size of an image, or change its color depth. When an image is enlarged, the density of pixels per inch decreases, making the color gradations between the pixels more noticeable. This also makes the edges of the image jagged.

Interpolation is a process performed by your software that makes extra pixels using a mathematical algorithm to reproduce the existing pixels. Interpolation looks at the existing pixels and carefully creates matching ones to fill the area. If one pixel is light gray and another is dark gray, interpolation creates a medium gray pixel to fill the intervening area.

Most scanner software applications include a feature that allows you to apply interpolation to your scanned images. When you purchase a scanner, and want to know its resolution capabilities, be sure you're distinguishing between standard and interpolated resolution. They're two different measurements.

Chapter 7

Troubleshooting Tips and Tricks

How To...

- Find basic information on how to work your scanner

- Deal with buttons that don't work

- Interpret a flashing lamp

- Respond when your computer doesn't recognize your scanner

- Speed up slow scans

- Save work in progress

- Deal with blurry and grainy images

- Find solutions to your problems on the Web

Did you think your scanner would be as easy to hook up and run as your printer? Guess again! Scanners are inherently more versatile, more complicated devices than home printers. Today's models are easy to use once you gain a little familiarity, but they have all kinds of quirks that can baffle you in the beginning. Before you pick up the phone to vent your frustration to the folks on the manufacturer's technical support line, try a few of the self-help hints offered in this chapter. In fact, most of the suggestions you find here are from scanner support staff who were kind enough to provide insight to me about the calls they receive most often.

Where Is the Manual?

Technical support personnel from every scanner manufacturer I surveyed told me a surprising number of callers are frantic that their scanner came "without instructions." Be assured, however, that virtually all scanner models *do* come with some sort of user guide or manual.

Locating Your User Guide

Gone are the days of paperbound user manuals; regrettably so, since it's sort of comforting to hold a nice, solid book in your hand when you're really confused.

These days, most manufacturers provide you with a single sheet of instructions telling you how to install your scanner software and hook up the cable connection from your scanner to your computer. For all the rest of the information you need about your specific model (and you usually need a lot), you must go to the user guide on your installation CD.

Try locating your user guide by doing one of the following:

Go to the Help menu of your scanner software   Most scanner manufacturers list the user guide as an option under Online Help, as shown in Figure 7-1.

Try the installation CD   Some scanner software (including a number of Visioneer Models) include their user guide on the installation CD. You can open and save it to your hard drive, but you can't access it directly from the software.

Get it on the Web   Many manufacturers, such as Hewlett-Packard, post the user guides for their various scanner models on the technical support pages of their websites. To see if your manufacturer provides your user guide on line, look for a search link on the site and enter the model number of your scanner as a keyword.

You generally must have Adobe Acrobat Reader software on your system to read the user guide. Fortunately, your scanner installation disk comes with the software you need to read an Adobe user guide document like the one shown in Figure 7-2.

7

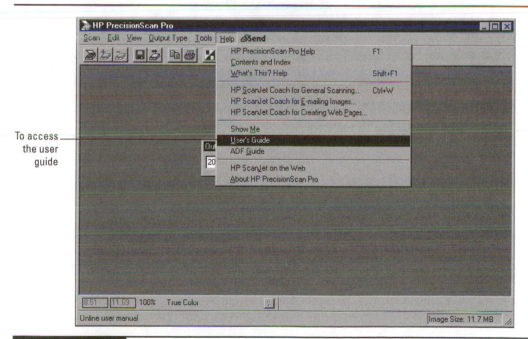

To access the user guide

FIGURE 7-1   The Help menu of your scanner software is the first place to look for your user guide.

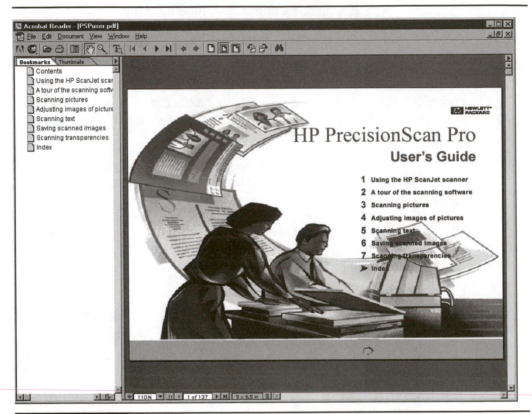

FIGURE 7-2   A sample user guide provided with the Hewlett-Packard 5370C model

Questions Answered by Your Guide

Your user guide is invaluable, and you'll most likely consult it many times over the life of your scanner. It's the most authoritative source for getting answers to certain types of questions. User guides commonly provide information about the following:

The basics of how to operate your scanner   How to operate the buttons, controls, and perform a basic scan.

How to send email and faxes with your scanner   Technical support personnel I spoke with told me they receive a lot of questions in this area, many of which are answered in the user guides.

Adjusting the settings and buttons on your scanner   Most user guides give you detailed, illustrated instructions as to how to modify resolution settings, configure buttons, adjust the color, and perform other tasks to refine your images.

How to scan text and transparencies   The attachments and software for scanning text and transparencies differ from scanner to scanner. The user guide is the best place to find illustrated step-by-step instructions.

Saving scanned images   The user guide tells you which file formats and software applications are available for saving your files, and how to use them.

When the Buttons Won't Do Anything

External buttons are the latest rage for scanner interfaces. They're efficient, convenient, and real time-savers—when they work.

If you have the disappointing experience of pushing promising-looking buttons that don't produce any results, you're not alone. If you have a newer operating system—such as Windows ME—you might have to download a special driver or patch from the Web. (The scanner was probably designed and packaged before the manufacturer had time to update the scanner software to be compatible with the new operating system.)

For nonfunctioning buttons, your first stop should be the manufacturer's website to check for drivers and updates. Hewlett-Packard, for example, provides a software patch that is *required,* as of the writing of this book, to make the buttons on its scanners operate under a Windows ME operating system.

To find a link to a patch, like the one shown in Figure 7-3, go to the manufacturer's website and look for a link labeled "drivers" or "updates." If you don't see a specific link on the home page, try looking for it on the technical support pages, or using any available Search feature provided on the website.

How to Interpret a Flashing Lamp

Some models of scanners signal for help by flashing the lamps under the glass. A logical interpretation of this would seem to be that the lamp itself is malfunctioning, but this is actually seldom the case.

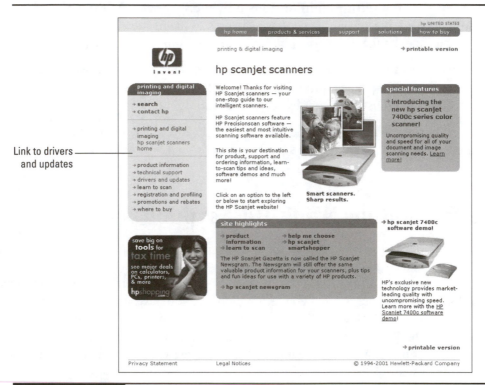

Link to drivers
and updates

FIGURE 7-3 Finding drivers and software updates on the manufacturer's website

Some, but not all, of the causes for a flashing scanner lamp include the following:

A locked scanner   Make sure that you've unlocked the carriage lock on your scanner. Chapter 4 tells you how to locate the lock and make sure it's been properly released. (The locking device is designed to protect the delicate sensors on the scanning device in transit.)

A stuck carriage   The sensor devices that capture image data are attached to a moving carriage within your scanner. Sometimes the carriage is stopped, and needs to be reset. To do this, simply unplug it from the power source to reinitialize the scanner motion settings.

Damaged or defective sensors   Occasionally the delicate sensors on a scanner carriage are damaged in transit. When this is determined to be the cause of the flashing lamp, your only recourse is to exchange it for an undamaged model.

When Your Computer Doesn't Recognize a Connection to Your Scanner

It might sound obvious, but loose cable connections are often the culprit for this error message. Even if you think you've checked all the connections, check again. Remember, your scanner needs a connection both to your computer and to its *own* separate electrical power source. In other words, be sure to check both the cable that leads to your computer and the cord that plugs into the wall.

If your cabling appears to be properly connected, try the following troubleshooting procedures in this section. A logical approach is to attempt them in the order listed here.

Restarting or rebooting your computer allows it to update its settings, and recognize new drivers and hardware such as a scanner. Use the Shutdown menu option, rather than Restart. Before you restart your computer, unplug the electrical connect to the scanner for a full 60 seconds. After you plug your scanner back in, restart your computer. This process should allow your computer to recognize your new scanner. If not, read on.

Look for a Conflicting Software Driver

Did you have another scanner installed before the one you're presently attempting to use? If so, the problem might be a conflicting software driver left over from the old scanner.

Basic Uninstallation Procedure for Old Drivers

Your first line of defense should be to properly uninstall the driver for the old scanner. Follow these steps to do so:

1. From the Start menu on your Windows taskbar, select Settings, then Control Panel. The Control Panel dialog box shown in Figure 7-4 appears.

2. Locate the Add/Remove Programs icon in the Control Panel dialog box and double-click it.

3. The Add/Remove Programs Properties dialog box, listing the software programs on your computer appears, as shown in Figure 7-5.

4. Locate the driver for the scanner that you no longer want to use and click the Add/Remove button. A message might appear telling you to restart your computer so the process can be completed.

5. After restarting your computer, check to see if your computer properly recognizes the new scanner.

Add/Remove Programs icon

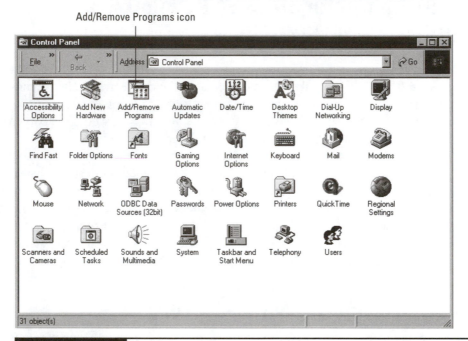

FIGURE 7-4   Access the Add/Remove Programs icon through the Control Panel.

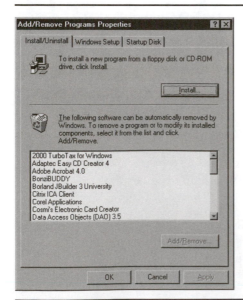

FIGURE 7-5   Scroll to the driver for the old scanner in the Add/Remove Programs
Properties dialog box.

Drivers that Don't Respond to the Standard Uninstallation Procedure

If after following the uninstall procedure above, your computer still gives you a message that it can't find the new scanner, you might have a stubborn driver that doesn't know when its welcome is up. You might have to delete the scanner from your computer's list of registered devices in the System Properties dialog box.

To look for the offending driver, follow these steps:

1. Right-click the My Computer icon on your Windows desktop and select Properties from the pop-up menu. The System Properties dialog box appears, as shown in Figure 7-6.

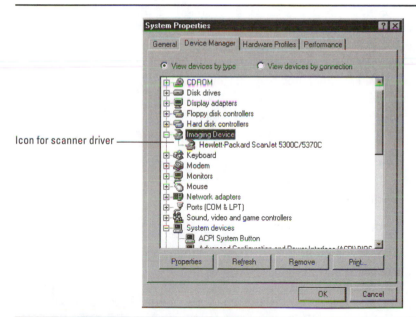

Icon for scanner driver

FIGURE 7-6   Look for a lingering driver using the System Properties dialog box.

2. Click the Device Manager tab and scroll through the dialog box to locate the Imaging Device icon.

3. Click the plus sign next to the Imaging Device icon to display a list of scanner drivers currently on your system. There should be only one. If more than one driver appears, delete the icon for the old scanner driver you're no longer using.

 *Most scanner manufacturers recommend that you install no more than one scanner driver on your computer at a time, since the potential for conflict between the two drivers is very high. There is a good probability that the resulting software conflicts will cause both scanners to malfunction, as they compete for computer resources and send and receive duplicate messages from the system.*

Exorcizing a "Ghost" Driver

Are you still getting a message that your computer can't recognize your software even after you've performed an uninstallation procedure and purged it from your System Properties dialog box? If so, you might be a haunted by what's colloquially known as a ghost driver. No one knows why; it's an unintended result. You usually can't see the ghost driver when your computer is running in its normal mode.

Safe Mode is a special diagnostic tool that allows your system to run using minimal resources and special diagnostic capabilities. While you're running your PC in Safe Mode, you're not connected to your network, and you don't have access to CD-ROM drives, printers, or other devices.

To detect and exorcize a ghost driver, you have to shut down your computer and reboot using the Safe Mode of operation. To reboot your computer in Safe Mode, follow these steps:

1. Click the Start icon on your Windows taskbar, then select Shut Down from the pop-up menu that appears.

2. Select Restart from the dialog box that appears on your screen, then click OK.

3. Press and hold CTRL until the Microsoft Windows Startup menu appears in white print on an entirely black screen.

 On some computers, you can continually tap F8 instead of CTRL to bring up the Microsoft Windows Startup menu.

4. The Windows Startup menu on the black screen will have several numbered options from which you can select; to make a selection, enter the number of the option.

5. Enter the menu option number for Safe Mode, then press ENTER. A message appears that your computer is running in Safe Mode and some of your devices or drivers might be unavailable. While you're in Safe Mode, however, you can access your Control Panel.

6. Click the Start icon on the Windows taskbar and select Settings, then Control Panel from the pop-up menu. Double-click the System icon. The System Properties dialog box appears.

7. Click the Device Manager tab and scroll through the dialog box to locate the Imaging Device icon.

8. Click the plus sign next to the Imaging Device icon to display a list of scanner drivers currently on your system. There should be only one, but you might be surprised to see a driver that did not show up in the Device Manager when your computer was running in Normal Mode. If more than one driver appears, delete the icon for the old scanner driver you're no longer using.

After you finish checking your system in Safe Mode, you need to restart your computer to run Windows in Normal Mode.

Slow Scans, Saves, and Edits

Is your computer suddenly running at a maddeningly slow pace when you try to scan, store, and edit images? This is particularly baffling if your computer was running just fine a few hours or days ago. The problem is most likely traceable to a shortage of a particular resource your computer needs to process tasks quickly. This resource, called random access memory, or RAM, handles the processing of all current tasks. The more available RAM, the more tasks can be performed simultaneously, speeding up the overall processing time.

Conflicting Scanner Drivers

Drivers for scanners you've previously installed can cause software conflicts as they compete for RAM resources with your new scanner. To remedy this problem, follow the steps in the previous "Basic Uninstallation Procedure for Old Drivers" section to correctly uninstall drivers for old scanners you're no longer using.

Other Programs Competing for Resources

Windows conveniently allows you to identify programs that you want to open every time you start your computer. The theory behind this is that it saves you time if you routinely use these programs.

The problem with this logic is that many software makers have designed their programs to run automatically every time you start your computer, often without your realizing it. (For example, I found an accounting program I haven't used in months included in my Start menu.) When several programs start automatically, they compete for system resources and slow your processing time. The solution is to decrease the number of programs that automatically open and continue to run when you boot up your computer.

To check for programs that start without your knowledge and remove the ones you don't want, follow these steps:

1. Click your Windows Start Menu button, choose Settings, and then Taskbar & Start Menu. A Taskbar and Start Menu Properties dialog box appears.

2. Click the Advanced tab. A list of each program on your system appears, with a check box next to it, as shown in Figure 7-7.

3. Delete any programs from the startup folder that you do not want to run automatically when you start your computer.

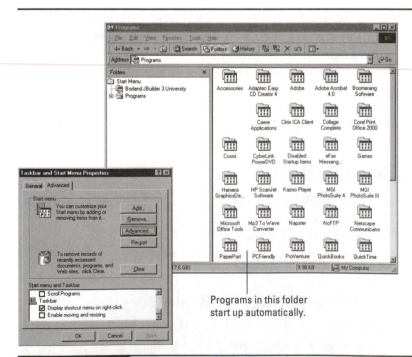

Programs in this folder
start up automatically.

FIGURE 7-7   Remove programs you don't want running in the background at startup.

Do not deselect programs that are necessary to run your system at startup.

4. Restart your computer to free resources from previously started programs, and to allow the new settings to take effect.

Checking Your System Resources

You can check your system resources while you're running your scanner and image-editing software to see if they're running low. According to Hewlett-Packard, your available resources should be about 85 percent of your total resources during the scanning process.

To check the resources available on your system for scanning and editing, follow these steps:

1. While your scanner and image-editing software are both open, right-click the My Computer icon on your Windows desktop.

2. The System Properties dialog box appears, as shown in Figure 7-8.

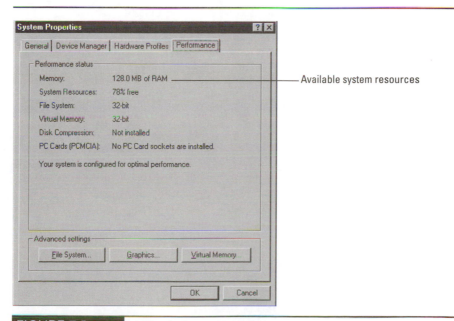

FIGURE 7-8   Check the available resources on your system.

3. Click the Performance tab to display the available system resources.

4. If your system resources are below 80 percent, limit the number of programs running in the background by following the steps in the previous "Other Programs Competing for Resources" section.

Recommendation for Cleaning Your Scanner: Don't!

If you're getting flecks of dust on your scanned photos or weird streaks, don't be tempted to resort to drastic cleaning measures. Scanner manufacturers unanimously concur that you should never attempt to clean your scanner surface with anything other than a dry cloth. More importantly, don't ever attempt to lift the scanner glass or take it apart for cleaning.

Chapter 8

Formats for Saving and Storing Files

How To...

- Understand the differences between various file formats

- Decide which format to use for sending images over the Web

- Balance file size and image quality considerations

- Recognize the benefits and effects of data compression

Scanners might signal the beginning of the end of bulky photo albums, with loose and disorganized photos stuffed between their pages. With digital imaging, storing and saving photos has taken a technological leap.

Central to the issue of storing image data are file format considerations. File formats that preserve a lot of data for high-quality images often take up impractical amounts of space on your hard drive. They can also take forever to send over the Web. This chapter helps you find a balance between the important considerations of image quality, storage space, and optimizing electronic-image transfers.

Files Saved on Your Computer Have Different Formats

Each time you save a document or project on your computer, you're saving it to a file. One way to locate the image, text, or other data you've saved is to right-click the Start button on the Windows taskbar, then choose Explore to open Windows Explorer, as shown in Figure 8-1.

When you look in the Explorer window, all the saved files look alike—identical yellow folder icons; however, if you access your files by clicking the My Computer icon on your desktop, you see something entirely different. Instead of a column of folder icons, you see icons for shortcuts to documents in different applications. For example, Figure 8-2 shows a window displaying icons in the Microsoft Word, Bitmap, WinZip, and other file formats.

Programs Write Files in Their Native Formats

Files might look alike when you view them in your Explore window, but in reality they're as different as the software that created them. Every software program, or *application,* stores files in its *native* format. For example, a Microsoft Word document creates a file with a native format that's different from a WordPerfect document.

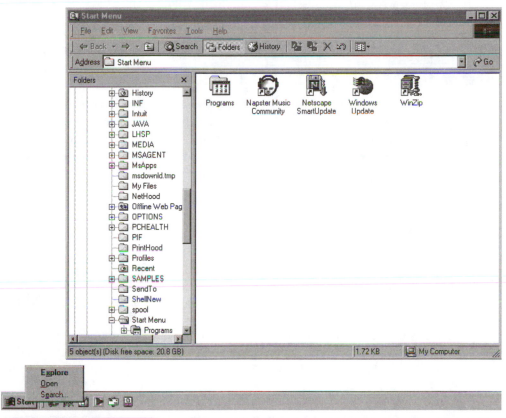

FIGURE 8-1   Locating a file from the Windows Explorer window

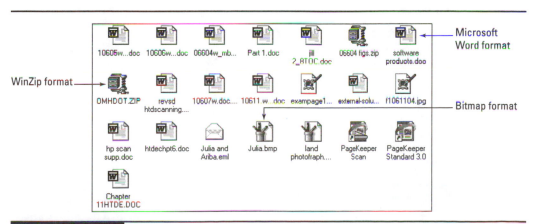

FIGURE 8-2   Locating a file using the My Computer icon

PhotoDeluxe writes files to its native PSD format. PhotoSuite uses JPEG as its native file format.

 *Different programs might have the same native format. For example, several image-editing programs might use JPEG as their native.*

Some formats are *proprietary,* which means you can open and use them only if you have the particular type of software for which they were designed. Other formats are extremely gregarious. You can easily transfer them into other applications, or send them to your friends over the Internet and know that they'll get along just fine with lots of other programs.

Image-Editing Programs Support Different Formats

In addition to their native file formats, most image-editing programs, such as PhotoSuite and PhotoDeluxe, support a smorgasbord of file formats. A particular image format, however, might have its own quirks and caveats. A program, such as PhotoSuite or PhotoDeluxe, might allow you to view but not edit or save files in particular formats. You might be able to perform some tasks, but not others, depending on what format you use to scan and save an image. Table 8-1 summarizes the file formats supported by PhotoSuite and PhotoDeluxe. PhotoSuite, for example, supports 18 different formats.

File Format	Extensions that Appear as Part of Filename	Can File Be Opened/ Saved in PhotoSuite?	Can File Be Opened/ Saved in PhotoDeluxe?
Joint Photographic Experts Group	.jpeg, .jpe, .jog	Y/Y	Y/Y
Portable Network Graphic	.png	Y/Y	Y/Y
Windows Bitmap	.bmp	Y/Y	Y/Y
FPX	.fpx	Y/N	Y/Y
Tagged Image File Format	.tif	Y/Y	Y/Y
CompuServe Graphics Interchange Format	.gif	Y/Y	Y/Y
Gem Image	.img	Y/N	N/N

TABLE 8-1   Common Graphics File Formats

File Format	Extensions that Appear as Part of Filename	Can File Be Opened/ Saved in PhotoSuite?	Can File Be Opened/ Saved in PhotoDeluxe?
PC Paintbrush	.pcx	Y/N	N/N
STING	.stn	Y/N	N/N
TrueVision Targa	.tga	Y/N	N/N
Sun Raster	.ras	Y/N	N/N
PhotoWorks	.sfw	Y/N	N/N
Konica	.kqp	Y/N	N/N
Encapsulated PostScript	.eps	Y/N	Y/Y
Floppy Shot	.pic	Y/N	N/N
Kodak Photo CD	.pcd	Y/N	N/N
Adobe Photoshop	.psd	Y/N	Y/Y
Windows Metafile	.wmf, .emf	Y/N	Y/Y
PICT	.pct	N/N	Y/Y
Simple Format Changeables	.ica	N/N	Y/Y

TABLE 8-1   Common Graphics File Formats *(continued)*

Identifying Image File Types

You can tell which file you're working with by looking at the filename. A period and three letters follow a file name. Those three letters, called the *file extension*, are an abbreviation for the type of file you're working with. For example, Figure 8-3 shows a .jpg and a .gif file, both of which are among the common formats discussed in the next section.

NOTE   *If you are unable to view file format extensions, an option might have been selected to hide them from view. To reveal them, choose View | Folder Options | View | Advanced Settings, and click to deselect the checked option box beside "Hide file extensions for known file types."*

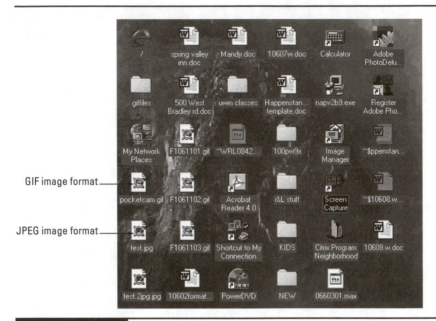

GIF image format

JPEG image format

FIGURE 8-3   Extensions for some common image formats

Selecting an Image Format

You don't have to specify a format when you save a file. The image-editing program will automatically do it for you. Image-editing programs such as PhotoSuite, PhotoDeluxe, Paint Shop Pro, and Photoshop save files to their own native format as a default.

If you don't specify a format when saving a file, the program you're using will save the file in its proprietary format. Using only the proprietary format will work fine for you if you want to edit, save, and print files using the same application, as many people do. You also need to be reasonably sure that anyone you send your images to can open them in the proprietary format. Also, some file formats allow you to save special effects, such as layers of text or graphics over a photo, that other formats do not.

Although you can accomplish many tasks using only the default proprietary format, you can sacrifice efficiency by staying in a file-saving rut. You achieve versatility and make life easier by choosing the appropriate format for the task at hand. For example, if you're sending a file over the Internet, you most likely want to opt for a format that economizes time and space by compressing data. If you're giving an image disk to a friend who doesn't have a copy of PhotoDeluxe, he or she won't be able to open the image if you've saved it in the default proprietary format (PSD) for PhotoDeluxe.

This section familiarizes you with some of the most commonly available and useful image formats. It also gives you a few pointers on how to select the one that best meets your needs.

JPEG: The Most Common Internet Format

The main advantage of the JPEG format is that it provides you with the ability to eliminate image information to reduce file size. This process is called *compression.* The advantage here is that smaller files transfer more quickly over the Internet.

Unfortunately, *overcompressing* a JPEG file can significantly reduce the detail presented in an image. The more a file is compressed, the more image data detail is eliminated.

If you save a photo in JPEG format and later want to make changes to it, rather then editing the JPEG file, rescan the photograph and make changes to the scan. This minimizes data loss.

8

GIF: The Graphics Interchange Format

The graphics interchange format, or GIF, is another type of format well suited for transferring files over the Internet. It's a file type designed for efficient compression, and also supports animation. PhotoSuite allows you to create animated GIF files, as explained in Chapter 17.

GIF is a favorite format because of its *lossless* compression scheme, which deletes only redundant data. This type of compression doesn't degrade image quality of the finished product. GIF is perhaps the most widely used format on the Web.

PNG: An Alternative Graphics Format

The PNG acronym stands for portable network graphic. This file type is an alternative to the GIF format. It also uses a lossless compression format.

There are times when PNG can be more desirable than GIF for two reasons. First, it is one of the only formats that allows you to save more than 256 colors. It uses a compression scheme that doesn't degrade the quality of the image files.

As you can imagine, this format produces large files because there are lots of color data and a compression scheme that retains a considerable amount of quality.

TIF: A Very Portable Format

The tagged image file, or TIF, format was developed by Microsoft and Aldus. It is a widely used format, which makes image files saved in this format very portable from application to application. It handles grayscale, 8-bit, and 24-bit color, and is compatible with a wide range of software programs. This makes it a good choice for swapping files among different image-editing programs, and sharing them among friends and family on a disk or CD. It's not, however, the format of choice for sending things over the Internet.

TIF compression does not reduce file size by very much, but this means it also doesn't result in a lot of data loss. In a nutshell, with the TIF format you get good image quality, but files that are a bit unwieldy for transferring over the Internet.

BMP: The Most Versatile Format

Windows bitmap, or BMP, is the native file format for Windows graphics. Every Windows-based software program supports this format. Unfortunately, this format does not support compression. You also cannot save more than 256 colors using this format.

The Costs and Benefits of Compression

Compression is the process of compacting data to save space. When I think of file compression, I always think of those packets of dehydrated food they sell in the camping stores. In both processes, you don't store what can be easily replaced: water or repetitive data.

How Compression Works

There are many forms of compression, but most of them work on a principle of identifying patterns of repetitive or similar data. The repetitive stuff is coded, rather than stored. The data that is not stored is either lost or replicated when the file is subsequently opened.

How much data you eliminate depends on the *compression ratio* that your image-editing program uses. Some programs, such as Photoshop, allow you to specify a compression ratio when saving a file to certain formats. PhotoSuite and PhotoDeluxe automatically determine the compression ratio for you. The higher the compression ratio, the smaller the file size and the more data is lost.

Compression Techniques

There are two types of compression: *lossy* and *lossless*. Lossy is very aggressive in discarding image data to reduce file size. Initially, the impact of this lossy compression isn't too devastating, but over time it takes its toll.

If you repeatedly save a file using a lossy compression scheme such as JPEG, each time you do so you recompress the file, eliminating more image data. Generally, the data loss isn't apparent to the naked eye. If you keep recompressing a file, however, you eventually might end up with odd effects such as a light border around a dark area in the photo, or a fuzzy image. If you're producing high-quality graphics for offset printing, you might notice these effects after only a few compressions. Figure 8-4 shows some effects of compression on a JPEG file that's been saved multiple times.

FIGURE 8-4   A 121KB JPEG image that has been saved 25 times

8

A lossless compression scheme discards only redundant data, which is data that's not actually used in producing the image. More importantly, data isn't lost each time you open and save the file. The disadvantage of lossless compression is that it's much less effective in reducing file size. The TIF format uses a lossless compression scheme. Figure 8-5 shows a TIF image after multiple saves. It is sharp and clear, but the file is about two-and-a-half times the file size of a similar JPEG image.

FIGURE 8-5   A 3.3MB TIF file that has been saved 25 times

Choosing the Right File Format

Choosing the right file format is a tradeoff between image size, quality, and compatibility with other programs. The BMP format, for example, is compatible with all Windows-based programs, but it is an unwieldy format for sending photos by email because it does not allow for data compression.

Similarly, TIF is an excellent format, since it uses a lossless compression scheme. It's the format I used to produce and submit most of the images that appear in this book. Your friends, however, might balk at downloading TIF-sized files, which are only slightly smaller than the BMP variety.

JPEG, GIF, and PNG formats are convenient for sending and downloading images, but the compression schemes they use result in data loss that might or might not be apparent over time. All in all, the format you choose depends on whether you'll be sending the format over the Internet and to what extent you're concerned with data loss.

Chapter 9

Selecting the Right Image-Editing Program

How To...

■ Evaluate the software bundled with your scanner

■ Distinguish the different types of image-editing programs

■ Decide which editing programs have the features that meet your needs

■ Experiment with shareware you can download for free

Start by Looking at Bundled Software

Bundled is a term for the software that comes with your scanner when you buy it. In the process of deciding which software to include with a scanner, scanner manufacturers strike deals with software manufacturers. Bundling provides advantages to both manufacturers.

The scanner manufacturers figure bundling image-editing software enables you to perform more projects and increases your satisfaction with their product. It generally makes their scanners competitive with other models on the market. The software manufacturers want to acquaint you with their particular product, in the hope that you become comfortable and familiar with its interface and features. The idea is that you'll likely be in the market for subsequent scanning software upgrades in future.

Decide Whether the Bundled Software Is a Bargain

Bundled software can be a really good selling point when you're choosing a scanner. For example, Photoshop is a high-end program that currently costs around $600—but it comes as a freebie with some high-end scanners. If you were planning on purchasing Photoshop, you might be financially ahead by opting for a high-end scanner and getting the program as a bundled add-on.

Something very important to keep in mind, however, is that very often scanners don't come with the latest versions of a software program. The idea might be to encourage you to go out and buy a later version of a product after you've become familiar with the bundled version. For example, if your scanner comes bundled with PhotoSuite 3, and you really like the product, you might be very motivated to upgrade to the added capabilities of PhotoSuite 4 because it is a relatively inexpensive software program.

Graduating from the Bundled Software

Just because a scanner comes with a particular image-editing application, it doesn't mean you're married to it. For example, many users find that PhotoDeluxe, which comes bundled with a number of scanners, provides a great introduction to image editing. The product has a short learning curve, but its features are limited. After getting up and running with PhotoDeluxe, you might want pay $50 (as of the writing of this book) to get the hundreds of project templates and more extensive capabilities with PhotoSuite, or you might want more the more sophisticated editing tools of Photoshop or Photoshop Elements. The features of all these programs are discussed below.

Shopping for the Right Program

You might be surprised to learn that, as of the writing of this book, I was able to locate more than 30 different image-editing programs just by surfing the Web. Some programs clearly have more to offer than others, but it can be a close race when you narrow it down to the finalists. In the end, the goal is to make sure the software you choose offers all the features you need to complete your projects, but that you aren't paying for features you don't use. Fortunately, you can choose from many programs on the market to strike the right balance.

Make a Shopping List of Features You Require

The best way to decide which features are useful to you in an image-editing program is to take a look at the types of projects you plan on doing. Here's a brief overview of what today's image-editing programs have to offer:

Photo-editing tools   If you just want to retouch, repair, and correct apparent flaws in photos, opt for a program with basic editing features that are simple and convenient to use.

Sophisticated color correction and enhancement   If you plan on correcting and editing color for publication purposes, you need a program that offers more sophisticated and technical editing tools such as separate color channels and CMYK adjustments.

Albums and archiving   It costs you nothing to scan a photo, but the downside of this freedom is that images tend to accumulate and take up a lot of space on your hard drive. If you're a "collector," take a good look at an image-editing software's options for organizing and archiving photos.

Website creation and optimization   Many image-editing programs have wizards, templates, and other features that allow you to create your own website easily, even if you have no prior experience in doing so. More sophisticated programs have tools for optimizing the images you post on your website.

Photo-sharing on the Web   If you're not interesting in creating your *own* website, programs such as PhotoSuite and PhotoDeluxe allow you to share photos on their websites for access by your friends and family with a special password.

Animation capabilities   You don't have to be a professional graphics artist to create animated effects from your photos. For example, PhotoSuite, a program for hobbyists, allows you to create animated GIF files that work sort of like those books that give the effect of animation as you quickly flip past a series of images. More sophisticated programs, such as Photoshop, have the capability to create professional-looking animated effects.

Read the Reviews

The Internet is a veritable convenience store for all different types of image-editing programs. You can read reviews and get product-specific information. Figure 9-1 shows an Amazon.com screen providing such information about PhotoSuite. You'll also find excellent software reviews at ZDNet.com and About.com, shown in Figure 9-2.

Survey the Software Market

There are literally dozens of image-editing programs on the market, some of which are used for special purposes or have an industry niche. This section explores the capabilities of the most popular programs available today that are intended primarily for home use. Most of the programs discussed in this chapter are available bundled with scanners, although the bundled version isn't always the most current version of the product.

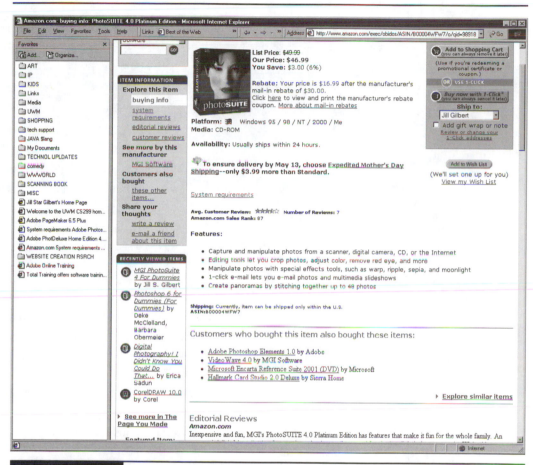

 Read about different image-editing programs on Amazon.com.

CAUTION *If you're considering Adobe products, be sure to pay attention to the widely varying system requirements. For example, Photoshop requires about 128MB of RAM to run its full range of features, while PhotoSuite and PhotoDeluxe will run on a lean 32MB.*

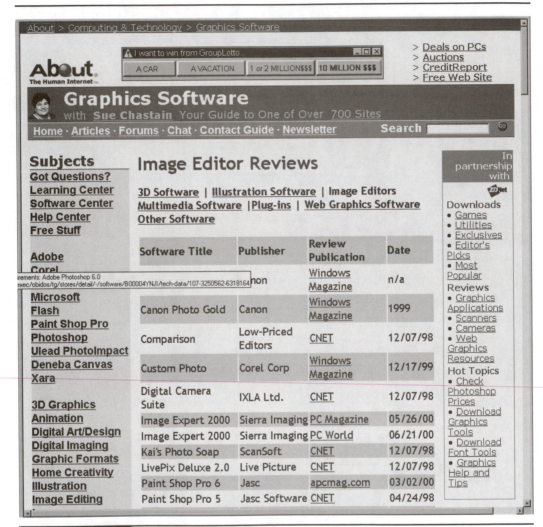

FIGURE 9-2   About.com contains links to reviews of popular image-editing programs.

Adobe: Targeting Three Different Types of Users

Adobe has, for many years, enjoyed a reputation as the premier manufacturer of image-editing software. The company's current marketing strategy is to target three different levels of consumers: experts, serious hobbyists, and entry-level users.

Photoshop is the high-end program aimed at professionals and serious hobbyists. It comes bundled with a few high-end scanners, and has a current retail price of about $600. Photoshop Elements is a pared-down version of Photoshop, aimed at the relatively sophisticated digital-camera and scanner user. As of the writing of this book, it costs around $100 and is not bundled with too many scanners, although it might appear as a bundled product in the future. PhotoDeluxe is a simplified, relatively limited image-editing program aimed at the entry-level user. PhotoDeluxe currently comes bundled with a number of scanners and is a great starter program for the beginner.

Photoshop: Powerful but Complex

Photoshop is considered the program of choice among graphics professionals. It's a high-end program, currently retailing at $609 as a download from the Adobe website. It has a wide range of capabilities and is considered one of the most powerful image-editing programs available—but its learning curve can be daunting. The sheer number of features can be overwhelming, and probably more than you'll ever need.

Even many professionals opt to use a simpler program, such as PhotoSuite, to accomplish routine touchup tasks quickly, since they find the program less cumbersome to work with. They break out Photoshop only when they need to delve into its more extensive editing features for a particular project.

9

Photoshop Features   If you're fortunate enough to purchase a scanner that has Photoshop bundled with it, don't be intimidated from giving the program a try. Free tutorials to help you use this program are available on the Adobe website at www.adobe.com/products/tips. The Web page shown in Figure 9-3 has links to tutorials ranging from how to perform basic correction and editing tasks to how to make sophisticated animated effects for use on the Web.

Some of the features that you get with Photoshop that you don't with most other programs include:

Highly sensitive correction tools   The image-correction tools in Photoshop are more extensive and sensitive than those found in other image-editing programs.

Extensive color-adjustment capabilities   Photoshop contains many sophisticated color adjustments, such as Levels and Curves, that can help you correct and fine-tune the balance of shadows, midtones, and highlights in your image. Other commands, such as Color Balance and Hue/Saturation, let you precisely adjust the color of an image.

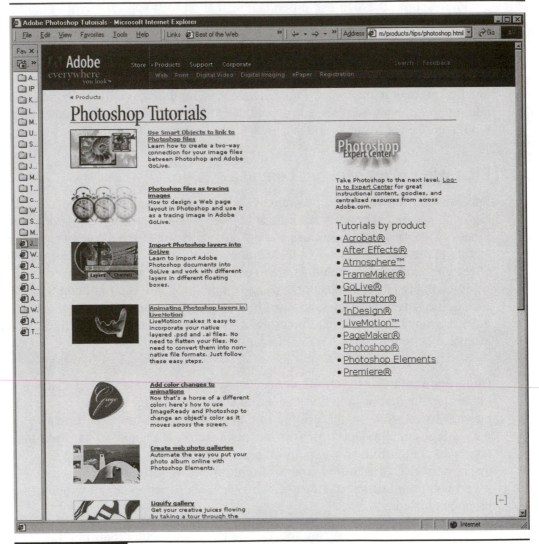

FIGURE 9-3   Adobe provides free online tutorials for Photoshop.

Histograms   These sophisticated graphs represent the mathematical values of light and dark areas in a photo, and allow you to make adjustments using the graph.

Sophisticated animation tools   Although PhotoSuite allows you to create animated GIF files, Photoshop offers you much greater control over the timing of your animation.

Vector drawing tools   The Photoshop vector tools let you draw crisp-edged shapes of various dimensions and colors. Unlike pixel data, such as a scanned photograph, these shapes are defined using the mathematical principle of vectors, which describe shape, size, and boundary properties of graphics with clean, resolution-independent precision.

Photoshop System Requirements   Photoshop requires greater system resources than other image-editing programs, primarily because of its sophisticated range of features. To run Photoshop your system must have the following:

- 128MB RAM
- 125MB hard disk space
- CD-ROM drive
- Monitor with 256-color (8-bit) or higher video card
- Monitor resolution of 800×600 or greater

Photoshop Elements

9

Photoshop Elements is a pared-down version of Photoshop that currently retails for less than $100. It's considered a mid-level program, aimed at the burgeoning market of scanner and digital-camera enthusiasts. It replaces the old Photoshop LE program.

Photoshop Elements lacks some of the more highly technical image-editing and color-correction features you find in Photoshop. For example, you can't do CMYK color specs and individual color-channel editing. If you have to ask what these features are, chances are you won't miss them.

Photoshop Elements provides a wide range of features at considerably less cost than Photoshop, but its interface can be difficult to navigate. Moreover, it doesn't have a wide range of project templates and wizards to help you quickly create a finished project. Consider purchasing Photoshop Elements if your needs run primarily toward image-editing rather than cards, calendars, or stationery. It has much of the sophisticated editing capability of Photoshop, at about one-fifth the price.

To run Photoshop Elements, your system must have the following:

- Pentium-class processor
- Microsoft Windows 98, 98 Second Edition, ME, 2000, or NT 4
- 64MB RAM (with virtual memory on)

- 150MB hard disk space

- Color monitor with 256-color (8-bit) or greater video card

- 800×600 or greater monitor resolution

PhotoDeluxe: Offering the Most Basic Features

PhotoDeluxe is a simple bundled product that allows you to get a taste of image editing. Many users outgrow it, and opt for a program with project templates and the capability to create sophisticated compositions and Web graphics. In the meantime, however, it's an excellent introduction.

PhotoDeluxe Features   PhotoDeluxe contains some basic templates for projects such as greeting cards and calendars, so you can get a feel for using these features. It also allows you to perform basic editing and layering effects, and to upload photos and display them on ActiveShare.com, a website for sharing photos.

The chief advantage of PhotoDeluxe is its comprehensive Help menu and simple interface, shown in Figure 9-4. You simply click the My Photos button to access saved photos, and the seven buttons at the top of the screen to access drop-down menus for all the program features.

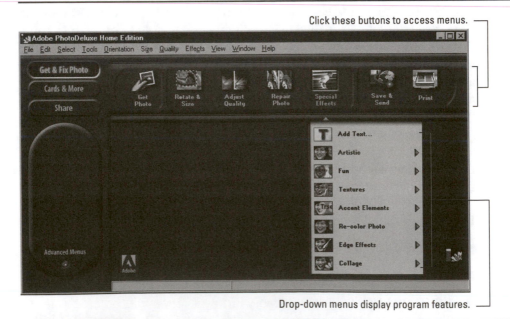

FIGURE 9-4   PhotoDeluxe offers a simple interface and basic features.

PhotoDeluxe System Requirements   PhotoDeluxe requires relatively minimal system requirements compared to other image-editing programs. To run it, your computer must have the following:

- Microsoft Windows 95, 98, or NT 4

- 32MB RAM

- 100MB hard disk space

- Monitor with 800×600 resolution and 16-bit color (thousands of colors)

PhotoSuite: Extensive Features and Versatility

PhotoSuite gives Adobe products a run for their money. PhotoSuite has lots of image-editing capabilities and features that make it easy to create a wide range of projects, combined with a simple interface. It's no wonder that it's currently the best selling image-editing program, and comes bundled with a number of scanners.

The PhotoSuite Niche

As of this writing, PhotoSuite retails for $49.95 at the PhotoSuite website located at www.mgisoft.com. In addition to the editing and correction tools you find with other image-editing programs discussed in this chapter, PhotoSuite comes with the following:

- Faux backgrounds and props to allow you to create interesting compositions like the ones shown in Color Insert Pages 1 and 2

- Dozens of greeting card, stationery, and calendar templates you can import your own scanned photos into

- Templates for creating novelty and gag items such as fake IDs, magazine covers, and sports cards with your own scanned photos

- A special easy-to-apply filter to simulate snow, rain, fog, tiles, crystallizing, and other effects, as shown in Color Insert Page 3

- Four different warp features that allow you to have fun with your scanned photos as shown in Color Insert Page 4

9

PhotoSuite also has features that allow you to create your own Web pages, even if you have absolutely no prior Web design experience. You can even create animations from a series of photos using the PhotoSuite wizard for creating animated GIF files.

PhotoSuite does not have the range of editing and color correction features you find in Photoshop, nor is it designed for extensive and sophisticated Web design. Most hobbyists, however, might not want to take the time to learn to manipulate these sensitive features and find the PhotoSuite wizards and templates a much easier route to accomplishing pretty much the same results.

PhotoSuite System Requirements

To run PhotoSuite 4 on your system, you must have the following:

- 32MB RAM

- 200MB hard disk space

- SVGA video card

- Monitor with 800×600 resolution and 24-bit true color

- 2MB video RAM

Other Good Imaging Products

Adobe products and MGI's PhotoSuite are the leading image-editing products both in terms of overall market share and what is most commonly bundled with today's scanners. There are dozens of other image-editing programs on the market as well. This chapter wouldn't be complete without the other notable mentions included in this section.

Paint Shop Pro: Another Image-Editing Alternative

Paint Shop Pro is another robust image-editing program, although it lacks the comprehensive tools of Photoshop and has nowhere near the number of interesting templates and project wizards of PhotoSuite.

Paint Shop Pro retails at an agreeable $109—or $99 if you download it directly from the manufacturer's website at www.jasc.com. It also offers Web graphics features and a pleasant interface.

Photo Soap: Companion Software to Organize Your Photos

Photo Soap is a slightly different type of image-editing program. It's designed to help you build and organize your library of scanned and other digital images. It addresses the issue that arises when you accumulate several gigabytes of scanned photos on your hard drive

Photo Soap includes tools for catalog and album building, as well as a basic array of retouching and editing tools. Photo Soap allows you to view your collection of photos by date, size, content, name, and color. It even includes a handy date-stamp feature not present in most other image-editing programs.

If you want to share your photos off line, Photo Soap can print album pages with headers, text, and captions. Photo Soap is a great companion software (or stand-alone program) to organize the legions of photos building up on your hard drive.

Photo Soap currently retails for about $20 and has the following system requirements:

- Microsoft Windows 95, 98, or NT 4 with Service Pack 3 or later
- 32MB RAM for Windows 95 or 98, 64MB for NT
- 100MB hard disk space
- 16- or 24-bit color display
- 800×600 screen resolution

9

CorelDraw and Photo-Paint

CorelDraw is a high-end graphics program, in the same league and price range (now around $500) as Photoshop. It has sophisticated and highly technical editing features, and gets rave reviews for its animation capabilities.

Photo-Paint retails now for about $350, and offers a Microsoft Office–style toolbar along the top of the screen. Photo-Paint can handle a greater number of image file formats than Photoshop, including AutoCAD file format.

You can learn more about Corel products on the company website, www.corel.com.

PhotoDraw

Microsoft offers its own image-editing software program, which is currently sold as a stand-alone product for just under $100. PhotoDraw gets rave reviews for its interface, which is designed to be intuitive to Microsoft Office users. It is second only to PhotoSuite in terms of templates and wizards, and offers a sophisticated range of features.

Exploring the World of Shareware

Shareware is software that you can download and try for free. Sometimes you get to use it indefinitely and other times you might be asked to pay a nominal fee to continue using the software beyond a trial period (usually 30 to 60 days).

A great place to look for image-editing shareware is the ZDNet website, at www.zdnet.com/downloads/specials/free. This site, shown in Figure 9-5, contains links leading directly to graphics shareware programs, as well as a list of the 50 most popular shareware programs on the Web.

FIGURE 9-5   The ZDNet site contains links to free graphics shareware.

The following are just a few examples of the interesting free graphics programs you can learn about on ZDNet:

MediaSpyder   A free tool that finds and downloads photos, clip art, and animations from the Internet. Searches using this program are automatically archived, with the ability to group images in collection folders.

FotoAlbum   Retrieves photos directly from your scanner and lets you organize, view, print, and share them with others on a free website. You can organize pictures into albums, set images as wallpaper, and print multiple-picture layouts.

Photocopier   Scans your document or photo and sends it directly to your printer. You can choose color, grayscale, or black-and-white scanning at 100 percent or 70 percent; adjust the brightness; and quickly select the number of copies to print.

Screen Seize   Allows you to photograph your entire computer screen, an application window, a dialog box, a selected area, or an object.

Making the Right Software Choice

In summary, choosing the right image-editing software to complement your scanning projects involves asking yourself the following questions:

- Does any software come bundled with a scanner you're considering purchasing?

- Is the image-editing program bundled with the scanner adequate to meet your needs or should you consider purchasing other programs or downloading shareware with additional capabilities?

- Based on the types of projects you plan to undertake, which additional image-editing capabilities will you need?

- After narrowing down programs in your price range that have the features you want, which interface is most intuitive and appealing to you?

Do you feel you still need more information to choose an image-editing software? Chapter 10 takes a look at some of the most commonly used image-editing tools and what they accomplish.

Chapter 10

Which Photo-Editing Tools Are Useful for Specific Tasks

How To...

- Cut, crop, and rotate images

- Correct red eye

- Airbrush like a professional photographer

- Fix scratched, torn, wrinkled, and stained photos

- Correct under- and overexposed photos

- Make good use of other touchup tools

- Colorize and tint images

- Draw and paint with your editing software

- Make cutouts and logos

- Combine several photos into a single work of art

It's both a blessing and a burden that there are dozens of image-editing products on the market. While the proliferation of programs gives you lots of choices, it means you must carefully select among them, and have a good understanding of which features are useful to you. This chapter gives you an inventory of the different types of tools you might be interested in purchasing in a software package, and shows you what they're used for.

A Disclaimer about this Chapter

Please be aware that this chapter is intended to provide you with an overview of different types of image-editing tools that you might find useful. It is *not* the purpose of this chapter to provide you with detailed instructions as to how to use any particular image-editing program. You'll need to consult the Help menu or online help for the software for that.

As with any computer book, the objective of this one is to enlighten, not confuse; but a chapter providing an overview of various image-editing tools can become frustrating. For example, say you're working with PhotoDeluxe while the author is using illustrations and examples that apply to the PhotoSuite 4 program. The book might seem unrelated to the menus and features on your screen. That's why this chapter focuses on the tools themselves, rather than how they're presented in any particular program interface.

 *This chapter is intended to educate about different image-editing tools. The information presented here is not specific to the user interface of any particular image-editing program.*

An Overview of Your Image-Editing Toolbox

Image-editing is one of the most fun and creative activities you can undertake with your PC. You probably already have dozens of ideas as to the types of projects you'd like to accomplish with your scanner. In creating most of your projects, you'll make use of image-editing tools from one or more of the following categories:

Cropping and positioning tools   These types of tools allow you to cut off part of your photo, or resize the entire picture without losing any of its content. You can also reposition, rotate, and create a mirror image of your photo, depending on the range of these features your image-editing program offers.

Correction tools   You can virtually go back in time to fix what went wrong at the point you snapped the photo. Image-editing tools allow you to compensate for the effects of overexposed film or a blurry, unfocused image. A tool that corrects the red-eye effect from a flash is my personal favorite.

Repair tools   These program features allow you to take care of damage that can occur to a photo after it's developed—scratches, stains, wrinkles, spills, and other wear and tear.

Pixel cloning tools   Did you ever wonder what people meant when they talked about "airbrushed" photos? Airbrushing is taking colored dots (called pixels) from a surrounding area of a photo and using them to cover something you don't want to appear in the finished picture. The color insert illustrates the use of a cloning tool to take care of a model's bad hair day and smeared lipstick by covering the wayward locks and runaway makeup with pixels from surrounding areas in the photo.

Colorizing tools   These tools allow you to give subtle or bold impact to a photo by selectively applying color. You can also enhance or create a mood by tinting a photo. The color insert has examples of both these techniques.

Composition tools   These tools allow you to cut and paste photos on your screen, and create a single picture from multiple images.

10

Painting and drawing tools   Most image-editing applications have drawing and painting tools that allow you to superimpose lines, shapes, and other markings.

Other special effects   Some image-editing programs offer special effects that allow you to distort photos (as if you were looking into one of those fun house mirrors) and create interesting visual effects such as fog, wind, and rain. These features are not specifically discussed in this book, but if you're interested, you should look for these features when comparing image-editing programs. Also check to see if they're included with software you've already purchased.

Cropping and Resizing Your Photos

You can alter the size of your photos by cropping (cutting) material from around the edges, or by shrinking or expanding the entire photo without altering its content. The ability to alter the size of your photo is particularly useful when you're creating a project, such as a greeting card, for which you need a photo that fits nicely within the finished piece.

Locating a Cropping Tool

Cropping allows you to remove portions of the photo that surround your main subject. Cropping is such an important feature that your scanning software—as well as your image-editing software—usually comes with this capability. As you might recall from Chapter 2, scanner software is the program that allows you to control the functioning of your scanner using an interface that appears on your computer desktop.

When the Cropping Tool Is Useful

Lopping off part of your photo with a cropping tool can achieve the following:

Focusing more attention on your subject matter   By getting rid of extraneous background, your subject appears larger and more prominently in a photo of the same size.

Getting rid of distracting or irrelevant background   Is your picture of you and your fiancé on the sunset beach ruined by an unknown passerby you didn't notice at the time of the shot? You might be able to rid yourself of the unwanted intruder by simply cropping him or her out of the photo.

Correcting an off-center photo   Do you have trouble centering your subjects when you take a photo? Cropping allows you to change the center of the photo by lopping a bit off one side or the other.

Eliminating worn or damaged edges   Torn corners and frayed edges can be fixed using some editing tools discussed later in the "Fixing Scratched, Torn, Wrinkled, and Stained Photos" section; however, it might be easier to just trim them off with your image-cropping tool.

A Sample Cropping Job

Figures 10-1 and 10-2 show a photo before and after cropping. Notice how cropping the photo both gets rid of extraneous background and focuses more attention on the main subject of the picture.

FIGURE 10-1   A photograph before cropping

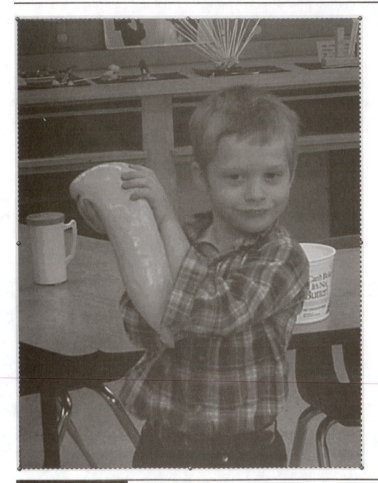

FIGURE 10-2   Cropping the photograph makes the subject appear larger and more prominent.

Cropping Tips

Cropping is an easy job, regardless of which image-editing program you might be using. Consult the Help menu to find out how to locate the cropping tool. Most cropping tools display your photo within a set of boundary lines on the screen, and you indicate where you want to crop the photo by moving the boundary lines.

Here are a few tips to keep in mind when cropping a photo:

- Make sure that you've selected a cropping tool, rather than a resizing tool. Resizing will increase or decrease the size of the entire photo without removing any unwanted areas.

- Save your original image to a separate file before you begin cropping, and make sure you're satisfied with the effects of your cropping *before* saving the newly cropped image. Most image-editing programs have an Undo feature (like the one that comes with Microsoft Word) that allows you to restore your original photo; however, you cannot use the Undo feature once you've saved your cropped photo.

- When cropping an unwanted background object, don't crop so much from one side that your photo is off center. If you can't crop the offending object *and* keep your subject centered, consider using the clone tool, discussed later in this chapter, rather than the cropping tool, to remedy the problem.

- Remember that if you crop a photo, the size will not change. The remaining portions of your image will fill the same dimensions as your original photo, resulting in a lower overall resolution. This might be an issue affecting the quality of your final project if you crop a large area from a photo that was originally scanned at a low resolution.

Resizing a Photo

Resizing a photo is a process that involves a different tool from cropping. When you resize, you retain all the subject matter in the original photo, but change the size of it. Depending on the program you're using, you might have more than one option as to how to resize your photo.

Some programs have resizing tools that enclose your photo within a boundary box (like the cropping tools). You move the boundary lines around the photo to make the photo smaller. This type of resizing can be difficult to use because you have to adjust the height and width manually and in precisely the same proportions to avoid distorting the photo. Figures 10-3, 10-4, and 10-5 illustrate how this type of distortion alters the appearance of your subjects.

FIGURE 10-3 A scanned photo prior to resizing

FIGURE 10-4 A photo in which the height dimension has been increased in greater proportion to the width dimension

FIGURE 10-5   A photo in which the width dimension has been increased in greater proportion to the height dimension

Some programs, such as PhotoDeluxe and even Microsoft Word, have a utility that I find preferable for resizing photos without the risk of distortion. This feature allows you simply to double-click on the photo and reset all its dimensions at once by specifying the new size as a percentage of the original size. For example, a 50 percent size would mean you reduce all the dimensions by half. A specification of 200 percent means you double the size of the scanned photo. A Microsoft Word dialog box for resizing images with this type of utility is shown in Figure 10-6.

TIP   *The resizing feature is particularly useful when you're working with templates. It allows you to manually resize a photo until it fits perfectly within the cutout area of a template, as shown in Figure 10-7.*

10

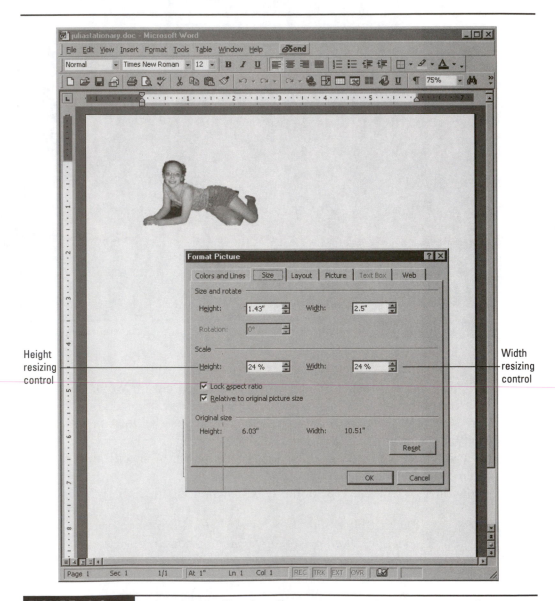

Height resizing control

Width resizing control

FIGURE 10-6
A resizing utility that allows you to exercise accurate control over photo dimensions

Resizing
boundary box

FIGURE 10-7   This photo needs to be resized to fit the greeting card template.

Altering the Angle and Inverting Your Subjects

Some of the most frequent editing tasks you perform might involve repositioning or inverting your photos. Fortunately, virtually all image-editing programs come with tools and utilities for straightening crooked shots or making your photo subjects face a different direction.

Straightening a Crooked Shot

In the excitement of getting a good shot, it's not uncommon to forget to hold your camera level. Fortunately most image-editing programs (and even some scanner software) comes with tools that allow you to reposition your photos. When used with the cropping tool, rotating a photo can be just the right remedy for a crooked shot.

Consider the photo in Figure 10-8. It's a great shot, but crooked. It looks like that computer is about to slide off the desk into the subject's lap! Using PhotoSuite 4, I carefully rotated the photo about 5 degrees to the left, as shown in Figure 10-9. Then I used my cropping tool to trim the photo so that it retained its original shape and dimensions. The finished result—rotated and cropped—appears in Figure 10-10.

FIGURE 10-8   This is a nice shot, but crooked.

Rotation tool

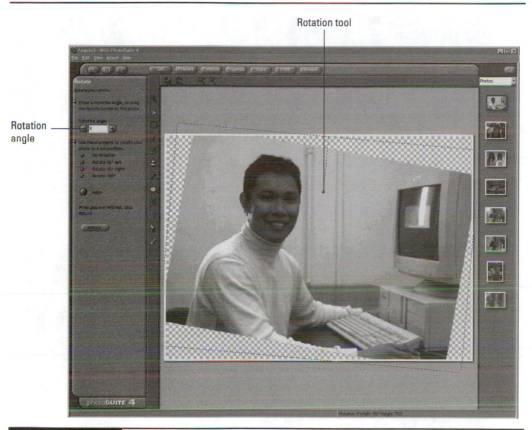

Rotation angle

FIGURE 10-9   Rotating 5 degrees to the left and cropping corrects the problem.

10

Creating a Mirror Image of Your Photo

This feature is particularly useful when you're importing cutout images into another photo (I tell you how to do this later, in the "Making a Cutout" section). Sometimes you need a subject to be facing left, when he or she is facing right in the original photo; or you might want to copy an image upside down to create a certain effect within a photo collage.

Many image-editing programs have features that allow you to do this. For example, PhotoSuite allows you to invert a photo or cutout from a photo both horizontally and vertically.

FIGURE 10-10   The subject now appears at the correct angle, and the computer does not look as if it's ready to fall into his lap.

This whimsical scene in Figure 10-11 would be a lot more collegial if the subjects were facing each other. It also might be a bit easier for the viewer to suspend disbelief if the giant butterfly were not flying upside down. In Figure 10-12, each of the animals and the motorcycle rider have been inverted using the PhotoSuite 4 horizontal flip tool. The butterfly has been placed in an upright position using the vertical flip tool.

In Figures 10-13 and 10-14, I have horizontally inverted an entire photo to make it appear as if the photo were taken from an entirely different vantage point.

FIGURE 10-11   In this scene, none of the subjects are facing each other, and the giant butterfly is flying upside down.

FIGURE 10-12   The horizontal and vertical flip tools allow you to reorient the subjects properly.

FIGURE 10-13   The original photo appears to have been taken from the right side of the stage.

FIGURE 10-14   Horizontally inverting the photo makes the vantage point appear to be to the left of the stage.

Correcting the Red-Eye Effect

Red eye (that *is* the actual technical term) is a well-known unwanted effect that's caused when the light from the flash is so strong that it actually penetrates your subject's eyeballs. It then reflects the red color of the retina.

This effect occurs most often in blue-eyed people or in dimly lit environments. In dim lighting, the subject's pupils dilate, exposing more of the red retina.

Prior to the advent of scanning and digital imaging, amateur photographers had only two alternatives for reducing the red-eye effect, neither of which was very desirable. The first involved purchasing a special red-eye reduction flash system that would emit a pre-flash before the actual flash. This would cause the subject's pupils to contract, but you ended up with a lot of squinty-eyed subjects, as well as people who stopped smiling or blinked after the initial flash. The other alternative was dabbing a blue marking-pen over a subject's eyes, but that could be tedious if you needed multiple copies of the shot, and it could obscure a subject's true eye color.

Most image-editing programs have a special feature for correcting the red-eye effect, which you can locate by checking the Help menu of the software under the keyword "red-eye."

Generally, the repair process for the red-eye effect involves the following steps:

1. Locate the red-eye correction tool in your image-editing software.

2. Use the zoom tool to enlarge the area with the red pixels, as shown in Figures 10-15 and 10-16.

3. Paint over the red pixels using the red-eye correction tool or other touchup feature provided with your image-editing program for this purpose.

 *If your image-editing software does not have a tool specifically for correcting the red-eye effect, you can enlarge the photo as described above and apply a gray tint to the red pixels.*

Airbrushing Flaws from a Scanned Photo

Airbrushing is a term that's historically been applied to image-editing technology that simulates the effect of using a paintbrush to cover up flaws and unwanted effects in the picture. Generally, with modern scanning and image-editing technology, you can achieve an airbrushing effect by creating patches of pixels (colored dots) from areas in the photo surrounding the flaw. You cover the flaw using pixels matching the surrounding background.

FIGURES 10-15 AND 10-16 Both of these subjects suffer from the dreaded red-eye effect caused by an indoor flash (left). Most image-editing programs allow you to zoom in on the eye area and correct the color of the pixels.

This process involves a feature that's generally referred to as a *cloning* tool because you copy (clone) pixels from the surrounding area of the photo. Cloning pixels is a simple (and fun) process once you get the hang of it, but you might need to use your Undo button and repeat the process a few times to get a final result that bears no telltale traces of editing.

How Cloning Works

Regardless of which image-editing program you're using, you generally follow these guiding steps to complete the cloning process:

1. Locate the cloning tool provided with your image-editing software using the Help menu for the program. Try using the keywords "clone" or "repair."

2. Zoom in and enlarge the area you want to cover or repair. In Figure 10-17, we need to repair the model's "bad hair day."

Hair needs fixing!

Smeared lipstick

FIGURE 10-17   This model's hair and smeared lipstick need airbrushing.

10

3. Use the cloning tool to take some source pixels from the surrounding area, and deposit them over the flaw that you want to cover, as shown in Figure 10-18. Follow the directions for your particular image-editing program to do this. Figure 10-19 shows the completed product.

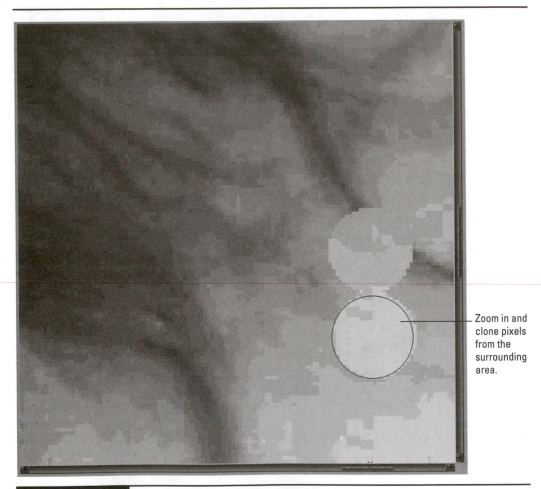

Zoom in and clone pixels from the surrounding area.

FIGURE 10-18   The editing can be accomplished by zooming in and cloning pixels from the surrounding area.

Who needs expensive and confusing lenses? You can apply filtering effects like the ones here using your scanner. These sophisticated effects make it hard to tell amateurs using disposable cameras from the professionals who own a suitcase full of expensive lenses.

Professional photographer Ian Britton took this incredible photo, called "Sunrise." I borrowed it from his website at http://www.freefoto.com to illustrate the dramatic effects you can achieve with filters.

Applying a blue filter entirely changes the mood of this shot.

Applying a gold filter can give a scanned photo an antique appearance

A sepia filter sets the sky on fire.

Once you become familiar with the capabilities of your scanner and your image-editing software, you can create fascinating pieces like these by layering and cutting portions from multiple photos. I used opacity tools that come with most image-editing programs to make some portions of these photos transparent.

These two photos were created by Chris Taylor using the cutting and tracing tool in PhotoSuite. First Chris traced a silouette of the cowboy in the center of a photo, and made the silhouette transparent. Then he filled in the silhouette with another edited photos to get this interesting result.

Chris used the transparency and cutting tools in PhotoSuite to artistically combine photos of the Statue of Liberty, the Lincoln Memorial, the Capital and, of course, the American flag.

This picture captures the important moment of Brett's successful performance in the school assembly. But the school lighting is harsh and unflattering to both her and her mom.

Harsh lighting casts creates unflattering shadows and glare on Mom's face

Distracting background

Glare on the glasses

I scanned the original photo and applied simple image-editing tools from PhotoSuite. I was able to downplay the distracting background using the cropping, blurring, and tinting tools, and I used the Touchup tools to get rid of harsh shadows and glare on my subjects' faces.

Enhancing the brightness and contrast settings to compensate for the poor lighting

The Soften Touchup Brush got rid of the glare on mom's face and the unflattering effects of harsh lighting.

The Blemish Touchup Brush eradicated the glare on Brett's glasses

The Blur and Tint Touchup Brush tools downplayed the distracting background

Here's an almost-but-not-quite photo. The red-eyed baby against the heavy red curtain here looks like something out of a horror flick. Just about every image-editing program has a red-eye correction tool that let's you salvage those almost-perfect photos. I also used the cutting tool here to cut the baby from the existing photo and place her on the softer, pastel background. The PhotoSuite 4 edge fading tools helped fade the cutout into the background I selected, turning a photo previously destined for the trash into a much better looking image.

Red eye

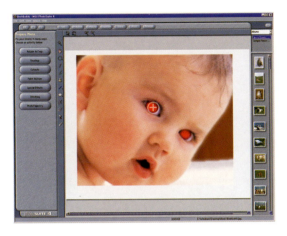

Zoom in and paint over the red pixels

No red eye

I scanned and colorized this black and white photo using the image-editing software that came with my scanner (PhotoSuite).

Here's another dramatically colorized scanned photo from a vacation to New York. It takes only a few minutes to do this!

Here's a more sophisticated example of how you can cut, crop and combine multiple scanned photos into a single composition. It's easy to switch heads and bodies as I've done here once you get the hang of it!

PhotoSuite, the image-editing program that came with my scanner has dozens of backgrounds. I also like to scan my own backgrounds using travel brochures, magazines and scenes from other scanned photos. In these images, I sent Professor Levine, from the University of Wisconsin Computer Science Department, to conduct some research on a few remote locations.

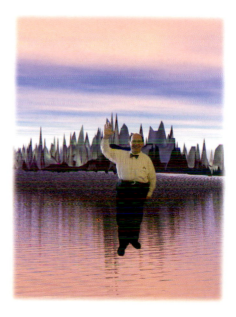

Our family uses our scanner to create personalized photo greeting cards, like these, for just about every occasion. We've also made shirts by scanning the photo onto a sheet of iron-on transfer paper available at any office supply store.

My image-editing software also comes with lots of fun templates that allow me to do fun and professional-looking projects with my scanner. I used this fake newspaper template to create a birthday invitation from a scanned photo of my daughter and some of her friends and used the magazine template to place another picture in a fun contect.

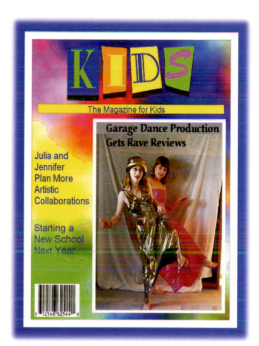

Our family has a lot of fun cutting, cropping and importing images into Microsoft Word documents. Here's a report my daughter wrote for school. Our image-editing software lets us create and save our own library of cut-out images we've made from our scanned photos to enhance letters, resumes and other Microsoft Word projects.

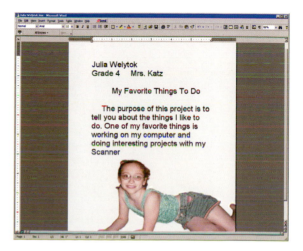

Another artistic use for scanned images is to crop, copy and paste them to create an interesting border effect, as I've done with this photo.

Your scanner is an invaluable tool for repairing and restoring precious family photos that have become damaged over the years. The photo on these next few pages was restored using PhotoSuite.

This scanned photograph of an old house (taken in the 1940's) hadn't weathered well in a shoebox. It was badly yellowed and had tattered edges and torn, missing pieces.

First, I tinted the photo to restore its original black-and-white appearance.

I cropped the photo to eliminate some of the damaged areas, and focus more attention on the house.

I used the PhotoSuite Enhance tool to properly balance the light and dark areas of the photo. This required just a single mouse click!

Getting rid of the torn spot was easy, I used the Clone tool to take some color from the surrounding sky and painted over the damaged portion.

Finally, I fixed the worn spot in the middle darkening it just a bit, using the PhotoSuite Touch-up tool.

The photo is now restored to the way it looked more than 50 years ago!

Here a just a few more samples of the thousands of unique special, stylized and personalized items you can create using your own scanned photos. The possibilities are endless!

Business cards, stationary and promotional items

Illustrated gift tags, signs, and labels

Calendars

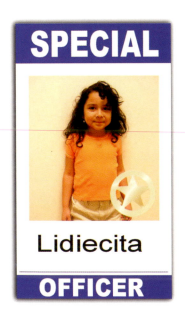

Make novelty items such as fake IDs, sports cards, and magazine covers using your own scanned photos and text

FIGURE 10-19   The completed, cloned result

10

Tips for Making Retouching Less Obvious

Retouching photos using a cloning tool can give you dramatic and flawless results. It's definitely a skill you'll want to master for improving on your scanned photos. It does, however, take patience and practice.

Here are a few tips to help you improve your cloning and retouching skills:

- Clone the smallest area necessary to achieve the desired camouflaging result. The smaller the area you clone, the more difficult it is to detect.

- Use as small a cloning brush (or other tool) as possible. Repeatedly cloning a smaller amount of pixels rather than trying to clone a large amount all at once results in a better overall match and less detectable result.

- Take pixels from a destination area as close as possible to the flaw you're trying to conceal. This usually results in a better color match.

- Pay careful attention to changes in color tone in the surrounding background, and try to get source pixels as close to the shade you need.

- Use the soften tool, discussed later in the "Improving Photos with Soften and Blur Effects" section, to blend the patchwork of pixels you've created and make the retouching less obvious. The photo in Figure 10-20 was edited to get rid of some of the distracting objects in the background, but the retouching is readily apparent in Figure 10-21. Figure 10-22 shows how a bit of blending with the softening tool obscures the otherwise obvious retouching.

- If your software allows you to adjust the opacity, which is the level of transparency, of the pixels you're depositing, experiment with this feature to achieve a better blending effect.

FIGURE 10-20   This photo has some distracting objects in the background that can be airbrushed away.

FIGURE 10-21   A retouched photo before the softening (blurring) tool is used for blending

FIGURE 10-22   The softening (blurring) tool makes the retouching less obvious.

Fixing Scratched, Torn, Wrinkled, and Stained Photos

Fixing scratched, torn, wrinkled, and stained photos is just a matter of applying the cloning and retouching process described in the previous section. Some programs, such as PhotoSuite 4, have special utilities and wizards to fix these types of flaws; however, you can treat them just as you would any other cloning and retouching job.

Figures 10-23 and 10-24 illustrate the process of repairing a scratched photo. The result of the repair process appears in Figure 10-25. Simply zoom in on the scratched, torn, stained, or wrinkled area, and begin cloning and covering it with pixels from the surrounding area.

FIGURE 10-23   This photo has an obvious scratch.

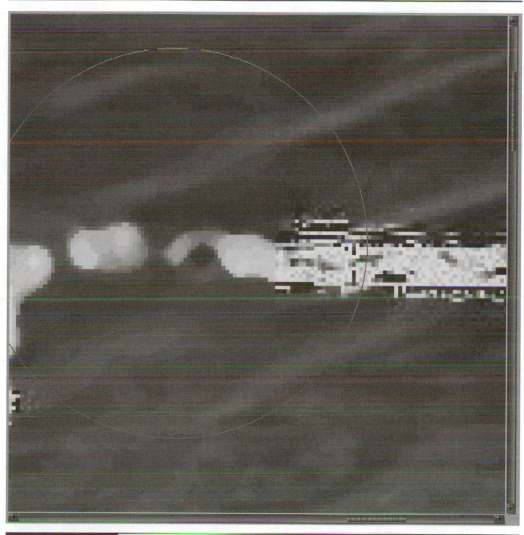

FIGURE 10-24   Image-editing software allows you to zoom in and clone the surrounding pixels.

10

FIGURE 10-25   After editing, the repair is barely noticeable.

Other Useful Touchup Tools

Depending on the sophistication of your image-editing software, it might include dozens of image-editing tools having a wide range of complexity. You might have the patience to research and master these tools, but if you're like most scanner users, you want to hone in on those tools that are most useful and versatile for enhancing your photos. You're more interested in a finished photo that captures a mood and a moment than one that reflects the maximum amount of cutting-edge technology. This section tells you about three powerful tools that can help you achieve a variety of professional effects with a minimum of techno-fuss.

Sharpening Blurry Photos

A sharpen tool is useful if you photograph people who move—and don't they all? It's a feature that corrects the blurriness than can result from a moving subject.

Blurriness results when a photo subject is captured at too low a *shutter speed*. The shutter speed of a camera determines the amount of time the film (or computer chip in a digital camera) is exposed to light by the shutter being opened. The faster your shutter speed, the better the ability of your camera to capture fast-moving objects.

A sharpen tool creates an illusion of sharper focus by adding small halos of light along the borders of an image. The darker side of the border gets a dark halo, while the lighter side gets a light halo. The greater contrast along the borders gives an overall impression of a less blurred image. Figures 10-26 and 10-27 show a photograph before and after sharpening.

FIGURE 10-26   A blurry photo before the sharpening effect is applied

10

FIGURE 10-27   The same photo after the sharpening tool is used

Improving Photos with Soften and Blur Effects

There are times when you might actually *want* to blur a photo to achieve a certain effect. Most image-editing programs come with softening and blurring tools that are useful for the following purposes:

Creating the effect of motion   Slightly blurring a portion of a photo can create the impression of motion. I've used this technique on the batter's feet in the photo in Figure 10-28 to create the illusion that she's about to run to first base.

FIGURE 10-28   Blurring the area around the batter's feet creates an illusion of motion.

Obscuring background and emphasizing your subject   In Figures 10-29 and 10-30, I've used this technique to make the subject stand out against the relatively uninteresting backdrop of the computer lab.

FIGURE 10-29   An attractive subject against a busy, uninteresting background

FIGURE 10-30   Blurring the background enhances the subject of the photo.

Making photo retouching less apparent   It's generally impossible to get a perfect match when using the clone tool described previously in this chapter to retouch a photo. Using the softening tool to blend the retouched area can make it nearly indiscernible. See Figures 10-21 and 10-22 earlier in this chapter.

Correcting Under- and Overexposed Photos

Do you have photos of meaningful memories—but the memory is obscured or ruined because the photos came out too light or too dark? Scanning and editing can salvage your precious memories. It's simply a matter of correcting the effects of the initial under- or overexposure.

How Exposure to Light Affects Photo Quality

Regardless of what type of camera you use to take a photo, the brightness and darkness of your shot are controlled by a measurement called *exposure*. Exposure refers to how much light reached the film inside the camera at the time you took the photo.

Two factors determine the level of exposure:

Camera shutter speed   Your camera has a component, called a *shutter,* that covers the lens. The shutter allows light to travel through the lens to the film when the shutter is opened. Shutters are set at different opening and closing speeds. The faster the shutter speed, the more quickly the shutter opens and closes and the less light is allowed to enter.

Film sensitivity   If you look at any box of film, the packaging displays a rating, for example, 100, 200, or 400. This rating tells you how sensitive the film is to light. The higher the rating, the more sensitive the film is to light.

The more exposure the film has and the higher the sensitivity of the film, the lighter and brighter the final picture. Too much light, and the image appears washed out, or overexposed. Too little light, and the image appears dark, or underexposed.

 When you're taking a picture and not sure of the shutter setting to use, it's generally better to err on the side of overexposing rather than underexposing. Overexposed photos have more stored image data, and can be corrected more effectively using your scanner and image-editing software than underexposed photos.

Enhancing an Entire Photo

Image-editing programs have a variety of different tools to allow you to compensate for the under- or overexposure of a photo. These tools might be called *gamma adjustment, enhancement tools,* or *histograms.* They vary in complexity depending on your image-editing program.

Generally, these tools work on the mid-range areas of your photo, leaving the light and dark areas alone. These tools can be very effective for scanned photos.

PhotoSuite 4 has an Enhance feature that allows you to perform this type of adjustment with a single mouse click. Figures 10-31 and 10-32 illustrate the use of this tool.

FIGURE 10-31   A photo before the light and dark areas are enhanced

10

FIGURE 10-32   A photo after the light and dark areas have been enhanced using the PhotoSuite 4 Enhance feature

Working on Light and Dark Areas of a Photo

There might be times when you want to apply a correction tool to specific areas of a photo to make that portion lighter or darker. Image-editing tools that allow you to do this are sometimes referred to as *touchup brushes*.

For example, if you've photographed a scene with a recessed area, it might work well simply to lighten the shadowed portion. This process can be tricky. Save the photo *before* experimenting with the tool, so you can use the Undo button to restore the photo to its original light and dark area. In Figure 10-33, the brightness and contrast settings are set at an optimum level for displaying most of the photo; however, more detail is apparent in the recessed areas of the motorcycle when a touchup brush is used selectively to lighten that area, as shown in Figure 10-34.

10

FIGURE 10-33   Much of the detail in the dark areas of the photo is lost.

FIGURE 10-34   Lightening with the touchup tools brings out this detail.

To locate tools within your image-editing program that allow you to lighten or darken an area of your photo selectively, try consulting the Help menu using the keywords "lighten" or "darken."

Colorizing and Tinting Images

Color tools allow you to both better capture images as they actually appear, and to artistically enhance photos to reflect your own interpretation of scenes and subjects. As with most of the other techniques discussed in this chapter, color correction and enhancement requires patient trial and error. Just a few years ago, this technology was the exclusive purview of professional photographers with high-end equipment. Now the tools contained with most mid-level software (such as PhotoSuite and PhotoDeluxe) are amazingly simple to master.

Using a Color Adjustment Filter

A color adjustment filter tool allows you to compensate for green or red tones on your subjects. It can also compensate for a reddish cast that might appear on incorrectly processed photos. You can even compensate for tonal differences that appear between a scanned original and a copy you produce on your color printer.

Correcting Color with the RGB Tool

If your original photo has an odd color cast—say a green tint from poor indoor lighting or a red tint from incorrect processing—you can correct it using an RGB filter. Most image-editing programs include this tool. Try searching the Help menu of your image-editing program under "RGB."

A picture of the RGB color adjustment filter included with the PhotoSuite program appears in Figure 10-35. This filter has three slide bars allowing you to adjust the levels of the following hues:

- Cyan-Red

- Magenta-Green

- Yellow-Blue

10

FIGURE 10-35   The color-adjustment tool found in the PhotoSuite 4 program

The actual adjustment process can be a bit tricky initially. For example, if you decide your photo is a bit too green, it's not quite as simple as merely adjusting the magenta-green slider. You have to adjust some of the *other* colors too. For example, if you decrease the magenta-green level, you actually have to increase the cyan-red and yellow-blue levels manually by half as much to keep all the colors in your photo in balance.

Table 10-1 summarizes the adjustments you need to make to keep the colors of your photo in balance.

Color Problem	Adjustment
Blue tone (common with digital cameras)	Decrease the blue; then increase both the red and the green by half the amount you decreased the blue.
Red tone (can be the result of artificial lighting or improper chemical processing)	Decrease the red; then increase both the blue and the green by half the amount you decreased the red.
Green tone	Decrease the green; then increase both the red and the blue by half the amount you decreased the green.

TABLE 10-1   Color-Balancing Adjustments

Adjusting Your Printer Tones

Although your scanner and computer monitor use the red-green-blue primary color group to create images, your printer uses a different scheme. Most color printers (and professional printing presses) apply dotted layers of cyan, magenta, yellow, and black (CMYK). If you find that your printed copies are off-color based on what appears on your monitor, you can tweak them using the color correction filter.

You should be aware, however, that CMYK can't precisely replicate the vibrant colors you see on your monitor. Printed images always appear a little duller than the ones on your computer screen.

Adjusting the color tones of your printer to produce a particular image is a matter of trial and error and personal judgment. Since you can never exactly match what appears on screen, you need to produce the colors in a way that appears representative and pleasing to your eye.

Cyan, magenta, and yellow have negative values, so you need to *decrease* the number to *increase* the value. For example, a –28 rating is higher than a –2 or +28 rating. Unlike RGB, you can work by adjusting one color at a time, without making simultaneous adjustments to the other two colors.

Artistically Colorizing Your Photos

One of the best ways to enhance a photo artistically is to apply color to it selectively. To determine which color tools your particular program has, search the Help menu using the keywords "color" and "tint." Your program might have one or all of the following color tool options:

Tint an entire photo   Tinting an entire photo sets a mood and makes an artistic statement in itself. The color insert illustrates several examples of the dramatic effect that can be achieved with a color tint.

Convert a photo to black and white   Some photo subjects such as old movie stars and jazz musicians actually look better in black and white. You can create a black-and-white photo from a color one by applying a gray tint to the entire photo.

Selectively apply color to portions of a photo   After you've turned a color photo to black and white, try selectively colorizing and tinting portions of it. Or experiment by adding sections of dramatic color to a photo that is already in color to make a more dramatic statement.

Adjust the opacity of the applied color   Most image-editing programs allow you to make the color you apply appear more or less transparent. A high opacity level means that when you apply the color, it will be opaque, and you might not be able to see the underlying color tones and details of the original image as well. In contrast, colorizing an area using a low opacity level means that you're effectively applying a transparent tint to the area.

10

Trying Your Hand at the Drawing Tool

Drawing tools are often overlooked in the image-editing arsenal; however, they can be very powerful and produce high-impact effects. Figure 10-36 shows an example where I've hand-drawn the black arrows pointing to the cow, as well as the spots, using filled and unfilled shapes.

Your image-editing program might include the following drawing tools:

Freehand   Allows you to draw lines of varying colors and thickness.

Unfilled shapes   These tools might allow you to draw squares, rectangles, ellipses, and other unfilled shapes with precision.

Filled shapes   This particular tool allows you to fill a shape with color.

FIGURE 10-36   This cow is modeling the effects of the PhotoSuite 4 drawing tools.

Cutting and Combining Photos

One of the most powerful capabilities your scanner affords you is to combine content from multiple photos into a single image. You might create cutout images that you can paste onto other photos and background scenes, or "stitch" several photos together to create a panoramic effect.

Making a Cutout

A cutout is a portion of an image you cut from a photo and save to a file or the clipboard. For example, I've made a cutout of the girl in the center of the photo in Figure 10-37 and pasted my cutout onto the photo background that appears in Figure 10-38.

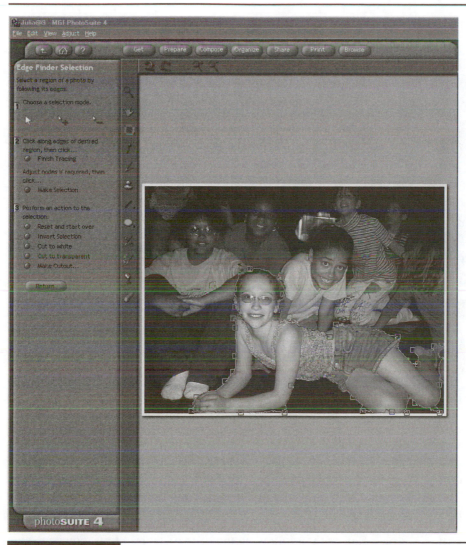

FIGURE 10-37   Cutting tools allow you to transport an image or figure from one photo
to another.

FIGURE 10-38   An image from one photo transplanted to another

Most image-editing programs allow you to create cutouts using a variety of tools. PhotoSuite, for example, includes the following options for making a cutout:

Freehand cutting tool   This tool allows you to trace around the edges of the image you want to cut out.

Edge finder   This tool is an improvement over the standard freehand cutting tool. It allows you to click gently at intervals around the image you want to cut out, and automatically finds the border of the image. It finds the edge of the photo by identifying an abrupt change in the color value of the pixels that represents the border of an image.

Cut to shape   Rather than following the edge of your cutout, you can select a portion having a regular predefined shape, such as a rectangle or ellipse.

Be sure to follow the directions provided in the Help menu or manual for your particular image-editing software for making a cutout. In particular, pay careful attention to the steps for saving, cutting, and pasting the cutout. There's nothing more frustrating than losing an image you've spent 20 minutes painstakingly cutting out.

Stitching Photos Together for a Panoramic Effect

Many image-editing programs, such as PhotoSuite, allow you to stitch several photos together to create a single, continuous image. If your particular image-editing program offers the capability to stitch or blend several photos together, you can achieve excellent results by following these guidelines:

Overlapping subject matter   Try to take and use photos that have an overlap in the subject matter. The manufacturers of PhotoSuite recommend that you use photos with at least 30 percent overlapping subject matter. In the stitching process, you'll be aligning the areas with the overlapping subject matter.

Size   Make sure all the photos you're planning on combining are the same size.

Zoom level   Remember to take all the pictures you plan to combine into a panorama using the same zoom level on your camera.

Variation   Keep in mind that there should be enough color variation to give the program a clue, just as you'd need if you were doing a jigsaw puzzle. The image-editing program needs to be able to figure out exactly where to splice your photos together. This works sort of like a jigsaw puzzle. It's hard for a program to figure out how to piece together photos of a blue sky or open ocean.

10

Artistically Layering Photos

Most image-editing programs on the market today provide you with the capability to create dramatic photo collages by layering multiple photos and adjusting the transparency of the various layers. The color insert provides two striking examples of this technique. In those particular photographs, the artist created a dramatic silhouette effect using the cutting tools, described previously in the "Making a Cutout" section.

Image-Editing Continues to Evolve

It was only a few short years ago that virtually all the image-editing techniques described in this chapter were the exclusive domain of professional photographers and image-editing labs. Scanning technology has given us all the ability to repair, edit, enhance, and artistically combine our photos in our own homes with an investment of only a few hundred dollars.

Scanning and image-editing technology continues to evolve, and software manufacturers continually introduce new and exciting features. A good way to keep up with what's happening in this area, assuming you've now adopted it as your hobby, is to check the software reviews on the Amazon.com website. Since this website sells a wide range of image-editing programs, the company has every incentive to induce you to purchase an upgrade by keeping you abreast of the latest software innovations.

Increasing Your Skill with Image-Editing Tools

Chapters 15 through 17 of this book tell you how to use the image-editing tools discussed in this chapter to create professional-looking printed projects and Web layouts. As you continue to undertake scanning projects of increasing sophistication, your proficiency with the tools in this chapter will increase. In no time, you'll be able to identify what's needed to edit and enhance a particular scanned image properly with a single intuitive glance.

Part III

Practical Uses for Your Scanner

Chapter 11

Scanning Instant Images: JoyCam, i-Zone, and Other Polaroid Products

How To...

- Understand why instant imaging works
- Identify when instant imaging can be most useful
- Decide which type of instant-imaging camera to buy
- Edit and enhance instant photos using your scanner
- Use special online resources for i-Zone owners

Do you remember those clunky Polaroid cameras from your childhood that fascinated you by spewing forth a thick sheet of film that materialized into a photograph before your eyes? The photo was amazing, but unfortunately there was no practical, economical way to reproduce and share it, since it did not yield a negative to make copies from.

This chapter revisits a technology from your youth that's being reinvigorated because of scanners. Instant images from Polaroid cameras used to be sort of one-of-a-kind objects that were difficult and costly to reproduce. Scanners have solved that problem more effectively than anyone could have imagined a decade ago.

Today, Polaroid cameras are inexpensive, streamlined, and simple to use. The emergence of scanners gives you the ability to enhance, copy, and share your instant images with the world. Even more exciting, Polaroid has even developed its own mini-photographic scanner—Webster—to be used with its instant-imaging cameras and film products.

How Does Instant Imaging Work?

All instant imaging is based on a technology of treating paper inside the camera with layers of light-sensitive chemicals that you activate when a picture is taken. As you'll notice, the finished Polaroid pictures are thicker than those developed by other processes.

When you take your photo, the camera quickly spreads a reactive layer of chemical across the paper on which your finished picture appears. This first chemical layer, called the "timing layer," disappears after 30 seconds. Behind the timing layer is an acid that reacts to the unexposed and exposed portions of the photo to create the finished color image.

The Interesting Development of Instant Imaging

The creator of instant-imaging technology, Dr. Edwin Land, recounted the inspiration for his idea, which came to him in 1944, as follows:

> I recall a sunny day in Santa Fe, New Mexico, when my little daughter asked why she could not see at once the picture I had just taken of her. As I walked around the charming town, I undertook the task of solving the puzzle she had set me. Within an hour, the camera, the film, and the physical chemistry became so clear to me.

The Land Legacy

In 1944, Land already had several hundred patents to his name. (He was the inventor of the famous Polaroid Land camera.) He was 35 years old; his daughter, Jennifer, was three. Her innocent question caused Land to commence three years of inspired research into the process of what is now known as a one-step dry photographic process.

One of the more interesting aspects of Dr. Land's creative process was that he commonly involved user testing in his inventing and testing process. He knew that for the cameras to serve the population for which he was inventing them, they had to be simple to use. He often provided housewives with prototype cameras, and watched as they read the directions he provided to process a photo. If they had trouble with a step in the process, Dr. Land scrupulously took that into account in his product design. On February 21, 1947, Dr. Land demonstrated his one-step instant camera and film before the Optical Society of America. Less than two years later, the Polaroid Camera Model 95 and Type 40 Land camera made their sales debut at the Jordan Marsh department store in downtown Boston. Each model cost $89.75—a staggering amount back in 1947.

Today's Instant Cameras

Today, you can pick up an i-Zone or a Polaroid JoyCam instant camera for a suggested retail price of less than $25. The original Polaroid camera weighed a full 4 pounds. The i-Zone and JoyCam weigh less than 10 ounces and easily fit in your purse or pocket.

The JoyCam, shown in Figure 11-1, is designed for teenagers, and comes in an array of fashion-conscious colors. It produces 4.4×2.5-inch instant photographs.

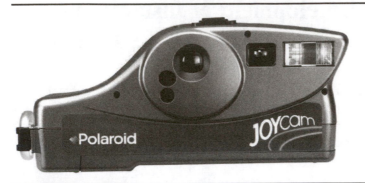

FIGURE 11-1   The Polaroid JoyCam

The i-Zone, which appears in Figure 11-2, one of Polaroid's bestselling cameras, is also designed for younger users. It instantly creates color photos and stickers that measure 1×1.5 inches. The camera itself is less than 7 inches, measured along its longest diameter. It has a flash range of 2.8 feet, for indoor photos and 2 feet to infinity for outdoor photos. This camera comes with two AA-size batteries.

The Polaroid Spectra 1200 FF, shown in Figure 11-3, is more appealing to adult users, without sacrificing any of the convenience of the JoyCam or i-Zone. It offers a sleek, modern design with auto-flash, built-in fill-flash, and folding lens hood. It includes two manually selected focus zones. Not surprisingly, I've found that it produces clearer, more vivid, pictures than the i-Zone and JoyCam. The camera has a suggested retail price of $90. It has a convenient collapsible design.

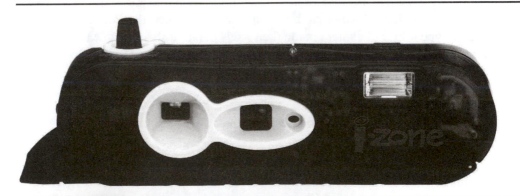

FIGURE 11-2   The popular i-Zone camera

FIGURE 11-3 The Spectra 1200 FF is less than 5×8 inches in size and offers high-quality 4-inch-square instant images.

11

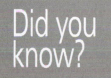

Polaroid Instant-Imaging Technology Is Unique

Patents on the instant color film process by Land was the basis of a well-publicized infringement suit that Polaroid brought against Kodak in 1976 and won in 1985. Land spent a year in court providing detailed testimony about his instant-imaging process and the relevant patents. Land retired from Polaroid in the summer of 1982, and sold his last stock in the company before the verdict in favor of Polaroid was reached. The verdict unequivocally required Kodak to withdraw the sale of its knock-off camera and instant-imaging film worldwide.

The Continuing Need for Instant-Image Cameras

While digital cameras are the latest rage, with price drops making them more affordable, instant cameras occupy an important niche for kids, teens, and a large percentage of the population that isn't able to access photos from a computer. Polaroid cameras also offer a convenient and cost-effective alternative to digital cameras in a variety of circumstances.

The Ideal Cameras for Teens and Kids

Would you trust a ten-year-old with a $300 digital camera? Most people wouldn't.

Digital cameras are complex and delicate. Polaroid iZone cameras were actually inspired by and invented for children and teens, and have the added advantage of providing them with the fun of an immediate result.

Not surprisingly, although Polaroid cameras have many scientific and business uses, their main following today is adults, kids, and teens. For a suggested retail price of less than $30, today's i-Zones and JoyCams are far more suited to the needs of these active users than digital cameras for the following reasons:

Cost   Parents are far more likely to spring for a JoyCam or i-Zone than for a digital camera for their kids. Even on sale or closeout, digital models still cost hundreds of dollars. Although a pack of Polaroid film might be pricier than a disposable camera or a roll of 35-millimeter film, you don't have any associated developing or processing charges. Most times you come out financially ahead with Polaroid film because you didn't have to pay to develop it.

Durability and portability   Parents can worry less about kids losing an instant camera, throwing them in their backpacks, or forgetting to cover the lens. The i-Zone and JoyCam cameras are clearly designed with the carefree (and sometimes careless) user in mind. The lenses are well recessed in the camera bodies, which are made of durable plastic. Both cameras are lightweight, have wristbands, and withstand a reasonable amount of bumping and jostling—although no camera is meant to be dropped on concrete from a moving bicycle.

Ease of use   My nine- and ten-year-old daughters had their JoyCam and i-Zone cameras out of the box, and the instructions read in less than 10 minutes. The cameras come with clear, illustrated directions and an automatic focus capability. (This is, of course, part of the legacy of their creator, Dr. Edwin Land, who tested each camera using ordinary folk.)

Sending Photos to People Who Don't Have Computers

Ten years ago, in anticipation of the birth of my first child, I bought a Polaroid camera to take to the hospital so that I could immediately mail photos of my new baby to my friends and family. Today, an expectant mother might bring a digital camera to the hospital.

But what about grandparents who haven't mastered the computer, and aunts and uncles with near-full hard drives, slow modems, and primitive printers? And what about siblings too young to log on and print out a shot to share around the nursery school? Instant imaging remains a quick and convenient medium for communicating with important people who don't have access to a computer.

Foreign Travel Adventures

When traveling abroad, an instant-imaging camera is a great asset. You might meet interesting new friends, and leave them with a photo of you as a memento. Instant imaging makes this tribute uniquely possible because all of the technology you need to produce the finished paper photo is contained within the camera. It's also nice to know that if you opt to take along *only* an instant-imaging camera, you can use a scanner back home to create future copies.

Scanning to Enhance the Quality of Instant Images

Although instant images have high resolutions identical to those you'd get with a 35-millimeter camera, the lenses are inexpensive and the focusing capabilities a bit more limited.

Be sure to consult the instructions to identify the optimum distance for shooting a photo. Your camera lens is designed to get the best results within this range. Since many instant-image users are kids, they tend to forget this. You probably will notice at least some occasional blurring and distortion in your instant-image photos. Here are a few scanning tips and tricks to make them look their best:

Use the sharpening tool   The sharpening tool is a Polaroid camera owner's best friend. It's a useful antidote for the "blurries." You can use the sharpening tool or filter in your scanner software when previewing the photo prior to scanning or apply it later in the image-editing phase. Applying it prior to scanning usually yields the best result. Figures 11-4 and 11-5 show an instant-image photo before and after the sharpening tools have been applied.

FIGURE 11-4   An instant-image photo scanned without editing

FIGURE 11-5   The photo after the sharpening filter-effect has been applied

Apply color-correction tools   I sometimes notice that my instant photos have a gray, blue, or reddish cast to them. I find it helpful to experiment with a correction filter that uniformly reduces the red or blue tones in the entire photo. I also lighten images when necessary. Chapter 10 covers these tools.

Enlarge within a reasonable range   Although JoyCam and i-Zone cameras produce photos at a resolution comparable to any 35-millimeter camera, the photos are smaller. This means that each time you double their size in the process of enlarging them, you cut the number of pixels per inch by half. The resolution is cut by a corresponding amount. Be realistic in your expectations for enlarging instant images. A good-quality 4×6-inch enlargement is probably the best you can hope for from a JoyCam or an i-Zone picture.

Cutting, cropping, and combining photos   Your image-editing software offers a solution to the problem of enlarging an i-Zone or JoyCam photo to fit into an 8×10-inch frame. If you want to create an image piece suitable for a larger frame, use your editing programs to cut, crop, and combine photos into a finished composition of the dimensions you desire. The larger the area you want to cover, the more images you might need to splice together. You might also consider using a standard photo or image template to provide a background for your photo, and enlarge the dimensions of the background media to fit your frame. Chapter 10 tells you how to use these tools.

Using the Polaroid Mini-Photographic Scanner

11

Polaroid, in continuing spirit of fun and practical innovation, has introduced a mini-scanner specially designed for i-Zone camera users. This amazing little device—possibly the world's most economical miniature scanning device—is called the Polaroid i-Zone Webster.

Webster, shown in Figure 11-6, sells for just $50, and allows you to instantly scan i-Zone photos, other images, or portions of images measuring 1.5×1.75 inches to the Web. This tiny scanner offers you a 352×288-pixel resolution. Since it's designed with kids and teens in mind, it's extremely easy to use.

It holds up to 20 photos, and runs on three AAA batteries. As is the i-Zone, it's meant to travel with you in a purse or backpack.

FIGURE 11-6   Webster miniature scanner

The i-Zone Website: A Perk for Young Scanner Users

If you enjoy scanning your instant photos, you should definitely pay a visit to the i-Zone website located at www.i-zone.com. The site is designed to provide a fun and creative outlet for i-Zone users who have access to Webster or any other type of scanner. It's specially designed with young users in mind, and provides loads of low-cost fun to kids without any cost to parents.

Site Safety for Kids

You can feel quite safe letting your kids roam the family-friendly i-Zone site, allowing them to edit, share, display, and chat about their photos. When you or your child creates a photo album or uploads photos, Polaroid provides you with a password to protect your privacy. If you're 13 years of age or older, you can create a special photo ID to identify yourself to other i-Zone users with whom you want to communicate (or with no one at all). You share and display only those photos you wish the world to see, and can do so without disclosing your family's identity, whereabouts, or email address.

The ID, as shown in Figure 11-7, can contain your child's photo or a cartoon logo, but rather a cartoon logo and nickname they select. They can choose to post this ID on the Web or to retain total privacy.

Registered users who are 13 years old and above can create an i-Zone crew. They can share photos and messages with friends that they specifically select to be part of their crew—a sort of online scanning club.

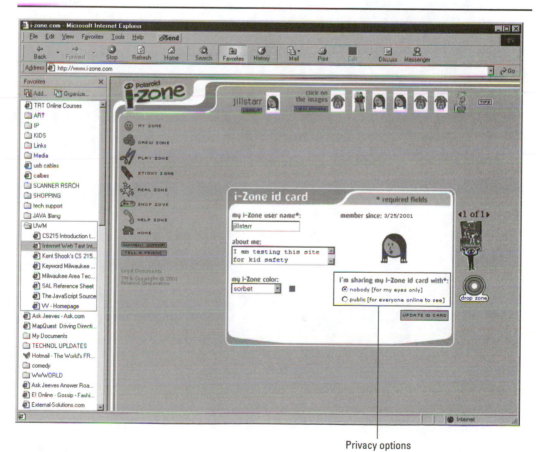

Privacy options

FIGURE 11-7   The i-Zone website provides an artistic outlet for scanner users.

Uploading Photos to the i-Zone Website

The i-Zone website provides a picture tutorial to teach kids how to upload photos to it, either from files on your computer containing a scanned image or directly from the Webster miniature scanning device. A page from the Webster upload tutorial appears in Figure 11-8. To upload a file containing a scanned image from your computer, all you need to do is click the large icon shown in Figure 11-9. This opens a browse dialog box from which you can select a photo.

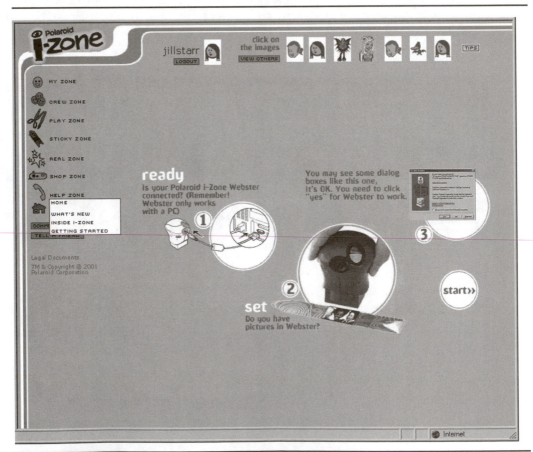

FIGURE 11-8   A tutorial for uploading photos to the Web from your Webster

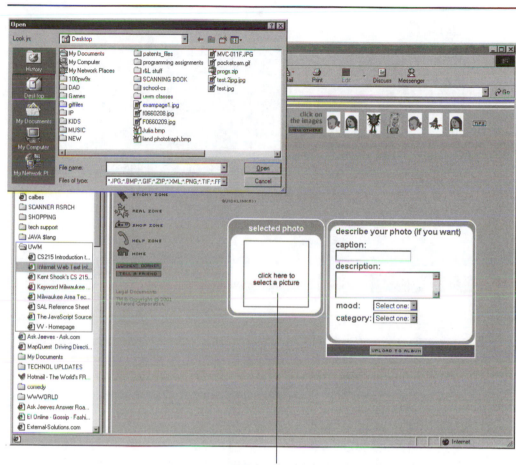

Click here to upload
image file from computer

FIGURE 11-9   The i-Zone (www.i-zone.com) screen for uploading other scanned files from your computer

Once you've uploaded your photos, the fun really starts. Here are just a few of the activities you and your kids can enjoy:

Create a collage   You can combine multiple i-Zone photos on the background of your choice, as shown in Figure 11-10. You can overlap them to create a collage effect. Once your collage is complete, you can save it or send it to a friend.

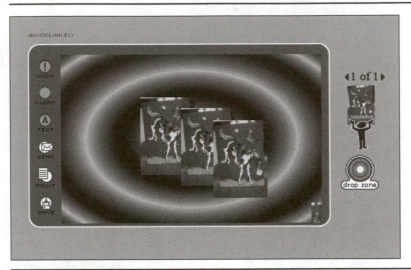

FIGURE 11-10   Kids can use the simple i-Zone tools to create a collage.

TIP   *The collage feature can be a little tricky to use in the beginning. You have to remember to go first to your photo album and collect the photos you want to use by positioning and clicking the i-Zone guy icon over them, then access the collage screen from the play Zone menu.*

Use simplified image-editing tools   The i-Zone site contains simplified image-editing tools that are perfect for kids who aren't ready to navigate PhotoSuite or PhotoDeluxe. They can simply drop their photos in the image-editing box shown in Figure 11-11, and access the tools (accompanied by illustrated icons) around the edge of the box. Kids can cut, crop, straighten, and resize their images in no time.

Create a card   The i-Zone offers special tools to allow kids to create and send cards they've made using their uploaded photos. You can access these templates from the menu that appears when you click the play Zone icon on any page of the i-Zone website.

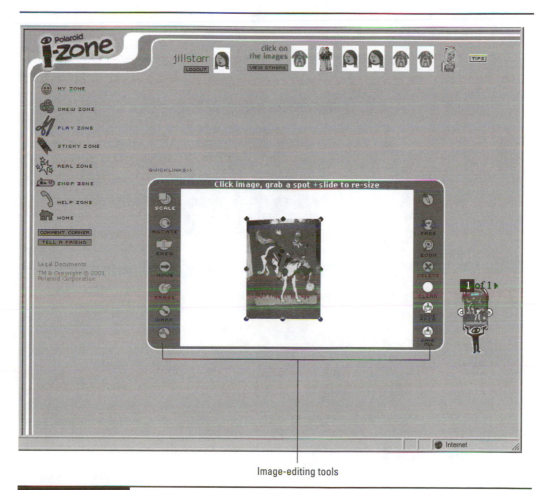

Image-editing tools

FIGURE 11-11   i-Zone offers simplified image-editing tools for kids.

Enter contests   Ready for photo fame? Submit your pictures to the i-Zone website, as shown in Figure 11-12. If the judges like your child's photo (or yours for that matter), they'll post it on the website for the world to see. This is really exciting for kids, and for the friends and family they direct to the website. You can also vote for your favorite submissions by other i-Zone users. Access this feature by selecting the Photo Fame option from the play Zone menu.

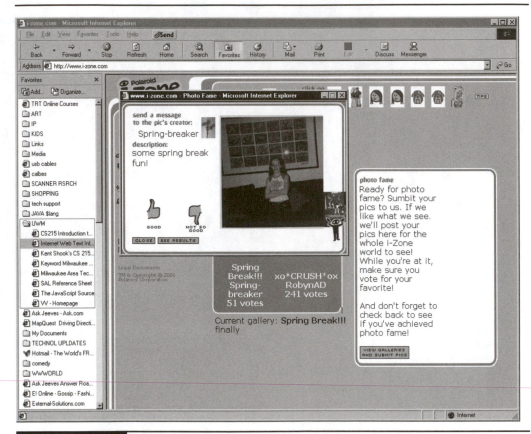

FIGURE 11-12   It's fun to compete in the i-Zone photo contests.

Create a private online scanning club   You and your kids can create an
i-Zone crew, which is like a private scanning club. To log into the crew "lounge,"
you must be a crew member who's been invited to join. Crew members can post
uploaded scanned photos, messages, and announcements for the rest of the crew,
as shown in Figure 11-13. A special dialog box tells you which crew members are
on line.

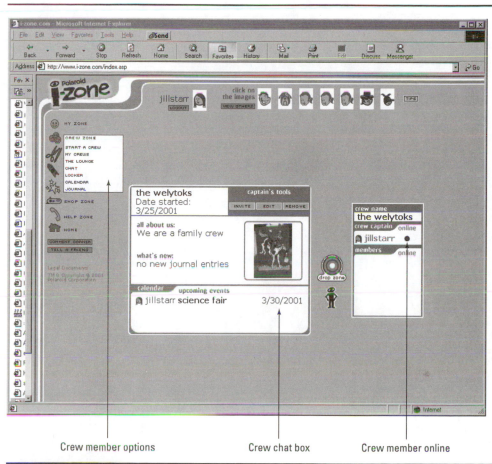

Crew member options   Crew chat box   Crew member online

FIGURE 11-13   Example of an i-Zone crew site

Chapter 12

Scanning Negatives and Slides

How To...

- Understand when it might be advantageous to scan a transparency

- Get the best results when scanning slides and negatives

- Decide if you should invest in a transparency scanner

- Choose a scanner that gives you good-quality transparency scans

The process of scanning negatives and slides is not terribly different than scanning photographs—but the end results can be dramatic. Negatives and slides give you truer colors and the benefit of starting from the original exposure rather than from a photograph that's already been processed.

Advantages of Being Able to Scan from Negatives and Slides

Printed photographs are often referred to as "originals." Although this book uses the term in this way, it's somewhat misleading. A "true" original is a negative or slide; a negative is the medium a photograph is produced from. Accordingly, a photo is properly regarded as a *copy* made from a negative. There are several advantages associated with being able to scan negatives and slides. Here are a few of them:

- Negatives and slides give you an original to match, which can yield sharp detail and high quality, as shown in Figure 12-1.

- Slide images are already in positive form, which offers you the opportunity to transform a wealth of information from old slide collections with your scanner.

- Scanning your own negatives provides an economical alternative to having printed copies made in a photo lab—although most home scanners cannot compete with a lab in terms of quality.

Understand More about What Transparencies Are

Transparencies—both negatives and slides—are produced from the film you load into your camera. Different types of film produce different types of media. Black-and-white pictures are produced from *black-and-white negative film,* color photos from *color negative film,* and color slides are made using *color reversal film.*

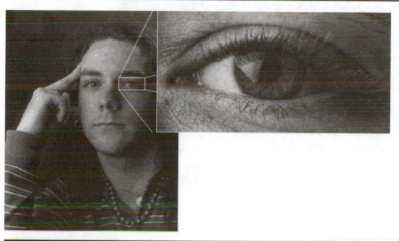

FIGURE 12-1   This photo, by Eric Boutilier-Brown, www.evolvingbeauty.com, shows the detail from a negative enlarged 10 times.

How Negatives Are Made

The *Encyclopedia Britannica* defines a negative as a "graphic image that reproduces the bright portions of the photographed subject as dark and the dark parts as light areas." Negatives are created using film, which is a type of thin plastic coated with chemicals that react to light. The film is exposed to light through a camera lens. When the shutter, which normally blocks the direct path of light between the film and the lens, is opened, light enters the lens for a precisely measured amount of time to expose the film.

When film is exposed, dark areas of the subject are reproduced as light areas, and the light areas become dark—hence the term negative. Notice how dark the lightest portion of a photo, a bonfire, appears in Figure 12-2. The developing process reverses these tones and produces a "positive" photographic print, like the one shown in Figure 12-3.

12

Lightest
portion
of photo

FIGURE 12-2   The process of creating a negative reverses the light and dark areas of an image.

FIGURE 12-3   A photograph processed from a negative

The Niche Filled by Slides

Historically, 35-millimeter slides have been the projection method of choice for creating dynamic, high-impact presentations. With the advent of the personal computer, programs such as PowerPoint, which create projection presentations from digital images, came into vogue. Nevertheless, slides and slide projection equipment continue to occupy a niche with to the following characteristics:

- Slides offer higher-quality resolution and color depth than images converted from scanned paper photos or the Web and imported into a program such as PowerPoint.

- Slides require the use of a special laptop projector, while digital images can be conveniently displayed using a laptop.

- Slides must be scanned and converted to digital images before they can be used for computer-based presentations such as PowerPoint.

The capability to convert slides to digital images offers you the best of both worlds: the quality of a transparency and the convenience of a digital image.

Tips for More Effectively Scanning Transparencies

Although scanning slides and transparencies can provide sharp color and heightened detail, it can be a tricky process. Here are a few tips to improve your batting average:

Pay careful attention to initial exposure when taking slides.   Slides have a narrow tonal range and are easily overexposed. When you're shooting the original with your camera, pay close attention to your shutter settings.

Use the color negative setting on your scanner.   Most scanners that offer transparency attachments have a special resolution setting, like the menu for the HP Scanjet 5370C, shown in Figure 12-4.

Scan at a high resolution.   If a menu choice is not available for scanning transparencies, scan at a high resolution. The chief advantage of scanning slides and negatives is that they allow you to capture so much detail at high resolution.

Opt for a brighter shot over a darker one.   If you have the choice between a too-bright negative or slide or a too-dark one, choose the light one. Overexposure is relatively easy to correct with your scanner.

Handle negatives and slides carefully.   This might seem obvious, but negatives and slides are very susceptible to fingerprints.

12

FIGURE 12-4   Your scanner might offer a special setting for scanning transparencies.

Clean your slides and negatives carefully.   If you forgot to heed the last tip, you might actually be able to clean your negatives and slides. You can use an antistatic brush and a can of compressed air to loosen dust and dirt. Both are sold at most photography supply stores.

Take the time to decipher processing markings on the negatives.   When you get a set of negatives back from the lab, they might have unobtrusive numbers or other markings. Look for these numbers and marks to help you identify and keep track of your negatives without having to hold them up to the light every time.

A Look at Some of the Top Flatbed Transparency Scanners

Until recently, devices that scanned negatives and transparencies were very expensive. It is only in the last couple of years that major scanner manufacturers such as Hewlett-Packard and Epson have been offering transparency-scanning attachments for their inexpensive flatbed scanners. Both manufacturers now offer scanners including transparency attachments for less than $300. Both scanners produce good, although not professional-quality, results.

The Hewlett-Packard ScanPro 5370C, shown in Figure 12-5, offers great image quality, good color balance, and sharp detail. The transparency-scanning device can be removed and stored when not in use.

| FIGURE 12-5 | The HP ScanPro 5370C with transparency adapter |

Similarly, the Epson Perfection 1240U Photo, shown in Figure 12-6, offers a transparency-scanning peripheral for about $90. The scanner itself has a base price of just under $200. This model has received many excellent reviews, and was used to create the photograph in Figure 12-1 shown at the beginning of this chapter.

| FIGURE 12-6 | The Epson Perfection 1240U Photo with transparency adapter |

If you're after professional-quality transparency scans, you might want to consider purchasing a scanner that performs that function solely. Favorites among experts who review these devices are the inexpensive PrimeFilm 1800 series models marketed by a company called Pacific Image Electronics. The 1800U model, shown in Figure 12-7, allows you to scan transparencies at 1800 dpi. It's the first dedicated film scanner to retail in the $200 price range. You can find out more about this product by visiting the company website located at www.scanace.com.

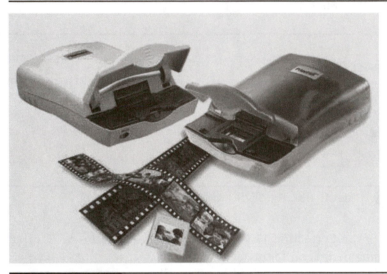

FIGURE 12-7   The PrimeFilm 1800U by Pacific Image Electronics is a popular, inexpensive film scanner.

 *Film scanners are sometimes called slide scanners, but while every film scanner scans both slides and negatives, some slide scanners might not do the job for both.*

Deciding Whether to Invest in a Transparency Attachment

It's a matter of individual choice as to whether you should invest in a transparency scanner. If your need for this capability is infrequent, you can find any number of services on line to scan negatives and transparencies. Labs can produce high-quality scans for less than a few dollars.

If you intend to make frequent use of a transparency adapter, consider some of the inexpensive, favorably reviewed models discussed in this chapter. You should, however, be aware that producing professional-quality transparency scans is a tricky proposition and might require a high-end scanner dedicated to this purpose.

Chapter 13

Scanning Text Documents Using OCR Software

How To...

- Understand how OCR software works

- Recognize the limitations of OCR software

- Properly prepare your original document for OCR software to read

- Optimize scanning of text documents

Installing Optical Character Recognition (OCR) software is sort of like teaching your computer to read and type text into your PC. It allows you to scan a document and convert it to a text file you can edit. This is a very useful feature, but the process can be plagued with inaccurately read characters and resultant errors. This chapter gives you a few pointers on how to make the process more accurate. Accuracy is the hallmark of effectiveness when scanning text documents.

What OCR Software Does

OCR software has the capabilities to do the following:

- Capture text images from your scanner

- Compare those characters to an existing database of characters and identify them

- Produce output that you can edit

OCR software looks at the millions of tiny dots that make up the characters on a page of text. It sifts to find characters that it recognizes, and converts those characters into a new, readable text file.

A Look at the Leading OCR Programs

Currently the leading OCR software is TextBridge Pro. Frequently bundled with scanners, TextBridge Pro converts scanned files into Microsoft Word. Once a file is in Microsoft Word format, you can covert it to other Microsoft applications, such as Access, Excel files, Internet Explorer, Netscape Navigator, and FrontPage. You can learn more about this popular program at the manufacturer's Website at www.scansoft.com, as shown in Figure 13-1. This program sells for about $80, as of the writing of this book.

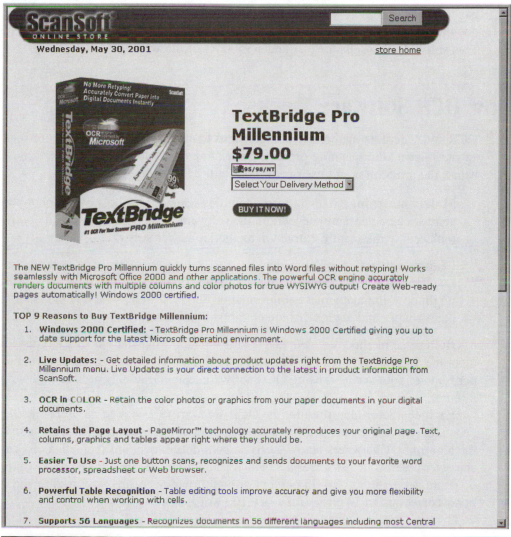

FIGURE 13-1   TextBridge Pro is a popular OCR program that comes bundled with many scanners.

A more sophisticated version, TextBridge Pro Millennium Business Edition, is intended to bridge the gap between bundled scanner software and a full-blown professional program. It comes with special tools for managing documents in a business setting, and sells for around $500, as of the writing of this book.

ScanSoft also offers another sophisticated program, called OmniPage Pro. In addition to offering basic text-reading and conversion capabilities, this product offers enhanced accuracy and automatic correction features for crooked and damaged pages. It also has more sophisticated capabilities to retain the original formatting of documents, such as Excel spreadsheets and magazine articles with multiple columns. This software also sells for just under $500, as of the writing of this book.

How OCR Software Works

OCR software uses mathematical algorithms to classify the characters your scanner extracts during the scanning process. Depending on what kind of software you're using, the program might use one or both of the following methods:

Matrix matching   This process identifies scanned symbols by matching them against character templates within the software. This process is gradually being replaced by the feature extraction method in newer software programs.

Feature extraction   This method analyzes each character extracted by your scanner using a mathematical algorithm (a formula). For example, the algorithm might describe mathematical information about a circle, which is the letter *o,* or other shapes and angles that are common to all letters.

Both these methods achieve fast results—much faster than having a typist simply input the documents into a PC. For example, an average typist can input about 60 words per minute. Your scanner, using OCR software, can extract upwards of 600 words per minute.

Each character identified by the OCR software is assigned a *confidence level,* depending on how closely the extracted character corresponds to the specifications of the algorithm. Characters below a certain confidence level are flagged, and a certain character is substituted, such as a ~, which you must hand-correct. Many OCR programs boast an accuracy rate of 90 percent or better, which means you might need to hand-correct up to 10 errors for every 100 words of text.

Recognize the Limitations of OCR Software

Optical character recognition is designed to read only text—sometimes referred to as *machine type.* It's important to understand that OCR software cannot read any of the following:

- Handwriting

- Data that must be extracted from boxes on forms such as tax returns (although high-end programs offer some capabilities in this area)

- Bar codes

Additionally, OCR software can be very finicky about the print quality it will convert. Carbon copies, newspapers, poor-quality faxes, and old documents typed on manual typewriters can pose problems for your OCR software.

Prepare Your Original Document for OCR Software to Read

When scanning a document prior to using your OCR software, always choose the best original available. Before scanning a paper document, inspect it carefully and attempt to fix the following:

Missing or broken characters   If your document has characters with small breaks or gaps, your eyes might be able to read it, but your OCR scanner might not. Look closely at the copy (maybe even with a magnifying glass). Try to find a copy with the least number of gaps, or reduce the brightness setting on your scanner to obscure them.

Dirt and smudges   You can keep these marks from confusing your scanner and OCR software by covering them with thin white correction tape.

Handwritten notations   Obviously you want to avoid writing on documents destined for OCR conversion. If someone has already done so, cover it up with white correction tape.

Staple holes and wrinkles   Cover these with correction tape as well.

Facsimile documents   If you plan to scan a facsimile document, ask the sender to transmit it using fine mode rather than standard.

Glossy paper   Glossy paper is less susceptible to clear, clean scanning. When an original has been scanned on glossy paper, a photocopy might work better for OCR conversion.

 *Don't try to fix a poor-quality original simply by photocopying it. A poor original simply makes a poor photocopy.*

Tips for More Accurate OCR Scanning

When scanning text, you are by and large limited by your software capabilities and the document quality; however, there are a few things you can do to boost accuracy:

- Scan at a high resolution to capture as much image data as possible. This facilitates the character-recognition process.

- If characters appear faint, broken, or jagged, reduce the scanner brightness level. Reducing the brightness can sort of reconnect the dots composing the character by minimizing the light areas between the dots. Darkening obscures detail.

- Keep your scanner surface clean and dust free. Particles on the glass bed of your scanner can interfere with character recognition.

- Use your search-and-replace feature after scanning to correct errors that occur when one character is consistently mistaken for another.

- OCR software sometimes has difficulty with crooked documents. Keep your original straight by scanning so that the lines of text are parallel to the top edge of the scanning surface.

The Future of OCR Software

High-end OCR software programs generally do not come bundled with scanners. Although accuracy and character confusion are presently nagging problems with bundled OCR software, they might soon be issues of the past. OCR software continues to become increasingly more reliable in all price ranges. Future bundled versions of these programs might even do spell checking and recognize words used in an incorrect context.

Part IV

Additional Scanning Projects

Chapter 14

Basic Scanning Projects for Home Hobbyists

How To...

- ■ Import a scanned image into your editing program

- ■ Organize scanned photos into an electronic album

- ■ Use templates and faux backgrounds

- ■ Create a slide show

- ■ Personalize your Windows desktop

Photos of family, friends, and favorite places are among our most treasured possessions. Being able to scan and print them is rewarding, but making copies is by no means the only way your scanner helps you share and save photos. Scanning technology, combined with a good image-editing program, allows you to organize and edit your images, and to display them in artistic and enduring compositions. This chapter identifies some basic ways you can use your scanner to archive and visually enhance your treasure trove of photos.

Understand the Role of Your Image-Editing Software

All the projects in this chapter and the subsequent chapters are made possible by the use of image-editing software. Before embarking on them, it's important to understand what image-editing software does.

First and foremost, it's important to understand the difference between *scanner* software and *image-editing* software. Scanner software runs your scanner, and always comes with your scanner. It directs your scanning device to perform the scanning function, and allows you to vary settings and preferences that enable the device to interface with your computer. The scanner software might offer you the capability to perform some limited editing, such as cutting, cropping, and resizing the image, but not extensive editing tools.

In contrast to scanner software, image-editing software has a vast range of editing capabilities. Image-editing programs, such as MGI PhotoSuite and PhotoDeluxe, allow you to apply a wide range of special effects and processes to an image that has already been captured and saved via the scanner software. Image-editing software also allows you to archive and display photos using special database features. Some programs even allow you to add effects such as fake backgrounds and props.

Image-Editing Software Used for Examples in this Book

There are a lot of different image-editing programs on the market. Chapter 10 gave you an overview, a sense that all image-editing programs perform the same basic tasks, with the more expensive, high-end programs offering you more options.

PhotoSuite and PhotoDeluxe are the two software programs that come bundled with most scanners. Other programs bundled with scanners, such as Paint Shop Pro, are remarkably similar to these two "industry standards." Consequently, these two programs are used to illustrate our projects in this chapter and subsequent chapters, but you'll find the steps are pretty much the same for other programs you might be using.

 *After you've mastered one image-editing program, you'll find it extraordinarily easy to master others.*

The Universal First Step: Importing the Image

With all image-editing programs, the first issue you face is importing a scanned image into the editing software. Does this mean you must first scan an image using your scanner software, then open it in your image-editing software? No!

Programs such as PhotoSuite and PhotoDeluxe actually open your scanner software and direct it to perform the scan. The image thus scanned is ready to be edited and saved in whatever image-editing program you're working with.

If you're working with PhotoSuite, simply follow these steps to scan an image and import it into PhotoSuite:

1. After opening the PhotoSuite program, click the Get button on the navigation bar. The navigation bar is located below the menu bar. The screen in Figure 14-1 appears, displaying an Activity panel on the left.

2. From the list of photo sources displayed on the Activity panel, select Scanner (TWAIN). A scanner list appears.

3. Select the scanner type from the scanner list. If the list is empty, the Scan button will be disabled.

Click to access
scanner software
interface.

FIGURE 14-1   You can access your scanner software from within the PhotoSuite image-editing program.

4. Each consecutively scanned image is assigned a default file name with the prefix "photo" added, for example Photo0001, Photo0002, Photo0003, and so on. You can specify a different file name, or change the file names later if you wish.

5. Click the Scan button to acquire the images. The interface of your scanner software becomes active, as shown in Figure 14-2. You can use this interface to perform the scan from within your image-editing program.

Similarly, if you're using PhotoDeluxe, the Get Photo button gives you access to all the ways you can import a digital photo into the program. Click the Get Photo button, then Scanners, and follow the onscreen instructions. When you finish, the photo appears in the photo window, ready for use in Home Edition.

NOTE   *You must click the Get and Fix Photo button before you can access the submenu containing the Get Photo command button.*

Activated scanner software interface

FIGURE 14-2   Your scanner software is operated from within your image-editing program.

Create Your Digital Photo Album

What good is a photo if you can't find it when you want it? Digital imaging programs not only allow you to edit photographs, they allow you to organize and display them conveniently and at will. Even better, digital albums never yellow, tear, or mildew.

What Is a Digital Album?

Just as paper albums allow you to store all your prized photos in a single location, digital albums allow you to store image files in a central location on your computer. Once you've done this, it's easy to display your photos, make slide shows, and copy them to CDs and disks.

14

You're probably familiar with one kind of database: the folders you use to organize documents and other files in Windows Explorer. A digital album is another kind of database. A database allows you to organize image files so you can access and retrieve them later. To retrieve a file from an album, you use a file name or path much as you would to access any other type of file on your computer.

Find out How Your Particular Editing Program Creates Digital Albums

You can find out whether your image-editing program allows you to create albums, and how to do it, simply by searching the program's help database by entering the keyword "album," as shown in Figure 14-3. Most image-editing programs use this term to refer to photo databases.

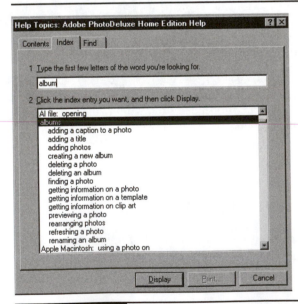

FIGURE 14-3   Enter the keyword "album" to find out how to create a digital album in any image-editing program.

A Look at How Some Popular Programs Create Digital Albums

The process of creating a digital album and viewing its contents is straightforward. Regardless of which image-editing program you're using, saving and viewing an album involves the following:

- Creating an album on your computer to save images

- Saving images to the album file

- Opening the album file and locating the image you want to view

Creating an Album in PhotoSuite

PhotoSuite is a particularly sophisticated and versatile program for creating image files. It has several features of interest. First, it allows you to view thumbnails (miniatures) of all the photos stored in an album, as shown in Figure 14-4. It also allows you to maintain a master album, which contains no pictures, but holds all your other albums. You can view all the photo albums you've created within PhotoSuite in the master album.

FIGURE 14-4   Some image-editing programs, such as PhotoSuite, allow you to preview the contents of your album on screen.

14

To create a new album in PhotoSuite:

1. Click the Organize button on the navigation bar. The Organize panel and Last Viewed Album contents appear.

2. Click the Albums button to open the Master Album dialog box, then click the New button.

3. Enter a name for your new album in the New Album Activity panel, then click OK to create the new empty album file.

Creating an Album in PhotoDeluxe

PhotoDeluxe also allows you to create digital albums. If you're working in PhotoDeluxe, follow these steps:

1. Click Get & Fix Photo, then Get Photo, then My Photos. The My Photos dialog box, shown in Figure 14-5, appears.

Click here to access
Create a New Album.   My Photos dialog box

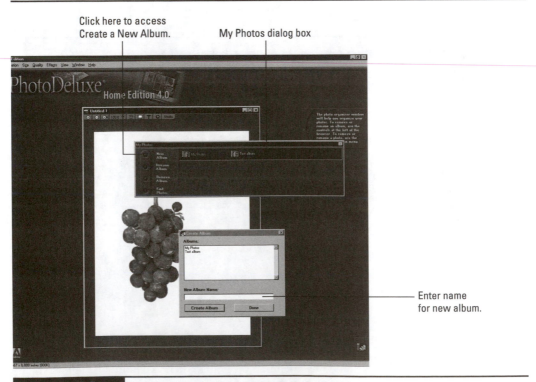

Enter name
for new album.

FIGURE 14-5   Creating an album in PhotoDeluxe

2. At the top of your screen, choose File, then My Photos, then New Album.

3 In the Create Album dialog box, type the album name in the text box, then click Create Album.

4. You can access your album by clicking Get Photo, then My Photos to display a list of albums across the top of the My Photos dialog box. See Figure 14-5.

What Can You Do with Your Digital Albums?

Digital albums are a great way to store and share scanned photos. Unfortunately, the technology is still not sufficiently advanced to allow you to email albums quickly using a standard dial-up connection. Uploading entire albums to send to a friend is time consuming and perhaps even impractical unless you and your friend have high-capacity, high-speed service such as cable or DSL lines. If you both have access to such service, you can email an entire photo album much as you would email any other text or graphics file, by attaching it to your email.

You can also copy your file onto a CD or high-capacity disk for sharing. Unfortunately, standard floppy disks just aren't up to the task of transferring entire albums; however, Zip drives, Jaz drives, and CD burners all allow you to conveniently store the large amounts of image data contained in an album. The U.S. postal service is more than happy to deliver albums stored on this type of media for the cost of a few stamps.

You can find more information about Zip drives and Jaz drives in Chapter 4.

Creating a Slide Show from Scanned Photos

Despite their bad rap, slide shows need not be boring. In fact, they're a great way to display your photos to an admiring (or at least polite) audience. Of course, you're not really displaying slides, but creating the digital equivalent of a slide show. Most image-editing programs allow you to create a digital show from an existing album, or import photos from different locations on your computer. You might even be able to add sound effects.

If you have existing slides you want to display using your computer, consider scanning them as discussed in Chapter 12, which explains how to scan transparencies.

14

To find out how to create a slide show using your image-editing program, search the Help index using the keyword "slide." This is a standard term, although not all programs refer to a finished project as a slide show. For example, when you search for the word "slide" in PhotoDeluxe, the Help menu displays "slide show (see Photo Parade)." While both PhotoShop and PhotoDeluxe have features that allow you to create slide shows with ease, PhotoSuite has a more sophisticated range of capabilities.

Creating a Slide Show Using PhotoSuite

You can create a slide show with PhotoSuite by following these steps:

1. Click the Share button on the Navigation bar, then the Slide Show button that appears on the left of the screen.

2. If you want to create a slide show from an album, click the Create from Album button on the left of the screen to display the screen shown in Figure 14-6. Alternatively, if you want to create a show using photos from different locations on your computer, click the Create from Scratch button, enter a name for the new slide show, set the Show Presentation options, and click OK. Click the Add Photos button to proceed to the next screen, and click the Computer button to browse and select the photos you want.

Select the album containing the photos you want to use.

FIGURE 14-6   PhotoSuite makes it easy to create a slide show from an album.

3. If you're creating a show from an album, select the album name from the drop-down menu in the Create Slide Show panel to display the album's current contents, and indicate whether you want to use some or all the photos in the album.

4. The photos you select for your show are displayed on the PhotoSuite desktop.

5. Choose a transitional screen to appear between displayed photos during the show using the drop-down menu in the transition screen.

6. Click the Create button, and in the dialog box that appears, indicate a name for your slide show, the duration you want each slide to appear on your screen, and the background color you want to appear.

Using PhotoDeluxe to Create a Slide Show

Although PhotoSuite allows you to create a professional-caliber slide show, PhotoDeluxe has a few features worth mentioning in this area. PhotoDeluxe allows you to select a theme, which provides graphics that surround and set off your photos. To use PhotoDeluxe to do this, follow these steps:

1. Click the Cards and More button, and click the PhotoParade button to access the PhotoParade menu commands. Choose Create a PhotoParade from the menu to display the PhotoParade menus. Follow the numbered steps by clicking the 1 Album tab, and then click Open Album. This opens the Photo Parade album within the My Photos Organizer window.

2. At the top of your screen, click the 2 Photos tab. Click Add Photo, browse to select a photo, and click Open. Repeat this for each photo you want to add to the album.

3. Click the Theme tab, and choose a theme from the Choose Theme menu.

TIP

PhotoDeluxe allows you to add captions to photos in your slide show. While you are creating a slide show, click the Captions tab, select the first thumbnail in an album, and click Add Caption. Type a title and caption for the photo, and click OK. Repeat this for each thumbnail in the album.

14

Adding Props, Shadows, and Faux Backgrounds to Your Photos

Some image-editing programs, such as PhotoSuite, come with a database of backgrounds and props that you can use to enhance your photos, like the ones shown in Figures 14-7 and 14-8. Other programs, such as PhotoDeluxe, don't come with these fun additions, but you can use the tips offered in this section to create your own database of backgrounds and props.

If you're in the market for an image-editing program, it's a good idea to compare the different software products on the basis of what backgrounds and props they provide. PhotoSuite comes with a separate content CD that is filled with props, backgrounds, and templates. Templates for frames and greeting cards are discussed in Chapters 15 and 16.

FIGURE 14-7   Thumbnails of some faux backgrounds you can use for your subjects

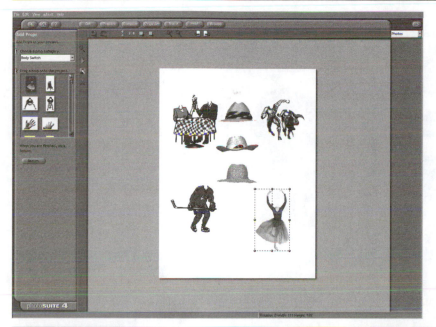

FIGURE 14-8   A sampling of hat and body props included with PhotoSuite

How to Add Props to a Photo

A prop is an image that you import into a photo from a database included with the image-editing software or from another source. Figure 14-9 shows a portion of the menu of props you'll find on the PhotoSuite content CD. In PhotoSuite, props are organized by category. Figure 14-10 shows a relatively uninteresting photograph of two subjects. Figure 14-11 shows portions of the same in a picture that uses the PhotoSuite "body switch" props imported onto a faux background. The same source photo is shown again in Figure 14-12 with a few randomly imported props from the PhotoSuite database.

If you're working with a program that doesn't come with a database of props, such as PhotoDeluxe, you can create your own using the cutting tools in your image-editing program. These tools are discussed in Chapter 10. Essentially, creating your own database of props involves scanning images and cutting out the portions you want to save and use as props.

14

FIGURE 14-9 PhotoSuite comes with an extensive props database.

Adding Props Using PhotoSuite

To add props to your photo, you need to locate the props database in your image-editing program, and follow the directions for importing the props. For example, if you're working in PhotoSuite, you'll follow these steps:

1. Click the Compose button on the Navigation bar, and then the Add Props button on the Activity panel that appears.

2. Choose a props category from the drop-down menu.

3. Drag the desired prop to the work area, and adjust the size and position of the prop by dragging the size handles on the bounding box.

FIGURE 14-10   A relatively uninteresting photo

FIGURE 14-11   Portions of the source photo used with the PhotoSuite
                    "body switch" props on a faux background

FIGURE 14-12   The same photo enhanced with some randomly selected props

   *After clicking the Compose button, you will not see the Add Props button unless you have an image open on your screen.*

Creating Your Own Props Using Other Programs

If you're working with a program that doesn't have a database of props, you can create your own by cutting and cropping images from existing photos. Chapter 10 tells you how to find and use the tools you need to do this in your image-editing program.

Here are a few tips for creating a database of fun props:

■ Don't limit yourself to photos you've taken yourself. Scour magazines for pictures of good props to print. Magazine printed media is of a sufficient quality to achieve good results for this purpose.

■ Glossy color catalogues from large department stores and retail outlets are also of good quality.

■ After you've scanned and cropped a prop, check to see if your editing program allows you to save the cropped image to your database. This way, you won't have to take the time to apply the cutting tool the next time your want to use it in a picture.

- Take advantage of edge-softening and blur tools to blend your prop more effectively into the picture.

- Some programs, such as PhotoSuite, allow you to create a shadow for the imported image. This is called a *drop shadow*, and adds authenticity. Check to see if this feature is available in your image-editing program. Also see the "Add a Drop Shadow" section later in this chapter.

Add a Faux Background to Your Photo

PhotoSuite comes with dozens of wonderful backgrounds you can use to enhance the subject of your photo. A couple of them appear in Figures 14-13 and 14-14. If you're using a program that does not come with backgrounds, you can easily create your own.

Photo subjects

FIGURE 14-13   A scenic faux background included with PhotoSuite

FIGURE 14-14   A surrealistic faux background

Using the PhotoSuite Database to Create a Background

To access the various backgrounds that come with PhotoSuite, follow these steps:

1. Click the Compose button on the navigation bar. The navigation bar is located directly below the menu bar.

2. Click the Fun Stuff button on the panel on the left.

3. Click Backgrounds to display a number of layout templates in the work area.

4. Double-click on the background template that you want to use. The background appears on your screen.

5. Import photos you want to superimpose on the background you've selected using the Activity panel on the left.

Create Your Own Background

If you're working in an image-editing program that doesn't provide a database of backgrounds, such as PhotoDeluxe, you can create your own. Here are a few suggestions for doing so:

- As with props, don't limit yourself to backgrounds you've photographed on your own. For example, try scanning a sunset or rainforest from a magazine such as *National Geographic*.

- Scour color travel brochures for high-quality images of faraway places that can serve as backgrounds.

- Eliminate unwanted objects from magazine and travel backgrounds, or from your own photos, using the clone tool in your image-editing program. This tool is discussed in Chapter 10.

- If your program has a "stitching" or other tool that allows you to combine photographs (see Chapter 10), consider combining multiple scanned images to create an interesting background.

Add a Drop Shadow

PhotoSuite allows you to add a drop shadow to add authenticity to imported images. The use of this interesting feature is illustrated in Figures 14-15 and 14-16.

14

FIGURE 14-15   An object without a drop shadow

FIGURE 14-16   After the drop shadow has been applied

To add a drop shadow using PhotoSuite, follow these steps:

1. Click the Adjust Objects button on the Activity panel, located directly below the menu bar. You must have an image open for editing on your screen, or the Adjust Objects button won't be available.

2. Click the Add a Drop Shadow button.

3. Select the object in your project you want to add a shadow to by clicking it. The selected item is enclosed within a bounding box.

4. On the Activity panel, choose a Shadow Direction, and adjust the intensity of the shadow using the Opacity and Diffusion sliders.

5. Click Return when you're finished.

TIP   *To check if your image-editing program allows you to add a drop shadow, try searching the Help database using the keyword "shadow."*

Personalizing Your Computer Desktop

Virtually all image-editing programs allow you to scan a photo and use it as *wallpaper* for your Windows desktop, as shown in Figure 14-17. To find out how to do this in your image-editing program, simply search the Help database using the keyword "wallpaper."

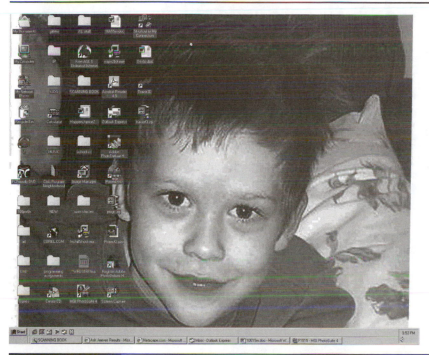

FIGURE 14-17   Using a scanned image as wallpaper

If you're working in PhotoSuite, you can customize your computer desktop by following these steps:

1. Open the photo you wish to set as wallpaper. The file should be visible in the work area.

2. Click the Share button on the navigation bar. The navigation bar is located below the menu bar.

3. Click the Windows Desktop button, then on the Activity panel, click the Set Photo as Wallpaper button. Your photo is automatically set as the background image on your desktop.

If you're using PhotoDeluxe, open Get & Fix Photo, click Save & Send, then Windows Wallpaper. Follow the onscreen prompts to retrieve or create an image you can designate as wallpaper.

14

Moving on to More Advanced Image-Editing Projects

The projects in this chapter introduce you to some of the simple, but powerful, features available with most image-editing programs. Albums and slide shows provide a convenient way to organize and display all your scanning projects. Your familiarity with the methods for creating backgrounds, props, and wallpaper will make you more comfortable with the advanced and multifaceted projects covered in the chapters that follow.

Chapter 15

Making Works of Art and Fun from Scanned Photos

How To...

■ Locate and use project templates in your image-editing program

■ Create a project without a template

■ Add artistic frames and borders to your photos

■ Add text, captions, and word balloons to photos

■ Design greeting cards

■ Make your own photographic calendar

■ Produce fake magazines and gag IDs

■ Make bookmarks, t-shirts, and refrigerator magnets

This chapter takes you well beyond simply using your scanner to copy images. You learn how to turn scanned images into artistic, fun, and useful objects. You can try your hand at designing greeting cards, calendars, gag items, and clothing. All you need to create the projects illustrated in this chapter are a scanner, image-editing software, and your own imagination.

Creating Useful Objects from Templates

Templates allow you to incorporate the capabilities of professional graphic artists and designers into your work, improving and personalizing a project with your own unique photos. The template is a ready-made format for a particular project. The purpose of a template is to save you time and give you the benefit of professional expertise in designing the initial layout of your project. Templates are designed to allow you to import scanned photos of your choosing easily.

You can create the projects discussed in this book using any image-editing program. PhotoSuite and PhotoDeluxe are used as examples, but tips and instructions are provided to allow you to accomplish the same results with other image-editing programs.

Many of the projects in this and the next chapter are created with templates. If your software doesn't offer a template for a project shown in this chapter, use the illustrations for ideas to create your own project layout.

How Templates Make Finished Projects Easier

Say you want to create a personalized greeting card or a calendar with pictures of your family. How do you get started? First, don't reinvent the wheel. For popular projects such as these, it's a safe bet that millions of people want to use their scanned images in the same way.

The designers of image-editing software such as PhotoSuite and PhotoDeluxe recognize this, and have included templates with their programs to help users easily accomplish popular projects. The software manufacturers employ skilled graphic artists and designers to come up with appealing and effective layouts.

Don't Be Afraid to Modify a Template

Don't worry that using a template will stifle your creativity. Most image-editing programs allow you to customize the standard templates quite a bit. Consider a template, like the one shown in Figure 15-1 (from PhotoSuite), as merely a starting point, not a cookie cutter, for your end result.

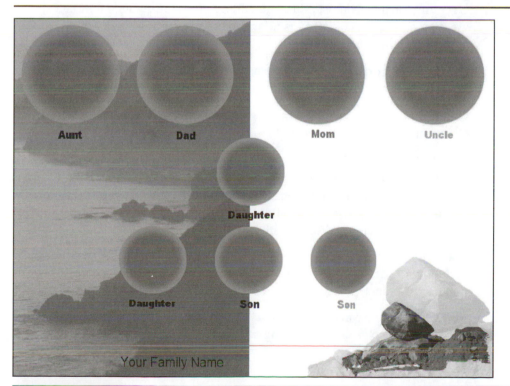

15

FIGURE 15-1   A sample PhotoSuite template for a family-tree project

Your personal enthusiasm and creativity are the ultimate determining factor as to how the finished project looks. For example, you can add or delete text on the template, add props, and vary the location of imported photos.

Projects You Can Create with Templates

PhotoSuite currently includes the largest selection of templates of any image-editing software. At a retail price of around $50 as of the writing of this book, it might be a good investment for the templates alone. Most other image-editing programs contain templates, although usually a considerably smaller selection.

Before embarking on a project you've envisioned, check the Help menu in your image-editing software to see what templates are available within that particular program.

Templates might be available in your image-editing software for a number of projects you can print and distribute. Projects discussed in this chapter and Chapter 16 include:

Greeting cards   Almost all image-editing programs include templates for greeting cards. These templates allow you to import your own photos and to include personal messages.

Frames and borders   Adding a decorative border to a photo, especially one that looks like an actual frame, gives it a finished look.

Calendars   Photo calendars make great gifts for family, friends, and business clients at a fraction of the cost charged by professional printers.

Family trees   These templates (see Figure 15-1) offer a great way to organize and display photos. Family trees reproduced on nice paper or laminated make terrific keepsakes for family reunions. PhotoSuite 4 includes four different family-tree templates, into which you simply drag and drop scanned images you've saved on your computer or a disk.

Stationery and note paper   Image-editing software makes it economical to include photographic images in your stationery and note paper. What better way to make a statement? These projects are discussed in Chapter 16.

Signs   Having a party? A yard sale? Announce the event visually. Chapter 16 tells you how to create signs using scanned images.

Fake magazine covers, sports cards, and gag IDs   It used to be that these kinds of items had to be specially produced. Now you can have fun doing them on your own, using the templates that come with PhotoSuite 4.

Business cards and brochures   Whether your business is a corporate conglomerate or an enterprise you operate out of a spare bedroom, image-editing software, quality paper, and a good printer allow you to produce items that convey the image you're looking for. Chapter 16 introduces you to these projects.

Name and gift tags   Even if you're all thumbs when it comes to wrapping, cute photographic gift tags make a clever statement. Chapter 16 tells you how to make them.

How to Locate and Use Templates

Templates are obviously very desirable features to have in your image-editing software. The more of them you have to work with, the better.

To see if your image-editing program offers a template for a particular project, search the Help database using a descriptive name for the project. For example, try "calendar" or "family tree."

If you search the PhotoSuite Help database using the word "template," you can view a list of all the available types of project templates included with the program.

Photoshop comes with a dozen or so templates for greeting cards, frames, and calendars, but it's PhotoSuite 4 that's the undefeated champion when it comes to providing templates. PhotoSuite comes with an entire extra CD filled with templates, props, and fake backgrounds—literally hundreds of templates.

Creating Your Own Project Template

15

Creating your own template requires saving a completed project to a file, and using that project as a starting point the next time you begin a similar one. This option works if you don't have a template in your image-editing program for a particular project, or you don't like the ones the manufacturer has included.

You can create a template simply by saving a completed project in a digital file format, such as JPEG, that allows you to modify it in the future. For example, suppose you create a cute greeting card for your mother, and a week later need to create one for your boss. Simply open the file in which you've saved mom's card and modify the text and images as necessary to create a proper acknowledgment for your boss. You can open the file and modify it again and again in the future as the birthdays of other friends and family members come up.

Add Frames and Borders to Scanned Photos

No one knows who started the custom of framing pictures, but adding just the right frame or border is an act of artistry in itself. Image-editing software allows you take this creative task to a new technological level.

Using PhotoSuite to Create Frames and Borders

PhotoSuite allows you to create two distinct types of frames and borders:

Templates that look like a frame   Since these are templates, you can't resize them. You need to resize your photos to fit into them. The PhotoSuite program CD offers dozens of frames from which you can choose. The PhotoSuite content CD that comes with the program offers more than 100 additional frame templates.

Borders that can be resized   Borders are frame-like effects that can be resized to fit snugly around photos of any dimension.

Working with PhotoSuite Frames

Generally you want your frame to enhance rather than overpower your picture, like the framing job shown in Figure 15-2. Other times it's the frame that gives the picture impact, as in Figure 15-3.

To access and use a PhotoSuite frame template, follow these steps:

1. Click the large Compose button on the Welcome screen, or the Compose button on the Navigation bar. The Navigation bar is located below the Menu bar.

2. Click Frames & Edges on the Activity panel displayed, then choose a category of frame or border types from the drop-down menu on the left side of the screen. A number of layout templates are displayed in the work area, as shown in Figure 15-4.

3. Double-click the frame template you want to use. An enlarged version of the frame appears in the work area.

FIGURE 15-2   A frame that complements a scanned photo

FIGURE 15-3   A frame with impact

15

FIGURE 15-4   PhotoSuite allows you to select from dozens of frame templates.

4. Click the Add Photos button, then the Computer button. Browse for the photos you want to add. Use your mouse to resize, rotate, and reposition your photos within the template.

5. When you're finished, click the Return button to return to the previous menu.

TIP   *When working with a PhotoSuite frame template, adjust the size of a photo by dragging the size handles located along the perimeter of its bounding box. To widen or lengthen a photo, drag the appropriate middle handles. To enlarge or reduce a photo proportionately, drag the appropriate corner handles.*

Adding a PhotoSuite Border to a Photo

PhotoSuite borders are a sort of one-size-fits-all frame. They have an advantage over frames because they shrink or expand if you resize your photo. To use and access a PhotoSuite border, follow these steps:

1. After you have opened the photo you want to use in PhotoSuite, click the Compose button on the Navigation bar, directly below the Menu bar, then the Adjust Objects button on the Activity panel.

2. Click the Add Borders button.

3. Click the photo on your work area so it's enclosed in a bounding box.

4. In the dialog box on the left side of the screen, choose a border category, as shown in Figure 15-5. The border styles contained within the category are displayed.

5. Drag a border from the Activity panel to the object or photo, and click Return when you're finished.

FIGURE 15-5   PhotoSuite allows you to drag and drop a decorative border onto your photo.

15

 *To remove a border that doesn't look just right, click your photo, then click the Remove button on the Activity panel. To adjust a border's width, select the object or photo the border currently encloses, and adjust the Width slider to make the border thinner or thicker.*

Frames and Borders Using Other Image-Editing Programs

If you're using a program other than PhotoSuite, you can generally find out which frame templates and border features are available by searching the keyword "frame" in the Help menu of your image-editing program.

PhotoDeluxe does not include frame templates; rather, the manufacturers of this software recommend that you create your own photo frame by using the tips and procedures described in the next section.

Creating Your Own Frame or Border Effect Without a Template

If your image-editing software doesn't include frame or border effects, don't despair. It's easy to create your own frames and borders using the two simple techniques described in this section.

Make a Frame by Layering

Many image-editing programs allow you to layer photos and backgrounds on top of each other and to add effects. By centering the photo you want to frame over an image you've scanned or imported, you can create an interesting framing effect, as I've done in Figure 15-6, in which I've layered a scanned photo over another copy of the same image, to create a dramatic frame without the use of my template.

To accomplish a frame or border effect by layering as I've just described:

1. Scan or import the photo or image you want to use as background into your image-editing software as an open project.

2. Scan or import the photo you want to frame as an object on top of the image in Step 1, and resize or adjust the photo until it appears properly centered over the image you're using as a border.

3. Save the newly framed photo in a project file.

FIGURE 15-6   A frame effect created without a template

> **TIP**   *If all you're after is a plain frame or border, try scanning a sheet of colored paper to use as a background. You can further adjust the color of the frame or border using the color adjustment tools included with your image-editing software program.*

Another great way to create a frame or border for a photo is to surround the photo with small images, as I've done in Figure 15-7. The technique for accomplishing this result was a simple matter of copying and pasting the image repeatedly around the border of the photo.

15

 FIGURE 15-7   Create a border by copying and pasting a small image.

TIP   *Does this frame effect seem a bit too basic? Try using the cutting tool and some of the other image-editing tools discussed in Chapter 10 to create a more sophisticated photo collage.*

Follow these steps:

1. Open the photo for which you want to create a frame or border, and then open the photo from which you want to create the border.

2. Cut and crop the image you want to use to create the border, using the image-editing tools described in Chapter 10 for cutting and pasting.

3. Shrink the cut and cropped image to the size you want it to be for the border.

4. Copy the resized image onto your image-editing clipboard by going to the File menu and selecting the Copy option.

5. Close the photo from which you've cropped the image you're using for the border.

6. Copy the resized, cropped border image repeatedly around the edge of your photo to get the desired effect.

Adding Text, Captions, and Word Balloons to Scanned Photos

A picture might be worth thousands of words, but a few well-chosen words can enhance an already terrific photo as shown in Figure 15-8. Fortunately, most image-editing programs have the capability to add text, word balloons and captions. If your particular program doesn't have this capability, Microsoft Word allows you to import photos into a document and resize your photo to get the same effect, as discussed in the next section of this chapter.

FIGURE 15-8   Adding text and captions can enhance an already great shot.

15

Adding Text and Captions to a Photo

Adding text and captions to a photo can add warmth, impact, and humor. A line of text or a caption adds an individual touch to your photos, and allows you to clearly convey a personal message. To locate the text and caption capabilities in your image-editing program, try searching "text" or "captions" in the Help database.

Using the PhotoSuite Text Editor

PhotoSuite has its own text editor built into the program. It's not quite as convenient to use or as intuitive as a word processing program, but it can be quite powerful once you get the hang of it. The PhotoSuite text editor allows you choose a font, resize your text, and position it anywhere you want on the photo.

To add text or captions to a photo using the PhotoSuite text editor, follow these steps:

1. Click the Compose button on the Navigation bar, directly below the Menu bar.

2. Click the Add/Edit Text button on the Activity panel located on the left side of the screen. A photo project must be open on your work area to access this feature.

3. Click anywhere inside the displayed photo, to specify a location for the text you're going to add.

4. Type your text in the Text Editor displayed on the left side of the screen as shown in Figure 15-9.

5. Select the desired font, style, and justification.

6. Adjust the size of the text by dragging the size handles on the text frame.

7. Click Return when you're finished adding text and captions to a photo, to display the finished result.

Creating a Caption with PhotoDeluxe

To create a caption using PhotoDeluxe, follow these steps:

1. With a photo open on the PhotoDeluxe work area, click the Text button at the top of the photo document window. The Text Tool dialog box appears.

2. Type the text in the text box.

3. Select a font type and font size.

4. When the text is the way you want it, click OK.

Enter text in text-editing window.

Resize and reposition text using handles on bounding box.

FIGURE 15-9   Image-editing programs have their own text-editing feature.

Inserting a Word Balloon

A word balloon is a type of prop you import into a photo and add text to. Not all image-editing programs specifically have the capability to allow you to add word balloons to a photo. However, you can create your own word balloon combining the text and line drawing program features as discussed below. To see if your program has a special feature for creating word balloons, try searching the Help menu using the keyword "word balloon."

15

Using PhotoSuite to Create a Word Balloon

PhotoSuite has a feature called a "prop," which is used specially for creating word balloons. To use the feature, follow these steps:

1. Click the Compose button on the Navigation bar, directly below the Menu bar, then click the Add Props button on the Activity panel that appears on the left side of the screen. A project must be open in the work area to access this function.

2. Choose Word Balloons from the drop-down menu.

3. Drag the desired word balloon to the photo on your desktop, as shown in Figure 15-10.

Select Word Balloons from the Props drop-down menu.

Drag and drop the word balloon prop you want to use onto your screen.

FIGURE 15-10   PhotoSuite allows you to drag and drop a word balloon prop onto your scanned photo.

4. Adjust the size of the word balloon or rotate it by dragging the size handles on the bounding box.

5. Rotate the prop by dragging the rotation handle located inside the bounding box. The vertical line indicates the orientation of the prop.

6. Click Return to save the word balloon to the photo, and then insert text in it by following the steps previously discussed in this chapter for adding text and captions to create a finished product like the one shown in Figure 15-11.

FIGURE 15-11   Use the text editor to add text to your word balloon.

Creating a Word Balloon from Scratch

If your image-editing program doesn't have a special prop to create word balloons, you can create the same effect using the drawing tools covered in Chapter 10. Simply draw a word balloon on the screen, and insert text as discussed previously in this chapter.

Using Microsoft Word to Edit Text

Adding text to photos is fun, but adding photos to existing text documents can be a lot more versatile, as a nine-year-old poet has demonstrated in Figure 15-12.

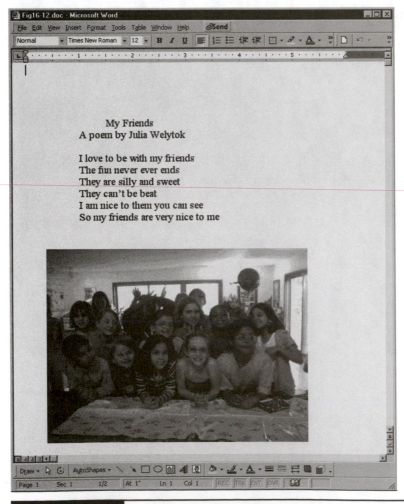

FIGURE 15-12   You can import a photo into a Microsoft Word document.

To import photos into Microsoft Word, follow these steps:

1. Save your photo, edited as you want it to appear, to a file.

2. Open a new document in Microsoft Word.

3. In Microsoft Word, click an insertion point using your text cursor, choose Insert on the Menu bar, and select Insert Picture.

4. Browse in the dialog box that appears for the image file containing your photo and open it. Your photograph appears in the Microsoft Word document.

5. Use the cursor to resize and reposition the photo as necessary.

Design Your Own Greeting Cards

The manufacturers of image-editing software know that one of the main reasons people buy their programs is so they can make personalized cards to send to friends and relatives, like the ones shown in Figure 15-13 and 15-14. That's why most of them offer at least a few greeting card templates, to help you get started.

FIGURE 15-13   A Christmas greeting using a scanned photo

15

FIGURE 15-14   A birthday greeting importing a scanned photo

   *When creating personalized greeting cards using templates, refer back to the instructions for accessing and using templates discussed earlier in this chapter.*

Create Hundreds of Greeting Cards with PhotoSuite

PhotoSuite contains literally dozens of greeting card templates, organized by the following categories:

Birthday   A great selection for all age groups.

Valentine's Day   Photo cards—the hit of any grade-school party—are simple and inexpensive to produce.

Christmas   Cards appropriate to insert photos of kids, adults, pets, and entire families for a seasonal update.

Easter   Cards with a spring look, perfect for inserting happy photos.

Father's Day   What Dad wouldn't want to skip the polyester tie in favor of a photo keepsake of the kids?

Mother's Day   Photo templates of cards that are gifts in themselves.

Other events   Includes Chanukah, Kwanzaa, and inspirational messages.

To create greeting cards using the PhotoSuite program:

1. Click the large Compose button on the Welcome screen, or the Compose button on the Navigation bar. The Navigation bar is located below the Menu bar.

2. Click Cards & Tags on the Activity panel.

3. Click Greetings on the next Activity panel displayed. Select a category of templates from the drop-down menu as shown in Figure 15-15. A number of greeting card templates appear on your screen.

4. Open photos you want to use and drag and drop them into the template, as described previously in this chapter.

Select a category of greeting cards from the drop-down menu.

Double-click any card template.

15

PhotoSuite 4 contains dozens of greeting card templates organized by category.

Making a Card with PhotoDeluxe

PhotoDeluxe includes a half dozen or so interesting greeting-card templates. To access these templates, simply click the Cards & More link located on the left side of the program screen, as shown in Figure 15-16. You can then drag and drop photos into the template layout, as described earlier in this chapter.

Click here
to access
templates.

Select a
template
category
from the
drop-down
menu.

FIGURE 15-16   Making a greeting card with PhotoDeluxe

Create an Illustrated Calendar

Calendars are a popular gift because they're functional and decorative even if you already have more than one. You can create them using a special calendar template, or create one on your own with a little help from a word-processing program.

Designing a Calendar Using PhotoSuite

The hardest part about creating a calendar with PhotoSuite is choosing among all the different template styles. Your first decision is whether you want to use the monthly or yearly calendar templates. Your first thought might be, "Why would I want to create a calendar for only one month?" The answer is that you can bind the monthly pages, like the one shown in Figure 15-17, to create a calendar with a different photo for every month.

FIGURE 15-17   Create a calendar from scanned photos.

To use any of the PhotoSuite calendar templates, follow these steps:

1. Click the large Compose button on the Navigation bar, directly below the PhotoSuite Menu bar.

2. Click Calendars on the Activity panel.

3. Choose 1 Month, Quarterly, or Yearly from the available options on the Activity panel on the left side of the screen. A number of thumbnail templates from the category you selected appear on your desktop, as shown in Figure 15-18.

15

Select from several calendar layouts and themes.

FIGURE 15-18 PhotoSuite offers dozens of templates and calendar themes.

4. Select the year and/or month you wish to display on the calendar.

5. Double-click the thumbnail of the template you want to use, then click Next to see it full size on your desktop.

6. You can return to the thumbnail view of the templates by clicking the Back arrow in the upper left corner of the screen.

7. Drag and drop photos from the Library to the template, or open photos from disks or your hard drive, and drag and drop them into the calendar template. You can resize and reposition the photos, as necessary, with your mouse.

8. When you've finished loading, resizing, and positioning your photos, click the Finish button.

TIP

Consider adding props from the PhotoSuite prop database to your calendar for added impact. The topic of adding props is discussed earlier in this chapter.

Creating a Calendar with PhotoDeluxe

PhotoDeluxe contains two templates for creating calendars: monthly and yearly. To access and use these templates, follow these steps:

1. Click the Cards & More link located on the left side of the program screen.

2. Select Month or Year from the Navigation bar, directly below the Menu bar.

3. Drag and drop photos into the template layout, as described earlier in this chapter.

Use Microsoft Word to Create a Calendar from Scanned Images

To create a basic calendar using the Microsoft Word Calendar wizard, follow these steps:

1. On the File menu, click New.

2. Click the Other Documents tab.

3. Double-click the Calendar Wizard icon in the dialog box, as shown in Figure 15-19. The Microsoft Word Calendar wizard appears.

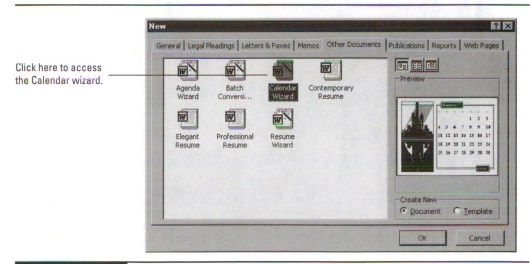

Click here to access the Calendar wizard.

FIGURE 15-19   Creating a calendar with Microsoft Word

15

4. Follow the steps in the wizard to create a Microsoft Word calendar document.

5. After you've created the basic calendar document, import image files from scanned photos by placing your cursor at an insertion point and choosing Insert | Picture.

6. A dialog box appears. Browse for the photo you want to import and open it. The photo appears in your document.

7. Resize and reposition the imported photos using your mouse to achieve a finished product, like the one in Figure 15-20.

FIGURE 15-20   A calendar created using Microsoft Word

Making Novelty Items

Scanning projects are so easily accomplished that most of the challenge is simply coming up with an idea. The purpose of this final section of the chapter is to provide you with some fun ideas and examples.

Templates for many of the projects included in this section are included with PhotoSuite. You'll also find templates for a couple of the projects in PhotoDeluxe and other image-editing programs. If your image-editing program doesn't come with a template for a project such as a gag magazine cover or fake sports card, don't let it deter you. Create your own template for these projects, using the tips provided in this section.

Produce Magazine Covers

Fake magazine covers, like the one shown in Figure 15-21, are fun and stylish. They make enjoyable projects for kids—something they can really show off. With a little imagination, you can also turn your fake magazine covers into announcements, invitations, and posters, like the example in Figure 15-22.

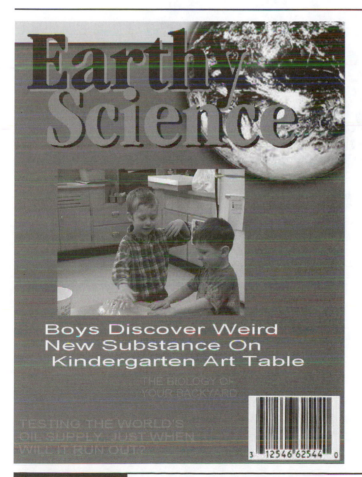

15

FIGURE 15-21   A fake magazine cover created with a PhotoSuite template and a scanned photo

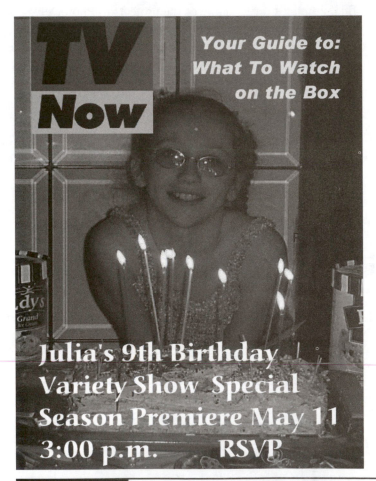

FIGURE 15-22   Fake magazine covers make great invitations.

Creating a Fake Magazine Cover with a PhotoSuite Template

You can access a special template in PhotoSuite for creating fake magazine covers by following these steps:

1. Click the Compose button on the Navigation bar. The Navigation bar is located below the Menu bar.

2. Click Fun Stuff on the Activity panel.

3. Click Magazine Covers on the next Activity panel displayed. A number of thumbnail pictures of layout templates are displayed in the work area.

4. Double-click the thumbnail of the magazine cover template you want to use. It then appears on your screen full size.

5. Click the Add Photos button to add photos to the template, and the Add/Edit Text button to add and modify the text and captions, using the text editor as discussed earlier in this chapter.

Creating a Fake Magazine Cover from Scratch

Creating a fake magazine cover without the aid of a template takes a little more time and effort. It also allows you a lot more flexibility, since you can pick just about any magazine cover to scan and reproduce.

The first step to creating your own magazine cover is to scan the cover of a magazine you're planning on spoofing. Save the scanned image of the magazine cover to a project file before you begin experimenting. Import pictures of people and objects you want on your cover, using your mouse to reposition and resize the imported images as necessary.

Some of the editing tools you'll probably find useful for this type of project, previously discussed in Chapter 10, include the following:

Cutting and cropping   These tools allow you to cut heads, faces, and bodies out of existing photographs, save them, and transplant them onto the magazine cover you've scanned.

Edge softening or blending   These tools help you make images you've inserted into a magazine cover look more realistic by allowing you to softly blend the edges of the imported image into the background.

Clone tool   This tool allows you to take samples of color from the background of the imported image and cover blank spots or portions of the photo you don't want in your image with an exact color-matched "patch."

All the above tools are discussed in more detail in Chapter 10.

15

Gag IDs

Creating a gag ID, like the one shown in Figure 15-23, is very much like creating a fake magazine cover.

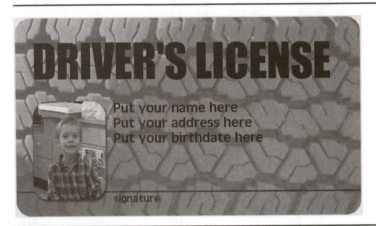

FIGURE 15-23   Try creating a fun fake ID from a scanned photo.

If you're using PhotoSuite, you can access the PhotoSuite templates for creating this project by following the steps for creating magazine covers above, except you must click the Fake IDs button in Step 3.

If you don't have PhotoSuite, you can scan an ID card and import face and body images onto it by following the same procedures for creating your own fake magazine cover without a template, as described above.

Bookmarks

Bookmarks make great party favors, promotional items, and thank-you items. You can experiment with different quality papers. You can also laminate them by taking them to your local photocopy shop or purchasing an inexpensive laminating machine from an office supply store or website. Currently, you can find laminating machines for less than $50 at www.pbplastics.com.

Figure 15-24 shows a bookmark created with a PhotoSuite template. To access the PhotoSuite bookmark templates, follow these steps:

1. Click the Compose button on the Navigation bar, located below the Menu bar.

2. Click Cards & Tags on the Activity panel.

FIGURE 15-24   Laminated bookmarks from photos make great keepsakes.

3. Click Bookmarks on the next Activity panel displayed. A number of layout templates are displayed on the work area. Then, click the Next button to open the template as a project file. Click the Compose button to prepare for the next step.

4. Click the Add Photos button to add photos to the template, and the Add/Edit Text button to add and modify the text and captions using the text editor, as discussed earlier in this chapter.

15

Making T-Shirts from Scanned Photos and Drawings

Making t-shirts from scanned photos and drawings is such an easy process you really don't need a book to learn how to do it. In fact, all you need besides your scanner is some iron-on transfer paper, a t-shirt, and an iron.

You simply print your scanned image or photo onto some iron-on transfer paper that you load into your printer as you would any other paper. Several companies manufacture the iron-on transfer paper you need for this project. You can find it at just about any office supply store, or visit the Avery website at www.avery.com. A six-pack of transfer sheets, as of the writing of this book, costs about $12.

 *T-shirts bearing photographs of the kids or scanned images they've drawn are gifts kids love to give to their friends, parents, and grandparents.*

Creating Customized Refrigerator Magnets

Refrigerator magnets are useful in any household. You can purchase sheets of magnetized plastic that can be cut to the shape of any image with regular scissors. Just glue an image onto the magnetized sheet and cut around the image.

You can find magnetized sheets at most office stores, or visit www.avery.com. A three-pack of transfer sheets, as of the writing of this book, costs about $6.

The Possibilities Are Endless

Is your head spinning from all the projects in this chapter? Is your to-do list growing longer and longer?

We've only scratched the surface of what you can create with your scanner. Templates expedite the process, but working without a template gives you unlimited flexibility. No doubt you're beginning to see your scanner as a tool of creative self-expression, as well as a handy peripheral device. The next chapter provides you with even more ideas for items that are practical as well as fun.

Chapter 16

Communicating Through Scanned Photos

How To...

■ Make personalized stationery and note paper

■ Design business cards and logos

■ Use scanned photos in a presentation

■ Make name tags, gift tags, and signs

■ Distribute coupons and certificates

We might operate on a paperless basis someday, but that day is far in the future. Most electronic communication is presently reduced to some form of paper.

Paper communication is portable and immediate in a way that electronic communication might never be. It doesn't require that the recipient be sitting in front of a computer to read it. Paper—in the form of cards, stationery, and brochures—can be distributed for reading on the fly. It can be passed by hand, posted on a wall, and stuck to a lapel as a name tag.

This chapter helps you combine some of the best aspects of both electronic and paper media.

Designing Stationery Using Scanned Photos and Images

Stationery can set the mood of the message, and make a personal statement beyond the words on the paper. Scanning technology allows you to create stationery and note paper ranging from high-impact to subtly elegant. This section offers a few ideas and sample layout illustrations to help you get started.

Designing Stationery That Makes a Statement

When you first rev up your scanner, it's tempting to design elaborate stationery for business or personal use, importing all sorts of images and interesting props—but showing off your new scanner's capabilities is not the goal of effective communication. More is not always better when it comes to making just the right statement, particularly for business communication.

When you design your own stationery, you don't have the feedback from a professional printer who can offer you a trained eye from developing hundreds of layouts—but you *can* borrow the following tips from the printing pros for a good layout design for a business:

- Select the color and quality of your paper carefully. Pay particular attention to the texture and thickness. Avoid paper that is thick and grainy or thin and glossy. Opt instead for a texture that falls between these extremes, to convey a confident, understated image.

- Pay the extra money for stationery bearing a watermark. It can make a good subliminal impression.

- Avoid trying to make too strong a statement with colored paper, which might distract from your graphics and undermine a professional image. Stick with off-whites, beiges, and grays. If you choose a stronger color, stay with pastel colors, although even these tones are not generally recommended. Follow this advice even if you're in a creative profession such as media relations.

- Remember to choose the color of your stationery to complement your logo and overall layout.

- Opt for smaller-scale logos and art on your stationery, without sacrificing legibility of text or clarity of any imported photographic images. Professional printers concur that less is generally more when it comes to conveying a professional image.

- Scan logos and other images you're planning on importing at slightly lower resolutions than you normally would, since they will be smaller than images you would use for other purposes. When the small-size image or logo is printed, too high a resolution can cause reduced clarity and smudging. (Smudging results from trying to print more image data per inch than your printer is capable of.)

- Experiment with different fonts. The text editor of your image-editing program probably comes with several. Figures 16-1 through 16-3 illustrate the dramatically different effects that can be achieved by changing fonts.

- Consider using a cutout image of yourself or your product. Chapter 10 tells you about the cutting tools you can find in your image-editing program.

16

Creating Professional-Looking Stationery from Templates

As with other types of projects, templates give you a running start. Figures 16-1 through 16-3 show you three different types of stationery created with templates included with PhotoSuite. Note the different impression each conveys with the graphic style and font, all of which can be very effective, depending on your intended purpose.

FIGURE 16-1   A capable and confident design

FIGURE 16-2   A letterhead that conveys an artistic touch

FIGURE 16-3   A bold letterhead using a cutout on neutral-color paper

Experimenting with the PhotoSuite Stationery Templates

PhotoSuite has the best selection of templates for creating stationery of any general image-editing program. You can choose from dozens of templates, organized by the following categories:

Education   These templates have school-related themes, like the one shown in Figure 16-4. You can communicate with the school in style, and give your kids notes they can't wait to deliver to their teacher.

FIGURE 16-4   Give your kids school notes they can't wait to deliver.

Letterhead   This category is where you'll find an array of professional-looking styles and designs, like the ones illustrated previously in this chapter.

Media   This template allows you to create customized CD labels, like the one shown in Figure 16-5.

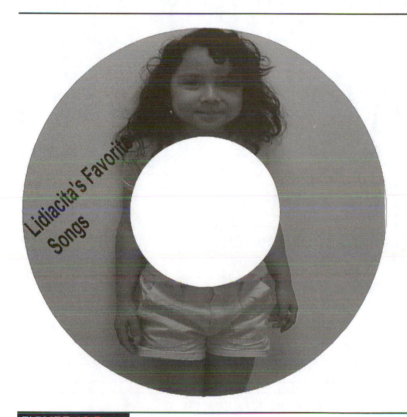

FIGURE 16-5   Create a customized CD label.

Notepads   Why settle for scratch paper? Opt for your own artistic notepads.

Recipes   Recipes are a personal art form. PhotoSuite allows you dozens of templates to personalize your recipes with your own likeness or a photo of a food or a special occasion as shown in Figure 16-6.

Miscellaneous   This category of templates includes bold stationery appropriate for personal rather than business use.

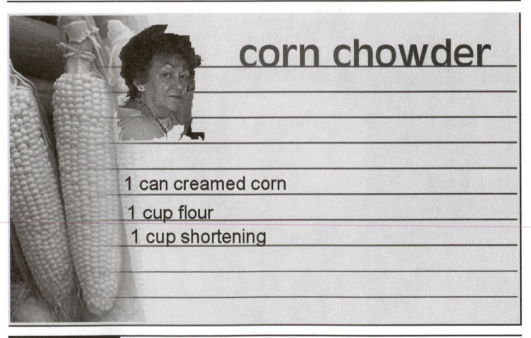

FIGURE 16-6   Hand out customized recipe cards.

Accessing the PhotoSuite Templates

To access and use the PhotoSuite stationery templates, follow these steps:

1. Click the large Compose button on the Welcome screen, or the Compose button on the Navigation bar. The Navigation bar is located below the Menu bar.

2. Click Business in the panel on the left side of the screen.

3. Click Stationery on the next panel displayed. You might be prompted to insert your PhotoSuite content disc into the CD drive to access the full range of templates.

4. Select a stationery category from the drop-down menu that appears on the left side of the screen. A number of layout templates are displayed in the work area, as shown in Figure 16-7.

Select ——
stationery
category.

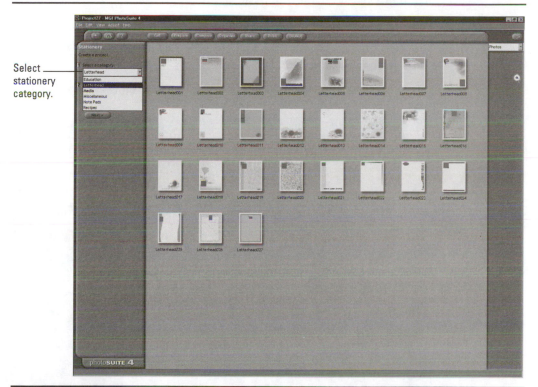

FIGURE 16-7   PhotoSuite comes with dozens of stationery templates.

5. Double-click the icon of the template you want to use. It appears full size on your desktop, ready for editing.

6. Click the Add Photos button in the panel on the left side of the screen, and specify a source you want to obtain the photos from: Computer, Digital Camera, or Scanner.

7. Resize and reposition the photos on the work area.

8. To save your project, select Save from the File menu. You are prompted to name the project if you've not previously done so.

Creating Stationery with PhotoDeluxe

PhotoDeluxe includes about a dozen basic stationery templates. To access and use them, follow these steps:

1. After inserting the PhotoDeluxe CD in your CD drive, click the Cards & More button on the desktop.

2. Click Pages & Certificates, and select Stationery from the drop-down menu, as shown in Figure 16-8.

3. Click the Choose Certificate tab, then the Choose Certificate button to view your stationery choices.

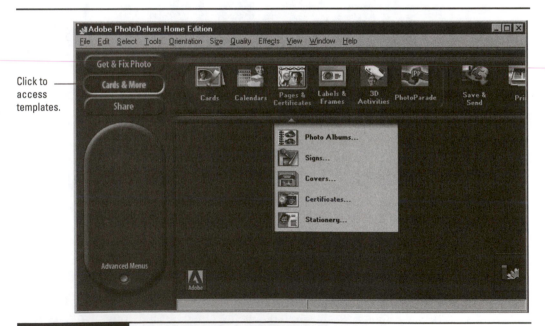

FIGURE 16-8   PhotoDeluxe has several stationery templates.

4. Double-click the icon for the stationery template you want to use. It appears full size on your work area.

5. Click the Add tab, then either the My Photos or Open File command button.

6. Click the Find Photos button on the left side of the screen to browse for the photos you want to add.

7. Reposition and resize the photos on your work area using your mouse.

8. Click Done when you're finished.

Designing Business Cards, Fliers, Brochures, and Logos

Designing your own brochures, business cards, and logos can save you a considerable amount of money—but you certainly don't want these items to be anything less than the highest professional quality. PhotoSuite comes with a range of templates for creating these materials that will represent you and your business well.

The professional layouts for business cards, brochures, and logos illustrated in this section were created with PhotoSuite templates, but can give you some ideas for creating your own layouts from scratch using similar fonts and graphic effects.

The Advantages of Making Your Own Business Cards

Business cards are generally so inexpensive to have printed, you might wonder why you even want to bother taking the time to create your own. But scanning software allows you a level of artistic control you could never get from a print shop.

Here are a few advantages of maintaining business cards you can edit and print on your computer:

- You can create several sets of business cards and tailor the text to types of clients or jobs you're hoping to attract. For example, you can print different sets of cards identifying specific types of services you provide, and omitting others that might be irrelevant in certain types of business settings.

- You can update your cards frequently, on a moment's notice, and never need to wait to get your cards back from the print shop.

- You can add a photographic image relatively inexpensively, and control the appearance and quality of the image by experimenting on your own. Most print shops can't allow you this degree of freedom.

16

TIP   *Consider making a set of personal cards with your name, address, and phone number, as well as business cards. These encourage people to stay in contact with you on a personal, as well as professional, level. For example, cards with personal information are handy for occasions such as your high-school reunion, a vacation, or if you're shopping and want salespeople to stay in contact with you as you gather quotes.*

Using PhotoSuite Templates to Create Business Cards

PhotoSuite comes with hundreds of business card layouts that you can import a photo or logo into. The card templates are organized into the following categories, by profession:

Entertainment   These card templates contain layouts with graphics appropriate for musicians and other entertainers.

Sales promotion   These layouts project a strong, direct image.

Services   PhotoSuite contains dozens of layouts with specific graphics for service professionals, including everyone from physicians to plumbers.

Miscellaneous   This category contains several attractive, general layouts.

Figures 16-9, 16-10, and 16-11 illustrate three different business card layouts. To access and use the PhotoSuite business card templates, follow these steps:

1. After inserting the PhotoSuite Content disc in the CD drive, click the large Compose button, located directly below the Menu bar.

2. Click the Business button in the panel that appears on the left side of the screen.

3. Select a business card category from the drop-down menu that appears on the left side of your screen. A number of business card templates from the category you've selected appear.

4. Double-click the template you want to use. It appears full size on your work area.

5. Click the Add Photos button and browse for the photo you want to include.

6. Drag, drop, and resize the photo you want to include in your business card. When you're satisfied with the result, click Create New Project.

FIGURE 16-9   An impressive business card with a photo

FIGURE 16-10   A card with personal information comes in handy.

16

FIGURE 16-11   A customized card for a clown with a photo cutout as a logo

Printing Your Business Cards

To print business cards properly and efficiently, you need good business-card stock. Avery is one manufacturer that makes printable business cards. Depending on which color and style you select, the cost is about $12 to $15 for 100 cards.

Printing on business-card stock is a procedure similar to printing on labels. You must properly center the text and graphics on each card.

PhotoSuite allows you to select a print option that corresponds to the Avery business-card size. Avery is a popular manufacturer of stationery products that supplies product lines to most major office supply stores.

Make Your Own Logo

It's very convenient to have a logo, saved to an image file that you can import into newsletters, business cards, websites, stationery, and other communications.

Use Your Photograph as a Logo

Image-editing software allows you to create your own logo from a scanned photograph by cropping the portion you want from the photo. For example, Figure 16-11 uses a scanned photograph of a clown that has been cut out and saved as a logo for stationery and business cards. Chapter 10 discusses cutting and cropping tools in image-editing software.

Adopt a Logo from a Prop Database

You can also "adopt" a logo from a prop database, which you might find in your image-editing software or on a clip-art CD at your local office supply store. Figure 16-12 shows a sampling of the images included in the PhotoSuite props database that can be used for logos.

16

FIGURE 16-12   Some PhotoSuite props that make interesting logos

 *To access the PhotoSuite props database, follow the instructions provided in Chapter 14.*

Import a Logo into a Microsoft Word Document

To import a logo image and make it the correct size for a particular project you're creating in Microsoft Word, follow these steps:

1. To open the image file containing the logo, go to the Insert menu and choose Picture, then From File. In the dialog box that appears, browse for and open the image file you want.

2. Right-click the logo, and select Properties from the pop-up menu. The Format Picture dialog box appears, displaying a representation of your photo. Click the Size tab, and adjust the height and width of the logo, as shown in Figure 16-13.

3. Click OK to close the dialog box, and use your mouse to drag and position your logo to the correct spot within your project.

Promotional Fliers and Brochures

Brochures and fliers give clients specific information about you and your services that they can retain and read at their leisure. Scanning technology allows you to add the impact of graphics to this valuable communication medium.

Designing Highly Professional Flyers

Fliers are not limited to informal communication and advertising. In fact, they can be highly polished pieces, and more dignified in appearance than glossy brochures. Fliers have several other advantages over brochures:

- Fliers are far easier than brochures to design and lay out because you don't have to worry about a multiple-panel format.

- An entire 8½-by-11-inch page is viewed at once, as opposed to a folded brochure.

- Graphic images can be larger and have more impact.

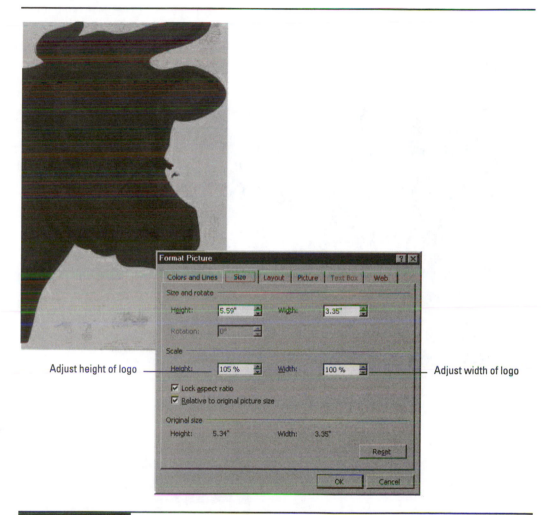

Adjust height of logo

Adjust width of logo

FIGURE 16-13   Resize your logo in a Microsoft Word document using this dialog box.

Your image-editing program might contain templates for designing fliers, but this is one project in which such a template can be a disadvantage. Flyers often contain a lot of text, and your image-editing program is designed only for editing images, not text.

Depending on how much text you decide to include in your flier, you might be better off importing your scanned images into a Microsoft Word document. Microsoft Word offers far more text-editing capabilities than any image-editing software.

16

On the other hand, if you're aiming for a high-impact flier with eye-catching graphics and little text, your image editor might be a better choice. The flier shown in Figure 16-14 was created using a PhotoSuite template, and contains very little text, so Microsoft Word's capabilities were not needed.

Company Name
(555) 555-5555

FIGURE 16-14 A PhotoSuite flier containing mostly graphics

Consider Whether to Invest Time in Brochures

Brochures are a nice way to present and organize information for the reader; however, this form of organization comes at a price. Brochures are relatively complex projects when it comes to designing a layout. In fact, standard image-editing programs, such as PhotoSuite and PhotoDeluxe, don't come with templates for creating brochures. This is because it's difficult to lay out text and graphics on the multiple-page panels required for a brochure.

If you want to create a brochure for your business or organization, you might want to consider providing disks with scanned images to a professional printer. You can coordinate with the print shop on the layout of your text and graphics, and the pros might be able to offer you helpful suggestions based on their experience.

If you do want to create a brochure on your own rather than having one profes-sionally printed, you can order special software that provides you with the templates you need to create a professional-looking layout. One program that you might find helpful is My Advanced Brochures, Mailers & More, shown in Figure 16-15. This program is specially designed to allow you to create layouts for hundreds of different brochures. You order it at www.click-here-now.com/software/mailinglists/ brochuredesign.htm. It's also available in many office-supply stores, along with other programs that are also designed to create brochures.

Draft Eye-Catching Newsletters with Microsoft Word

The popularity of newsletters is on the rise. Many clubs and organizations rely heavily on them; the newsletter is often perceived as one of the chief membership benefits. For businesses, they're a great way to touch base with current customers and to attract new ones.

Use the Microsoft Word Newsletter Capabilities

Microsoft Word has very sophisticated newsletter capabilities. Most image-editing programs do not contain templates for creating newsletters because the ones in Microsoft Word are so versatile and easy to use.

To create a newsletter using Microsoft Word, follow these steps:

1. Using the View menu at the top of the screen, select Print Layout View. From the Edit menu, choose Select All.

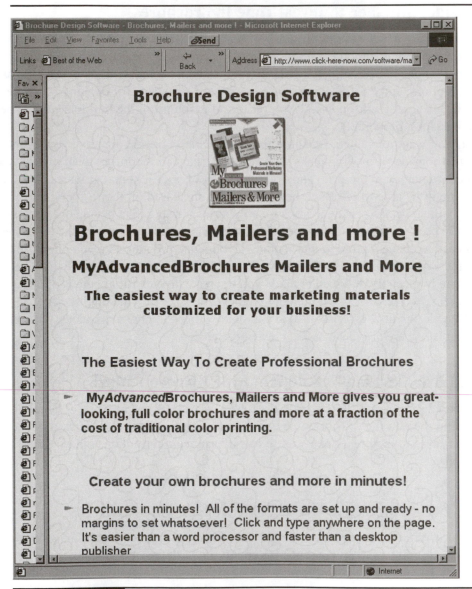

FIGURE 16-15 You can purchase a software program specially designed for brochures and mailings.

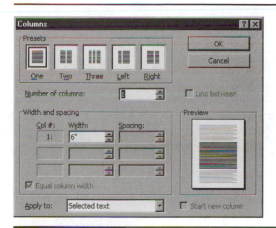

FIGURE 16-16   Format a newsletter in Microsoft Word using this dialog box.

2. On the Format menu, select Columns. The dialog box shown in Figure 16-16 appears. Select the number of columns you want to appear in your newsletter. You can then begin typing in the columns. As you reach the end of each column, the text will continue smoothly into the next column.

3. If you want to adjust the column widths and spacing, drag the column markers on the horizontal ruler at the top of your Microsoft Word document window.

4. Import a file containing an image file into the newsletter by going to the Insert menu and selecting Picture. Browse for and open the image file you want to include in the newsletter, using the dialog box that appears.

Add Stylistic Touches to Your Newsletter

Here are a few ideas for adding panache to your newsletters:

■ Don't forget to explore the database of interesting props that comes with many image-editing programs, such as PhotoSuite. Consider importing props from the prop library, as well as scanned photos, to add visual appeal to your newsletters.

■ Investigate software programs specifically designed to create sophisticated newsletters. There are many software programs on the market exclusively designed to produce professional-looking newsletters and mailings. You can usually find several such programs at your local office-supply store.

16

■ Microsoft Word comes with dozens of font types, and you can experiment
with the legibility and artistic effect of each. To change the font of your
newsletter in Microsoft Word, go the Edit menu and choose Select All. Then
select a font type from the drop-down menu, as shown in Figure 16-17.

FIGURE 16-17   Select a font type for your newsletter in Microsoft Word.

Name Tags, Gift Tags, and Signs

PhotoSuite contains templates for name tags, gift tags, and signs. These simple items
can be used to make creative and stylish statements when you spruce them up with a
scanned photo or two.

Enclose a Distinctive Gift Tag

Why not tag your gift with a picture of yourself? It's easy to make a distinctive
enclosure, like the one shown in Figure 16-18. Use the illustration here as a guide, or
access more than a dozen gift card templates in the PhotoSuite program by following
these steps:

1. Click the Compose button, directly below the Menu bar.

2. Click Cards & Tags on the Activity panel.

3. Click Gift Tags on the next Activity panel displayed. A number of layout
    templates are displayed in the work area.

Merry Christmas from
Lidiacita

To: Grandma

Create personalized gift tags.

4. Double-click the template you want to use. It appears full size on your
    work area.

5. Click the Add Photos button, and browse for the photo you want to include

6. Drag, drop, and resize the photo you want to include in your gift tag. When
    you're satisfied with the result, click Create New Project.

Make Photographic Name Tags

Name tags, like the one shown in Figure 16-19, are often laminated and used to
provide added security by conclusively identifying the wearer. To create one, follow
these steps:

1. After inserting the PhotoSuite Content CD in the CD-ROM drive, click the
    large Compose button on the Welcome screen, or the Compose button on the
    Navigation bar. The Navigation bar is located below the Menu bar.

2. Click Business on the Activity panel.

16

FIGURE 16-19   Make name tags for fun or security purposes.

3. Click Name Tags on the next Activity panel displayed. A number of layout templates are displayed in the work area.

4. Double-click the template you want to use. It appears full size on your work area.

5. Click the Add Photos button and browse for the photo you want to import into your project.

6. Drag, drop, and resize the photo using your mouse.

7. When you're satisfied with the result, choose Save from the File menu and name your project if you've not previously done so.

Illustrate Everyday Signs

You can create stylish signs with your scanner to direct clients, students, neighbors, and other attendees at an event. Why settle for something scrawled or hastily printed out, when you can create a high-impact sign complete with your scanned graphics, like the one in Figure 16-20?

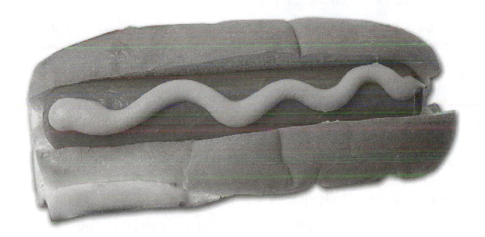

Office
PICNIC

Centennial Park
Friday June 23, 2001

FIGURE 16-20   Quickly create a high-impact illustrated sign.

To access and use the dozens of sign templates included with the PhotoSuite program, follow these steps:

1. Click the large Compose button on the Welcome screen located below the Menu bar.

2. Click the Business button located on the left side of the screen.

3. Click Signs on the next Activity panel displayed.

4. Select a category of signs from the drop-down menu on the left side of your screen. A number of layout templates from that category are displayed on your work area.

4. Double-click the template you want to use. It appears full size on your work area.

5. Click the Return button, then the Add Photos button.

6. Browse for the photo you want to import into your project. Drag, drop, and resize the photo using your mouse. When you're satisfied with your sign, click Create New Project.

Create Coupons and Certificates

Coupons and certificates are fun to create for personal as well as promotional purposes. Use the illustrations in Figures 16-21 and 16-22 as a guide, or access the PhotoSuite templates by following these steps:

1. After inserting the PhotoSuite Content CD in the CD drive, click the large Compose button on the Welcome screen, or the Compose button on the Navigation bar located below the Menu bar.

2. Click the Business button on the left side of the screen.

3. Click Certificates on the next Activity panel displayed.

4. Select a project category from the drop-down menu on the left side of the screen. A number of layout templates are displayed in the work area.

5. Double-click the template you want to use. It appears full size on your work area.

6. Click Return, then click the Add Photos button and browse for the photo you want to import into your project.

7. Drag, drop, and resize the photo you want to include on your project. When you're satisfied with your coupon or certificate, click Create New Project.

FIGURE 16-21   Coupons can be a creative gift.

FIGURE 16-22   Every child loves a certificate with his or her picture.

16

Add Impact to All Your Communication

Scanning technology allows you to add style and visual impact to your daily communication. Why settle for mere words on a page when it's so easy to scan and import images? Most of the projects discussed in this chapter are ultimately reduced to some form of paper, but if you feel you really want to go paperless, Chapter 17 shows you how to use scanning technology to create websites, enhance email, and complement presentations.

Chapter 17

Adding Scanned Images to Your Web Pages and Email

How To...

■ Email scanned photos

■ Post scanned photos on the Web with PhotoSuite and PhotoDeluxe

■ Create your own web page

■ Find free web hosting services to make your site accessible on the Web

■ Get started with Microsoft FrontPage

■ Send image files and upload web pages to a server using a file transfer program

What fun is a photo you can't pass around and share? Photos are meant to be viewed, not hidden away, and the reality of modern life is that a lot of our viewing now takes place over the Internet, via email and by surfing websites. This chapter is devoted to the subject of helping you share your photos with friends and family using today's efficient and instantaneous electronic communication media.

Choose the Best Way to Share Your Scanned Photos

The Internet and the World Wide Web are dynamic tools for sharing and transmitting photos. You have a number of options for using them, depending on your intended audience, your comfort level with technology, and the amount of time you want to invest.

This chapter gives you a whirlwind overview of your Internet-based photo-sharing options. At the simplest end of the spectrum, you can simply attach a photo to an email message.

Taking things a step further, you can post photos for friends and family to view on an actual website. You can use a service such as PhotoSuite's GatherRound.com or Adobe's PhotoShare.com. These communal websites allow registered users to post photos and provide friends and family with a password to access them.

If you're ambitious, creative, and have the time to invest, you can easily design your own website. You can choose from among a number of programs to help you do this, including PhotoDeluxe, PhotoSuite, Yahoo! GeoCities, and FrontPage.

A Word about the Internet

If someone stopped you on the street and asked you to define the term *Internet,* with a capital *I,* what would you say? Chances are you visualize the Internet based on the part you interact with: your own computer screen.

The Internet that brings a wealth of information to your screen is vast. It's made of hundreds of thousands of interconnected *networks* in more than 100 countries using large computers, called servers, to interconnect them. A network is a grouping of interrelated computers, such as those for commercial, academic, and business entities.

Originally developed as a tool for the U.S. military, the Internet has become a tool for communication and research that businesses, governments, and individuals now depend on.

A term closely related to Internet, but not synonymous, is the term *World Wide Web.* Figuratively speaking, it's a web of documents. The World Wide Web connects documents by the use of web-page links called *hypertext markup links.*

How Computers "Talk" on the Internet

Just as people must share language consisting of a common vocabulary and grammatical rules to communicate, computers must share common rules for transmitting and receiving data. A *protocol* is a set of programming rules and conventions that allow computers to "talk" to each other while sharing data over the Internet. Most computers use a protocol called *transmission control protocol/Internet protocol* (TCP/IP).

What You Need to Communicate on the Internet

To allow your computer to communicate with other computers on the Internet, you need to have web browser software and an *Internet service provider* (ISP).

Web Browser Software

Web browser software enables you to view web pages from the World Wide Web on your computer. To view a particular site, you type its address, called a *URL* (short for uniform resource locater), into the location field on your web browser software. Figure 17-1 shows a URL typed into the Microsoft Internet Explorer browser software.

17

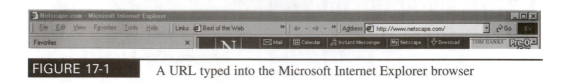

FIGURE 17-1   A URL typed into the Microsoft Internet Explorer browser

An Internet Service Provider (ISP)

An ISP is usually a paid service provider you contract with to provide you access to powerful computers called *servers*. A server is a computer shared by hundreds, thousands, even millions of users. It contains files, applications, and data posted to the World Wide Web, and allows you to connect to a backbone network of other powerful servers that comprise the Internet.

An ISP might also be an employer, educational institution, or free business-community service.

Attaching Scanned Photos to Email Messages

Email is perhaps the most frequently used feature on the Internet. In fact, so much written communication is now sent electronically that a venerable U.S. institution—the U.S. Post Office—has found itself financially threatened. Stamps and paper are simply at a competitive disadvantage with this new electronic medium. This is particularly true now that scanned images, such as photographs, can be beautifully and efficiently transmitted as email attachments.

How Scanned Photos Travel over the Internet

Images travel over the Internet much the same way as other types of email. When an email message is sent, regardless of whether it contains text or images, it's broken up into *packets* of data. These data packets can be transmitted over telephone, cable, and other lines, and ultimately to the destination computer.

What happens next depends on whether you're hooked up to a network of computers or a stand-alone PC. If your computer is part of a network, an internal routing device determines whether the email is addressed to someone on the same network as the sending computer. If the message is going to someone within a network, it's delivered and the process is complete.

If your email is not part of a network or is going to another computer outside its own network, a device called an *Internet router* performs the complex process of locating and directing your message to the network the destination computer resides at.

Once the Internet router directs your email to the appropriate destination network, you email might pass through both a *gateway* and a *firewall.* The gateway uses the TCP/IP protocol to reconstruct the data packets into a complete message. A firewall is a type of security device that shields a network from the Internet so unwanted intruders can't break in and cause damage. Occasionally, for security purposes, a firewall might be programmed so that no file attachments are allowed to pass through. For example, a network administrator might decide that image files have no legitimate business purpose, and take up too much space on the company's server.

When someone sends you an email message, the message is seldom delivered straight to your computer. Instead, the message usually passes through a computer called an email server. The email software on your computer periodically logs into the email server and communicates with it to see if you have any mail.

An Internet server might be programmed to reject email over a certain size, such as 1 megabyte, so the email server isn't overtaxed. A megabyte is a lot of text—about a thousand pages of text like this page—but a single high-quality image might be as much as 1 megabyte.

Emailing an Image Using Your Scanner Software

As you might recall from Chapter 2, your scanner comes with its own software that runs it. Your scanner software might have a feature that allows you to open your email program and send email. Check the documentation that came with your scanner or the scanner's Help menu to see if it has this capability. You might even have a special external button on your scanner that allows you to scan or email an image simply by pressing the button.

Let's look at an example of how scanner software that has email capability works. The Hewlett-Packard ScanJet ScanPro 5370C is an example of a scanner that offers this functionality. There are three phases to the process:

Configure the default email settings.   The first time you press the external email button on the scanner, the Scanner Button Settings dialog box, shown in Figure 17-2, appears. This dialog box allows you to identify the email program on your system you want the scanner software to use, and the type of scanned document you're sending. For example, the dialog box in Figure 17-2 is configured to send true-color

17

photographs using the Microsoft Outlook Express email program. After you've initially configured the external email button on the 5370C, it uses these default settings each time you press the scan button. You can reopen the dialog box and reset these specifications if you are, for example, scanning another type of document or using a different email program.

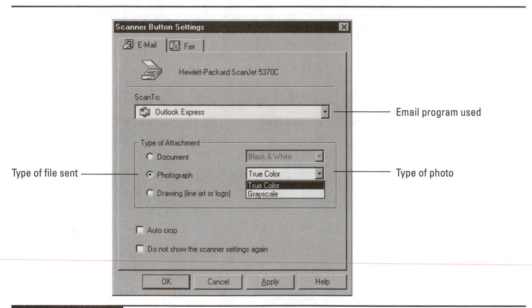

FIGURE 17-2   The dialog box used to configure the external email button on a Hewlett-Packard ScanJet 5370C scanner

Perform the scan.   After you've configured the default settings for your scanner software, you scan the image you want to send. The 5370C displays a status message, as shown in Figure 17-3, telling you the scanning process is in progress and the finished scan will be sent to the particular utility within the software that handles email. In this case, the email utility is called eFax Messenger Plus.

Send the email.   After the scanning process is complete, your scanner software automatically opens your email program and creates an email message document to send the scanned image, as shown in Figure 17-4. Simply enter a text message, and identify a recipient for the message as shown. If you're using the 5370C, you go to the File menu and select the Send To option.

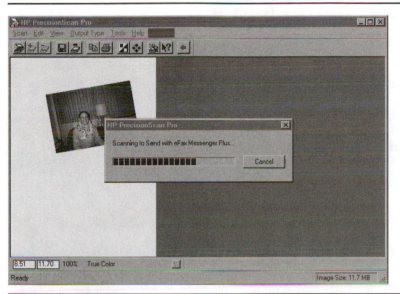

FIGURE 17-3   After configuring the external email button, scan the image you want to send.

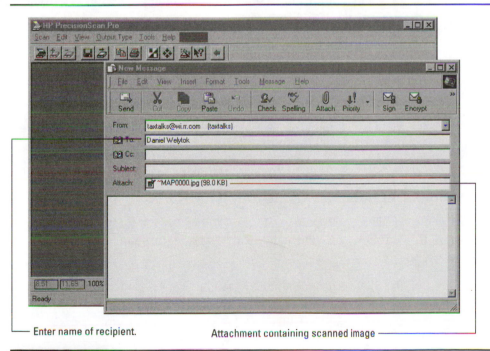

Enter name of recipient.   Attachment containing scanned image

FIGURE 17-4   Your scanner software might open your email software and attach the image to an email message.

17

Sending Email Directly from Your Image-Editing Program

After you finish editing an image or creating a project such as a greeting card, you might be able to open your email program from within your image-editing program. Both PhotoSuite 4 and PhotoDeluxe have this convenient feature.

Emailing Your Project from PhotoSuite 4

If you're working in PhotoSuite 4 and want to email one of your editing projects, follow these steps:

1. With the project file open on your work area, click the Share button, located directly below the Menu bar.

2. Click the Send E-mail button on the Activity panel that appears, or select Send via E-mail from the File menu.

3. Click the Return button from this Activity panel, then click Send Now or one of the other options.

4. Indicate whether you want to send your scanning project in its current format, or change it to the JPEG format.

5. Your email application/service is automatically launched, as shown in Figure 17-5, creating an email with your editing project as an attachment. The email includes a standard greeting, which you may include, or you may type your own. Enter the email address of the person you want to send your project to.

6. Click Send to send the message with your scanned and edited project as an attachment, then click Return.

Sending an Email Message from PhotoDeluxe

When you work with PhotoDeluxe, it's easy to email your completed editing project to a friend. Just follow these steps to open your email program directly from PhotoDeluxe:

1. Click the Share button, then the Email button. An Email Information dialog box appears, as shown in Figure 17-6.

Email option dialog box

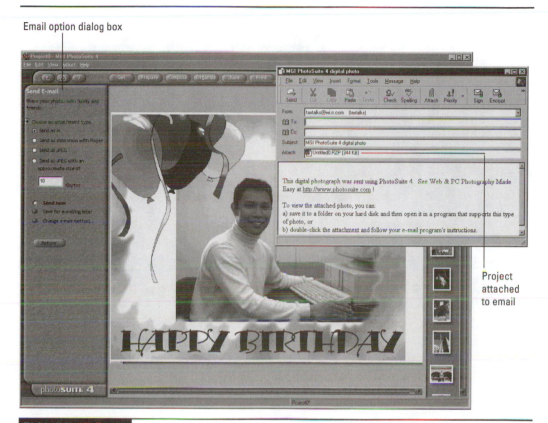

Project
attached
to email

FIGURE 17-5   Open your email program directly from PhotoSuite, as shown here.

2. Type complete email addresses in the Send To and From text fields. You can add multiple addresses, using a maximum of 255 characters per field, including commas and spaces.

3. Complete the information in the Subject and Message fields.

4. Click Attach File, browse for the PhotoDeluxe project you want to email, then click OK.

Attaching a File to an Email Message

It's not always convenient to send your photo directly from your scanning or image-editing software. If you're sending multiple image files, you might need to open your email program and browse for the files you want to attach.

17

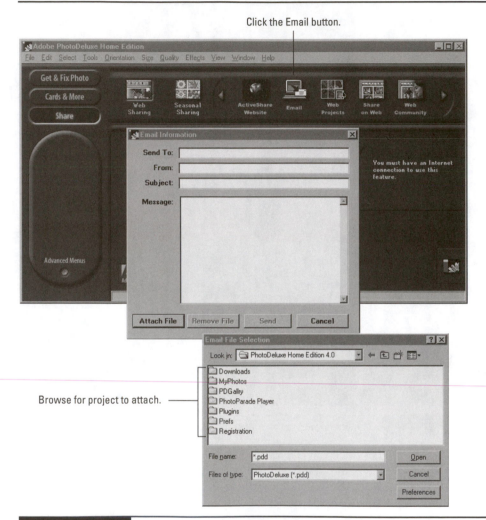

FIGURE 17-6   Email a scanned image directly from within PhotoDeluxe.

Attaching a File to a Microsoft Outlook Email Message

If you're working in Microsoft Outlook, follow these steps to attach a file:

1. Click the paper clip icon, as shown in Figure 17-7. A dialog box opens.

2. Browse for the file you want to attach, and select it.

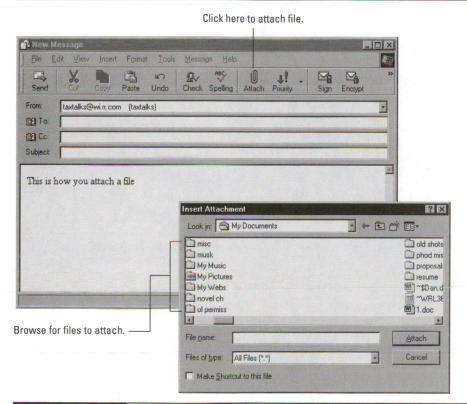

Click here to attach file.

Browse for files to attach.

FIGURE 17-7   Attaching a file to a Microsoft Outlook message

3. Click Attach. The file is now attached to your email. To attach additional files, select them and click Attach.

4. When you're done attaching files, save or send your email as you normally do.

Attaching a File to a Netscape Communicator Email Message

If you use Netscape Communicator to send image files, follow these steps:

1. Click the paper clip icon, as shown in Figure 17-8, and select File from the pop-up menu that appears. A dialog box opens.

17

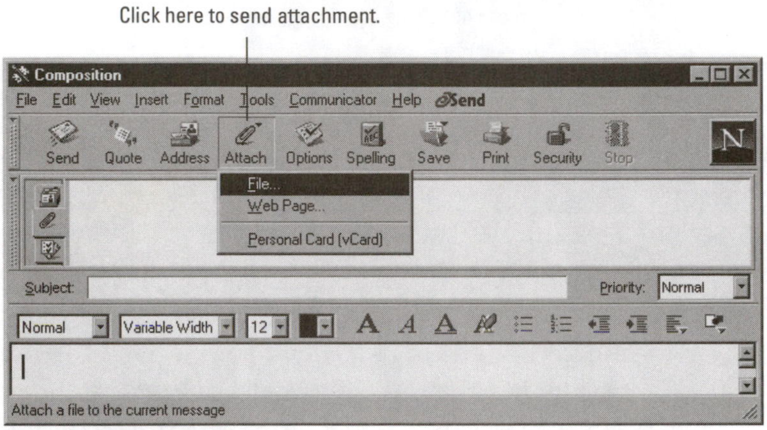

Click here to send attachment.

FIGURE 17-8   Add an attachment by clicking the paper clip icon.

2. Browse for the file you want to attach, and select it.

3. Click Attach. The file is now attached to your email. To attach additional files, select them and click Attach.

4. When you're done attaching files, save or send your email as you usually do.

Email Your Photos Faster and Save Computer Space

Emailing images is not much more difficult than sending simple text messages; however, the image files can take a much longer time to send and download. They can also take up a lot of space on the respective computers of both the sender and recipient.

Here are a few time- and space-saving tips to keep in mind when emailing images:

Delete sent messages to save space.   When you send an image as an attachment, most email programs, such as Microsoft Outlook Express and Netscape Communicator, keep a copy of the sent message, along with the attachment—unless you configure the programs not to save sent messages. If you don't actually need to save a copy of such email, it's a colossal waste of space. Delete unneeded copies of sent email as soon as practical.

Select your file format carefully.   Most image-editing programs allow you to select from a variety of formats for saving a file, as exemplified by the PhotoSuite Save menu shown in Figure 17-9. Some formats are decidedly more efficient for sending over the web. Chapter 8 provides you with information about various file formats and their relative advantages and disadvantages when it comes to emailing scanned photos and posting them to the web.

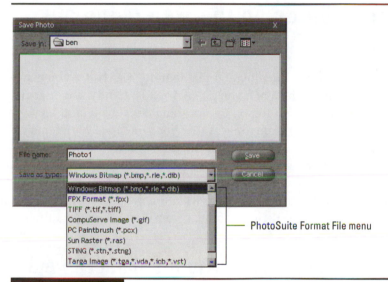

PhotoSuite Format File menu

FIGURE 17-9   Image-editing programs allow you to save files in a variety of formats.

Use compression software.   Compression is a process that reduces file size by eliminating redundant data. This is a particularly useful thing to do when sending large image files over the Internet. The redundant data is replaced when the file reaches its destination. A popular compression program is WinZip. You can download a trial version at www.winzip.com.

Spring for a faster Internet connection service.   While your dial-up connection might be great for standard email, images take more time to send and receive. If you plan on sending a lot of photos over the web, you might want to evaluate a high-speed Internet service such as cable or DSL (discussed in Chapter 2).

17

Consider a CD burner.   If high-speed Internet connections aren't available in your geographical area or in your budget, consider the advantages of a CD burner. You can burn several dozen photos onto a single CD and mail it to friends and family using a cardboard envelope you can get at any office-supply store and less than a dollar in postage.

Posting Scanned Photos on the Web Using a Communal Site

Even if you don't want to bother creating and maintaining a website, you can still post and share photos on the Web. When you do so, friends, family, and associates who have the correct password can log on to a designated website and view your photos. One of the advantages of doing this is that your intended recipients can circumvent their slow dial-up connections and the time spent downloading. They also don't need to dedicate any space whatsoever to view the picture. They can decide whether they want to download and store the posted photos on their own hard drives. Both PhotoSuite and PhotoDeluxe come with simple, uncomplicated features that allow you to upload photos to their communal websites in a matter of minutes.

Posting Your Pictures on PhotoSuite's GatherRound.com

PhotoSuite 4 allows you to create password-protected picture albums (photo databases) on its communal GatherRound site. You can upload your favorite photos and even entire albums to www.gatherround.com, and invite family and friends to see them. Best of all, this web service is totally free.

To share your work via GatherRound.com:

1. Click the Share button, located directly below the Menu bar, as shown in Figure 17-10.

2. If you're new to the service, after establishing an Internet connection, click the Create Account button. Type your name, email address, and an account password. If you're already a member, type your email address and password in the appropriate fields, and click the Login button.

Click here to access site.

FIGURE 17-10   You can access the GatherRound website directly from PhotoSuite.

 TIP   *If you want to view more information about GatherRound before you create an account, click the Go to GatherRound.com button to launch the GatherRound home page.*

3. On the next Activity panel that appears, either select an existing album or create a new album. If you're creating a new album, click the Create New Album button. In the dialog box that appears, type an album name and a brief description.

4. Click the Upload button. All photos currently displayed in the area are uploaded. Once the photos have been uploaded successfully, you are brought automatically to the GatherRound website, as shown in Figure 17-11. You can then view your album on the site. Figure 17-12 shows your guests' view of the site.

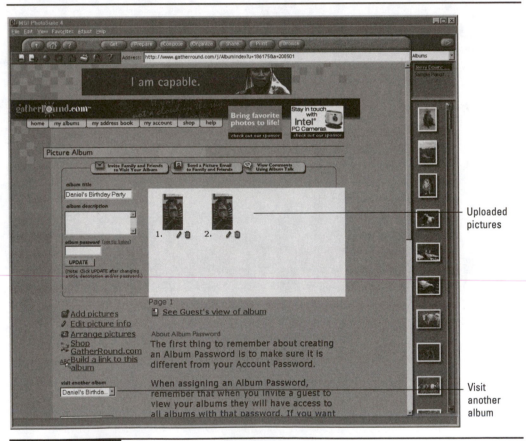

FIGURE 17-11   Your pictures uploaded to GatherRound.com

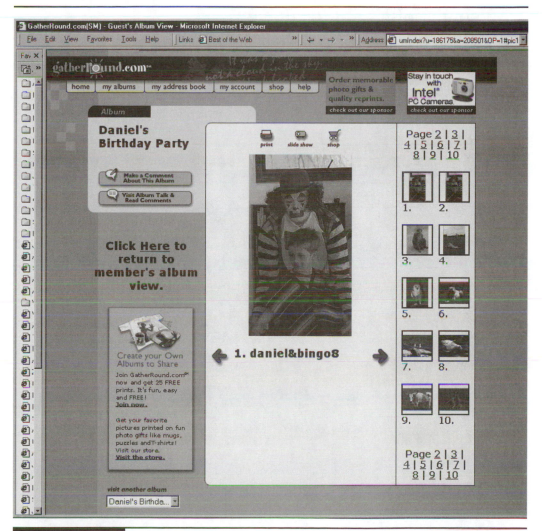

FIGURE 17-12   Here's what friends and family can view on GatherRound.com.

17

Using Adobe's Shutterfly.com

PhotoDeluxe used to have a feature called the PhotoShare website, which you might see referenced in the Help menu of the program. This is a bit confusing since that particular website no longer exists. It was discontinued as of April 13, 2001. Instead, Adobe now provides PhotoDeluxe users the Shutterfly website for posting and sharing photos. You can open an account on this site, which is shown in Figure 17-13.

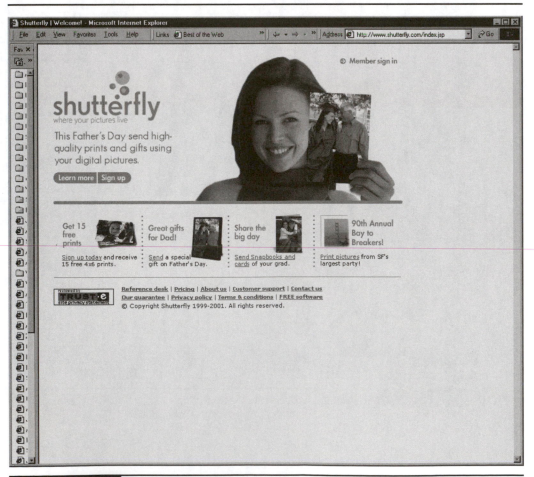

FIGURE 17-13   PhotoDeluxe users can post photos to the Shutterfly website.

After you've entered your user name and a password, you can browse for files to upload from your computer, as shown in Figure 17-14. You can provide your friends and family with your password so they can view the photos you've posted on the site as shown in Figure 17-15.

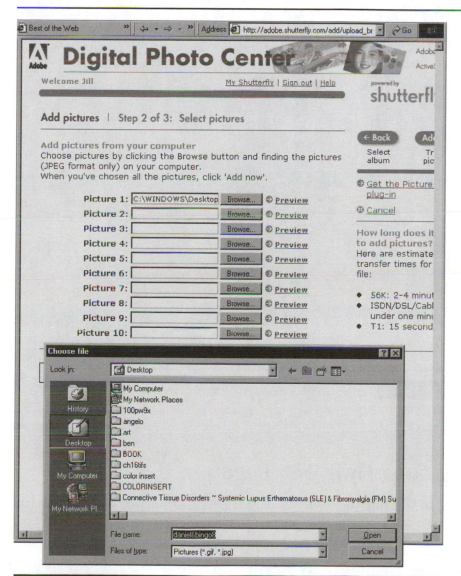

FIGURE 17-14   Use this page to browse for photos and post them to Shutterfly.com.

17

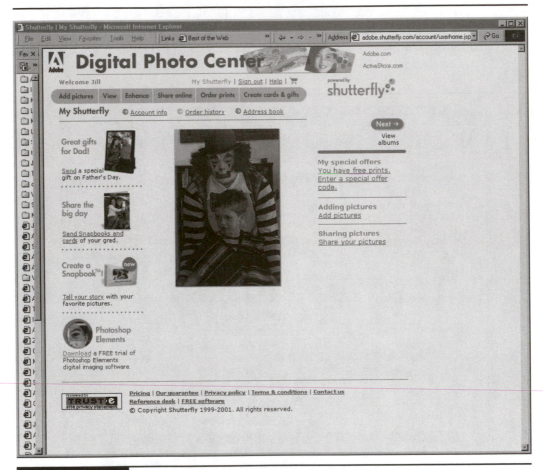

FIGURE 17-15
A photo posted on the Shutterfly website

Creating Your Own Web Page

Creating and hosting your own web page featuring scanned photos is simpler than you might think, and it's the perfect ongoing application for your new scanning skills. To host your own web page, you need three things:

A host server To be accessible on the World Wide Web, your page must be stored on a web server. Your ISP might provide this service, or you can use the services of a third party to host your page. Yahoo! GeoCities provides a free web hosting service, and is discussed later in this chapter.

Web editing software   You need to edit your web page on your own computer using a program that allows you to create and edit web pages.

Upload capability   You must be able to upload your edited pages and scanned images to the web server so they can be accessed and viewed by all interested parties surfing the Web.

There are a number of programs that allow you create, edit, and post web pages. This chapter explores the capabilities of the popular PhotoSuite and PhotoDeluxe programs that often come bundled with scanners. It also discusses the Yahoo! GeoCities service, which allows you to create and host a web page using free editing software and server space. Finally, we take a brief look at the ever-popular Microsoft FrontPage program, which is specifically designed to allow you to create and maintain a highly sophisticated website.

Finding Server Space to Post Your Page

If you already have access to the Internet, you need to find out if your ISP offers web hosting. Web hosting is the ability to publish your web page and store it on the ISP's server computer. If your ISP doesn't have this service, you need to shop around for a *web presence provider* (WPP), which will allow you to rent space on its server for this purpose. You can contract for the services of a WPP, such as www.addr.com, for less than $20 a month, or take advantage of a free service, such as Yahoo! GeoCities, discussed below.

Creating and Posting a Web Page Using PhotoSuite 4

The PhotoSuite program includes powerful but simple to use website creation capabilities. To create a web page featuring your scanned photos, follow these steps:

1. With the project file open in your work area, click the Share button, located below the Menu bar.

2. Click the Create Web Items button on the Activity panel.

3. Click the Web Page button on the next Activity panel displayed.

4. Click the Create New Web Page button. A number of web-page templates are displayed on the work area, as shown in Figure 17-16.

5. Select a template category from the drop-down list, then choose a template from the work area.

6. Click the Next button. Your work is displayed within the selected template, as shown in Figure 17-17.

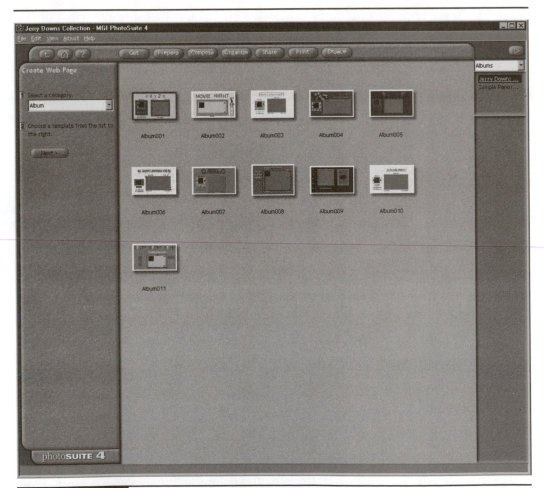

FIGURE 17-16   PhotoSuite allows you to select from a number of web-page templates.

Default text

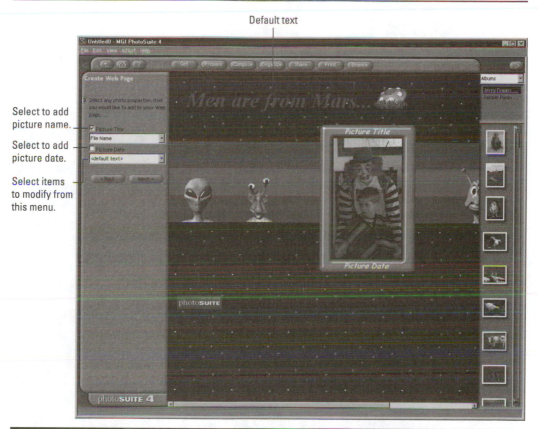

Select to add
picture name.

Select to add
picture date.

Select items
to modify from
this menu.

FIGURE 17-17   A web page in progress using a PhotoSuite template

7. You now have the option of using the template's default text or entering your
    own text. The default text indicates the photo's filename and the date the
    photo was saved to disk. You can also identify the album name by selecting
    the check box shown. Indicate what properties you want to modify by
    selecting the check box, and click Next.

TIP   *Consider using these captions to identify the people and places in your
    photos.*

8. The dialog box shown in Figure 17-18 appears, providing you with extensive options for modifying the web page. For example, you can modify and add text, photos, interactive panoramas, animation files, and web links. When you select any of these options, a special dialog box appears for editing the particular feature.

Edit text.
Add photos.
Add animation.
Add links to other Web pages.
Change background.
Add sound.

FIGURE 17-18   This dialog box provides extensive web-editing capabilities.

9. When you're finished editing your web page, click Next.

10. A dialog box prompts you as to whether you want to

■ View your web page in your browser so you can see how it will look

■ Save your web page as an HTML file

■ Send your web page to someone as an email

■ Post your page on the Web

If you choose to post your page on the Web, you're prompted to enter the necessary information about your web hosting service in the dialog box shown in Figure 17-19. Your web page is then uploaded to the server.

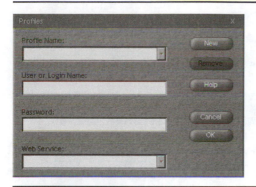

FIGURE 17-19   Dialog box for posting your newly created web page to your web host's server.

Creating Your Site for Free Using Yahoo! GeoCities

You can find one of the absolute best deals by logging on to www.geocities .yahoo.com, as shown in Figure 17-20. You can host your own website for free on the Yahoo! server, and you get access to state-of-the-art web editing software to boot.

At the risk of sounding like an infomercial for the free services on this site, here is a list of the services and capabilities you can find on it, with no corresponding financial obligation:

Free disk space   Yahoo! GeoCities provides you with 15 megabytes of space for your web page on its server. That roughly corresponds to anywhere from 15 to 40 scanned photos.

Wizards and templates   If you're a neophyte to web design, you can use the wizards provided to create an impressive-looking website.

Web-editing software   You can access the Yahoo! PageBuilder software for free. You don't have to have any prior experience with web design software to use it.

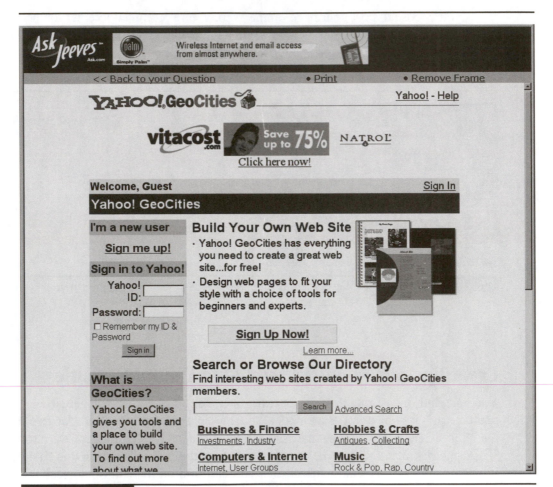

FIGURE 17-20   Website for the Yahoo! GeoCities free web-hosting service

Site statistics   Your site will have an automatic counter to track the number of visitors.

Add-ons and program extensions   Once you get your site up and running, you can add advanced preprogrammed features—stock quotes, games, news headlines, clip art, a guest book, email forms, countdown clocks, and much more.

FTP access   Transfer files using your favorite file transfer protocol (FTP) program. FTPs are discussed in the next section.

File Manager   This software allows you to create, edit, upload, delete, and maintain your files in directories and subdirectories.

Signing up for Yahoo GeoCities: Your Obligations

In exchange for the use of the free Yahoo! web-hosting services, you are asked to provide registration information about yourself, and you give Yahoo! the right to place some of its banner advertising on your website. They target the banner advertising that appears on your site based on the information you give them.

You are not asked to provide a lot of intrusive personal information. As with most free web-based services, you are automatically placed on some advertising lists unless you deselect the check box shown in Figure 17-21. Yahoo! also allows you to specify the types of advertising you want to receive.

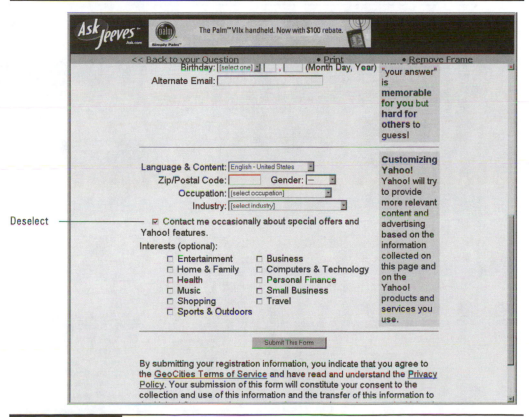

FIGURE 17-21   Deselect the check box to avoid being placed on Yahoo! mailing lists.

Creating a Yahoo! Web Page

Once you're registered with Yahoo!, you have access to their free web creation and editing software. In fact, you have three types to choose from. Depending on your level of experience and desire for control over the web-editing process, you can select from one of the following:

Yahoo! PageWizards   This is probably the way to go if you're a beginner to web design. Step-by-step instructions help you build your page quickly using a wizard format, as shown in Figure 17-22.

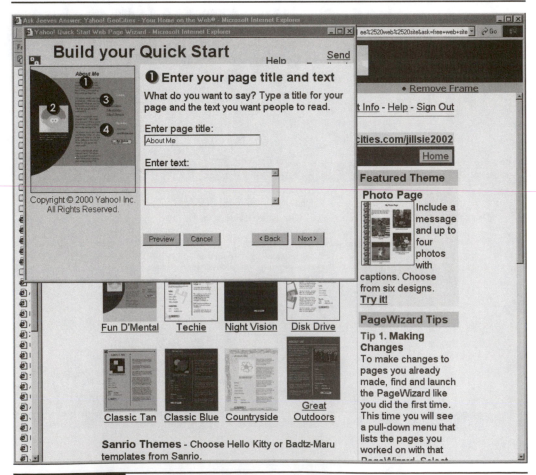

FIGURE 17-22   The Yahoo! PageWizards are great for beginners.

Yahoo! PageBuilder   Once you've established your site, you can use this straightforward and easy-to-master editing program to add graphics, backgrounds, and music.

Advanced Editor   If you're experienced at web design and are familiar with hypertext markup language (HTML), you can cut and paste the code you create yourself.

Viewing a Yahoo! Web Page

Yahoo! recommends that you name the first page of your site "index.html" and save it. After doing so, you can view your site on the Web immediately, by using the following naming convention to find the URL for the site:

www.geocities.com/yourYahoo!ID

The URL for your home page can always be found at the top right corner of the Yahoo! GeoCities home page.

Yahoo! also sends you an email telling you your URL.

Uploading Edited Pages and Scanned Photos to Your Yahoo! Account

Yahoo! allows you to use your own text editor and to upload pages to its server using the PageWizards or by accessing the Upload Files option from the PageBuilder File menu.

You can also upload your own image files to your web page. Yahoo! provides you with a file transfer program called Easy Upload. Alternatively, you can use a file transfer protocol (FTP) program of your own choosing. FTP programs are discussed in the next section.

Consider Microsoft FrontPage for Your Website

Microsoft FrontPage is the most popular web design software on the market today. It's designed for use by both beginners and professionals.

FrontPage uses drawing tools similar to the Microsoft PowerPoint program. It also includes templates and web content that you can add and use to develop your site to make the pages appear more professional and dynamic. If you're familiar with HTML

17

editing, there are lots of streamlining tools to help you format in HTML and its progeny language, XML (extensible markup language). The program even includes website management tools that store data about who accesses and uses your site.

This section tells you a little bit about what you need to know to get started using this program. The program has sophisticated capabilities and comes with an excellent online manual and Help feature. You'll need to consult these resources carefully if you plan to follow through on designing a website with FrontPage.

This chapter takes a quick look at how to

- Install the related Internet tools you need to use the program
- Create and save a home page
- Add text to your home page
- Upload scanned photos to your home page

Install the Related Windows Internet Tools Before Using FrontPage

If you're going to use this program to create a web page, you should first install two related Internet tools. Microsoft's Web Publishing wizard and Personal Web Server both come with Windows 98, Windows 2000, and Microsoft Internet Explorer. You can load these tools from the original program CDs if you haven't already installed them.

The Web Publishing wizard is a tool designed to help you upload pages to your ISP or WPP. After you have created your web page using FrontPage, follow the steps provided by the wizard to upload the pages. The wizard is effective for most ISPs and WPPs, but occasionally you might encounter a glitch. When this happens, you should call the WPP, and they can talk you through the process of uploading the web pages you've created.

The Microsoft Personal Web Server tool allows your PC to mimic a web server. Using this tool, you can create and test web pages on your own PC before you publish them on the Web by uploading them to a server maintained by your ISP or WPP.

Creating and Saving a Home Page with FrontPage

The first step in launching your own website is creating a home page. It's the first page visitors see when they come to your site. Once you've created a home page, it's easy to create links to other pages you set up using the same tools and procedures you used for creating your home page.

To create your home page, open Microsoft FrontPage. The screen shown in Figure 17-23 appears, displaying code to create a blank web page.

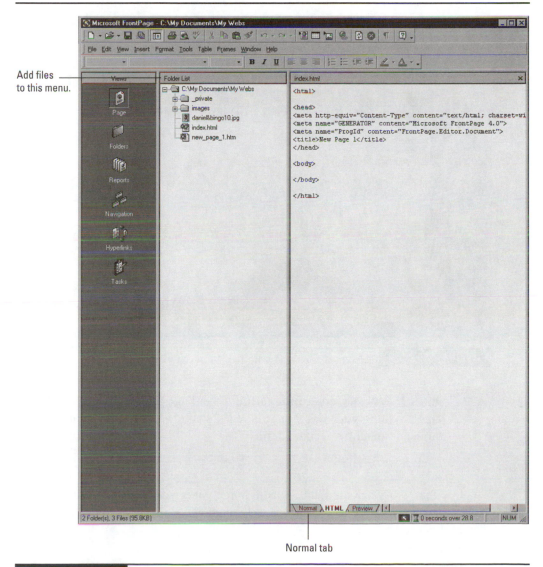

Add files to this menu.

Normal tab

17

Before you begin typing any text onto this blank page, which will become your home page, you need to give it a title and save it so it has a filename. To give your home page a proper title and save it to a file, follow these steps:

1. From the menu bar, choose File, then Save. The Save As dialog box appears, as shown in Figure 17-24.

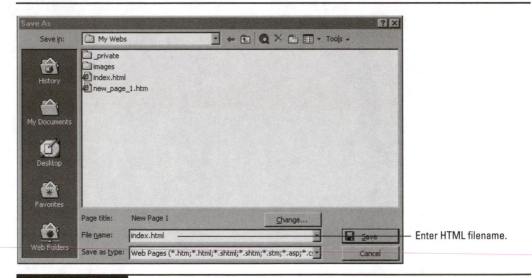

Enter HTML filename.

FIGURE 17-24   Enter a filename with the .html extension.

2. Under File Name, enter **index.html**. FrontPage allows you to name your home page anything your want, but many ISPs and WPPs require that you use the name and extension "index.html."

3. Click Save.

Now that you've created and saved a home page, you're officially up and running. You can proceed to add text, images, and increasingly sophisticated features as you master this program.

Explore FrontPage's Text-Editing Capabilities

When you create a Web Page using Microsoft FrontPage, the program is actually creating a hypertext markup language (HTML) document behind the scenes. HTML is a special language that defines text formatting for all documents that appear on the Web.

Perhaps the most attractive feature of Microsoft FrontPage is that it allows you to add and edit text using an interface similar to Microsoft Word. If you're familiar with Microsoft Word, editing with FrontPage is easy and intuitive. You can type, select, move, copy, and delete text in FrontPage exactly as you do in Word.

Formatting text is a little bit different. You can resize text, make it bold, underline it, align and center it, change the color, and apply a heading style using the dialog box shown in Figure 17-25.

FIGURE 17-25   The FrontPage Font dialog box

Adding Scanned Photos Using FrontPage

What can be duller than a web page that contains only text? Your scanned photos can make it a site worth visiting.

To add scanned photos to a web page you've created with FrontPage, follow these steps:

1. Right-click the Start menu on your Windows desktop to access the Explore window, then select the file containing the scanned photo your want to import.

17

2. Right-click the file you want to import, then click Copy on the pop-up menu that appears.

3. Open Microsoft FrontPage.

4. Click the Normal tab and the folder on the left side of the screen where you want to import the scanned image (see Figure 17-23).

5. Right-click in the pane containing the file list and select Paste from the pop-up menu. The image appears on the web page.

When you import an image onto a web page using the above steps, it usually isn't sized or positioned exactly the way you want it. You can resize the photo by following these steps:

1. Right-click the scanned photo, then click Picture Properties on the pop-up menu that appears. The dialog box shown in Figure 17-26 appears.

2. Select the Specify Size check box.

3. To maintain the height-to-width proportions, select the Keep Aspect Ratio check box.

4. Specify whether you want to change the size in pixels or percentage, then enter values in the Width and Height boxes.

5. Save the changes you've made to the web page.

Obviously, this chapter tells you only a fraction of what you probably want to know if you decide to create your own web page using Microsoft FrontPage. It's intended only to give you a feel for the familiar Windows-like interface, and to demonstrate how intuitive this program can be. If you think you'd like to use FrontPage to create a web page using your scanned photos, you'll find *How to Do Everything with FrontPage 2000* (Osborne/McGraw-Hill, 2001) to be an excellent resource.

Sending Large Image Files Using a File Transfer Protocol

It's often inconvenient to send large or multiple image files over the Web. That's why many ISP and WPP sites allow you to send files using a file transfer protocol (FTP)

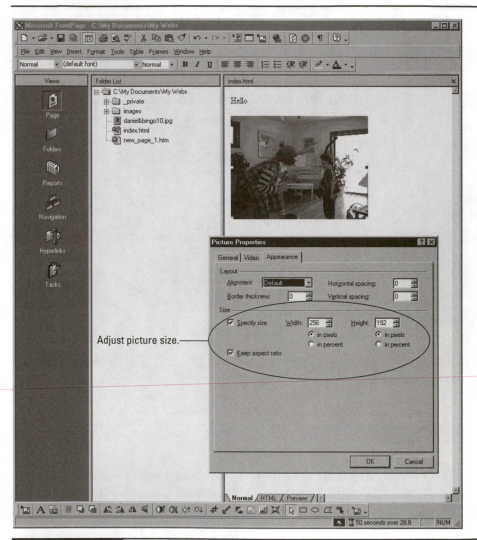

Adjust picture size.

FIGURE 17-26   Reposition and resize photos uploaded with FrontPage.

program. In fact, you should inquire whether your service provider allows you to use FTP to transfer files, and what programs are available for you to use for this purpose.

FTP programs are designed to facilitate and expedite the transfer of large files over the Web. Perhaps the most popular file transfer program is WS_FTP. You can download a free 30-day trial version for this program from www.ipswitch.com/ Products/WS_FTP, shown in Figure 17-27.

17

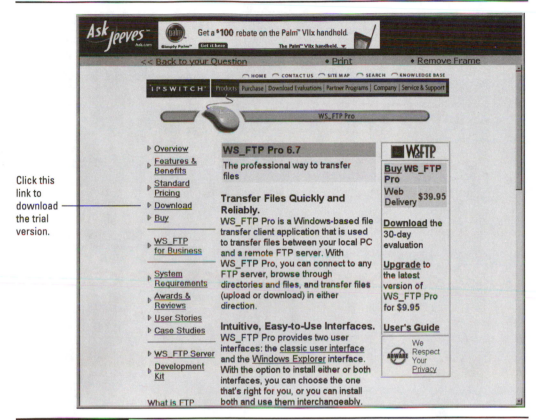

Click this link to download the trial version.

FIGURE 17-27   Download a free trial version of WS_FTP software from this site.

After you've downloaded this program, you can connect to another computer, such as the server for your ISP or WSP. To establish a connection with another computer from your own PC, you need the following three items of information to enter into the dialog box, shown in Figure 17-28:

- The name of the server computer
- A user ID that's recognized by the server computer
- A password

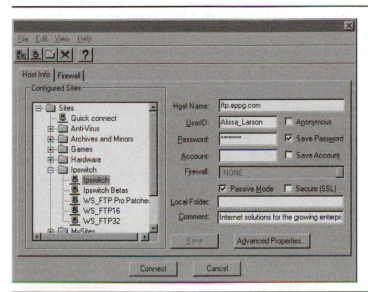

FIGURE 17-28 Enter information about the web server to connect to it and upload files.

Once a connection has been established, you can transfer files back and forth between the two computers by searching for the right directory and clicking on the arrows shown to transfer files to and from either computer (see Figure 17-29).

Click arrows to transfer the files you've selected.

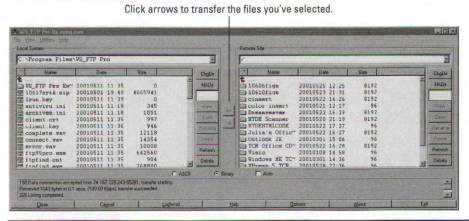

FIGURE 17-29   The WS_FTP File Transfer application window

17

Evaluating Your Photo-Sharing Options

You are the master of your own photos when it comes to sharing them over the Internet. You can decide whether to email them to a single person or to post them on a website for any number of people to access. You can even design your own website to display them. It's up to you to set your own creative goals. The technology to achieve them is accessible and inexpensive or even free!

Index

Z

INTERNATIONAL CONTACT INFORMATION

AUSTRALIA
McGraw-Hill Book Company Australia Pty. Ltd.
TEL +61-2-9417-9899
FAX +61-2-9417-5687
http://www.mcgraw-hill.com.au
books-it_sydney@mcgraw-hill.com

CANADA
McGraw-Hill Ryerson Ltd.
TEL +905-430-5000
FAX +905-430-5020
http://www.mcgrawhill.ca

**GREECE, MIDDLE EAST,
NORTHERN AFRICA**
McGraw-Hill Hellas
TEL +30-1-656-0990-3-4
FAX +30-1-654-5525

MEXICO (Also serving Latin America)
McGraw-Hill Interamericana Editores S.A. de C.V.
TEL +525-117-1583
FAX +525-117-1589
http://www.mcgraw-hill.com.mx
fernando_castellanos@mcgraw-hill.com

SINGAPORE (Serving Asia)
McGraw-Hill Book Company
TEL +65-863-1580
FAX +65-862-3354
http://www.mcgraw-hill.com.sg
mghasia@mcgraw-hill.com

SOUTH AFRICA
McGraw-Hill South Africa
TEL +27-11-622-7512
FAX +27-11-622-9045
robyn_swanepoel@mcgraw-hill.com

**UNITED KINGDOM & EUROPE
(Excluding Southern Europe)**
McGraw-Hill Publishing Company
TEL +44-1-628-502500
FAX +44-1-628-770224
http://www.mcgraw-hill.co.uk
computing_neurope@mcgraw-hill.com

ALL OTHER INQUIRIES Contact:
Osborne/McGraw-Hill
TEL +1-510-549-6600
FAX +1-510-883-7600
http://www.osborne.com
omg_international@mcgraw-hill.com